The Social Dimensions
of International Business

The Social Dimensions of International Business

An Annotated Bibliography

Compiled by JON P. ALSTON

Bibliographies and Indexes in Economics
and Economic History, Number 12

Greenwood Press
Westport, Connecticut • London

Library of Congress Cataloging-in-Publication Data

Alston, Jon P.
  The social dimensions of international business : an annotated
bibliography / compiled by Jon P. Alston.
    p.   cm.—(Bibliographies and indexes in economics and
economic history, ISSN 0749-1786 ; no. 12)
  Includes bibliographical references and index.
  ISBN 0-313-28029-0 (alk. paper)
  1. Communication in international trade—Bibliography.
  2. Intercultural communication—Bibliography.   I. Title.
  II. Series.
  Z7164.C81A46   1993
  [HF1379]
  016.3888'8—dc20   92-29466

British Library Cataloguing in Publication Data is available.

Library of Congress Catalog Card Number: 92-29466
ISBN: 0-313-28029-0
ISSN: 0749-1786

First published in 1993

Greenwood Press, 88 Post Road West, Westport, CT 06881
An imprint of Greenwood Publishing Group, Inc.

Printed in the United States of America

Dedicated to the "thunderbirds" of the American
Graduate School of Management and all expatriates
everywhere, the Center for International Business
Studies at Texas A&M University, the Department of
Sociology, Beijing University, Beijing, of the
People's Republic of China, and my French relatives
and cousins.

Contents

Acknowledgements

I wish to acknowledge the assistance of the personnel of the Interlibrary Loan office at Texas A&M University. I also benefited from the support and encouragement of Kerry Cooper, director of the Center for International Business Studies. Others at the College of Business Administration gave me valuable knowledge and advice whenever needed. John Boies and Laurie Silver were always willing to help with programming problems.

Introduction

This bibliography presents over 1300 annotated citations of material concerned with the cultural and social dimensions of international business. These publications are meant to alert readers to the social issues involved in cross-cultural business situations, whether a person wishes to live in a foreign country or deal in any fashion with those from other cultures. I assume that knowledge of one's own and other cultural patterns makes cross-cultural business-related interaction more comfortable and more likely to be successful.

Each culture has unique patterns of business-related behavior, including managerial behavior, superior-subordinate relationships, negotiating strategies, and business communication. In some cultures, managers avoid giving direct orders and criticisms. Those who come from more aggressive cultures can offend foreign colleagues without meaning to do so. In Asia, where maintaining social harmony is more important than being honest, a "yes" may actually mean "no." Those expecting to do business throughout the world must be familiar with a wide range of foreign customs and patterns of thinking. Unfortunately, business persons from the United States are generally unprepared to deal adequately with foreigners.

The selection of citations is based on three general guidelines: (1) the material deals with the social and/or psychological dimensions of international issues; (2) the material includes discussion of national character; and (3) the material was published during 1980-1991. The first guideline is that to be included, a book, report, or journal article in the English language must deal with national patterns of managerial and work-related behavior or attitudes/values in the work place. I am concerned with material that describes, explains, or compares managerial behavior or its social and cultural origins, between and among cultural areas. All materials in this bibliography deal with selected aspects of the social/cultural/behavioral elements of international business.

An example of this emphasis on the cultural dimensions of international business is Robert Doktor's carefully developed studies on how senior-level managers use their time (905-7, 1217). Doktor found that, contrary to all expectations, Japanese chief executive officers (CEOs) did not spend more of their time working with others than U.S. CEOs. On the other hand, American CEOs divided their time into shorter units. This research was later extended to compare time use of CEOs in Hong Kong and Korea.

Another approach comparing work-related behavior among different nationalities is found in the work of John L. Graham and his associates (314-22), who observed negotiating behavior of subjects from five cultures under laboratory conditions. The literature indicates a number of other research streams that analyze a behavior or attitude using respondents from a number of different countries. These are truly comparative analyses on a global level.

I excluded technical analyses of business procedures throughout the world when they did not also illustrate cultural patterns. I omitted, for example, studies on global taxation practices, or marketing procedures per se. How the French and Japanese negotiate and communicate is relevant; how their accounting and taxation systems differ is not.

The second guideline for inclusion is that materials deal with descriptions of national character or social values, especially those influencing national managerial styles and work behavior. Generally, international business research focuses on actual business-related behavior, and then infers general societal values from that behavior. This strategy is most common in comparative research, where the author(s) compare two or more national samples. The differences in work behavior are generally interpreted to be caused by cultural differences. Work-related behavior (including managerial practices) are seen as more specialized examples of general cultural patterns.

The second criterion for inclusion also demands that a work offer knowledge on the work-related behavior in one or more cultures. This material, more commonly known as "how-to" information, offers practical advice on how to work with, or manage, persons from other cultures. Many of these "how to" guides prepare future expatriates for living in unfamiliar social environments. The practical benefits of such knowledge include a reduction of early returns from a foreign post and better work performance.

This knowledge is often "soft" in the scientific sense. That is, the information is often anecdotal, unsystematic, or based on personal experiences. Some presentations focus on business-related behavior, while others include general etiquette information useful to those conducting business in foreign countries. The implicit assumption of these works is that cross-cultural relations become more pleasant and productive when parties are considerate and aware of each other's social norms and customs.

The instructions vary from which colors are seen as offensive when selecting flowers to offer a hostess (yellow flowers in France denote death) to which gestures are defined as obscene in one country and not in another. During his 1992 visit to Pacific Rim nations, U.S. President George Bush inadvertently made a gesture defined by his Australian hosts as obscene. While in Japan, he interrupted a classic game of kickball (not allowed) to join the players. He used his head (against the rules) to move the ball, thereby disrupting an ancient and highly formalized activity. The equivalent in American culture would be if a member of the audience at an operatic spectacle started singing with the cast. Americans are famous throughout the world for not knowing how to behave properly in other cultural settings.

This knowledge also avoids cultural misunderstandings. What does a Thai or a Latin American, for example, mean when he says "the report will be done in a few days"? When should a "yes" spoken by a Japanese, Indonesian, or South Korean be understood as a "no"? When an American says "it will be difficult to meet this schedule," she probably means that the schedule can be met with some effort. By contrast, this statement when spoken by a Chinese or Japanese most likely should be interpreted as a "no."

Many of these works point out the differences in how a culture defines space and time, peer relations, behavior during meetings and negotiation, etc. Others define a culture's patterns of authority and managerial styles. In some cultures, subordinates are not expected to use any initiative or independence of thought. They will follow direct orders even when they know they are counter-productive. In other cultures, a manager expects self-direction from subordinates.

Readers of such works will quickly notice a wide range in quality. Some reflect current fads, such as the on-going interest in Japanese work practices. Other works are based on little more than a rewriting of previously-published works. Still others are highly impressionistic and resemble tourist tracts. Nevertheless, many offer valuable, though often repetitive, advice on cross-cultural behaviors. Most "how-tos," however, are written in a theoretical vacuum. There is little cumulation of knowledge, nor is there much systematic presentation of facts.

Some "how-to" works are little more than boosters for a country; others are extended travelogues. I have excluded these since they often contain misleading material. Material that is too uncritical and diverge too much from practical experience has also been avoided. These criteria eliminated many articles, often sponsored by government agencies, from magazines and more popular periodicals. Citations are primarily from academic sources, although exceptions were made in the case of a number of excellent journalistic reports on China and Japan.

Yet other "how-to" works are sensitive, filter out the non-essential elements of a foreign culture, and prepare the foreign visitor for adjustment to new etiquette and protocol standards. They range from whether (and how) to shake hands with Japanese, how to "listen" to what is being meant rather than said, or what degree of formality is proper with a German or Latin American. Such works describe the minutiae of proper behavior. Others offer practical advice, such as how to find an English-speaking doctor in a foreign country.

The third criterion for selection is that the material be published during 1980 through 1991 and be easily available to scholars and the general public. The field of international business gathered momentum during the 1970s, and experienced a virtual explosion during the 1980s. Scholars and readers became much more international in their interests during the latter decade, especially in the United States. The 1980s also experienced a mushrooming interest in Japanese and Chinese material.

There are, however, a number of pre-1980 works that are included in this bibliography. Some of these began a research stream of influence that continued during the 1980s. I include these partly as a tribute to their significance. In addition, the materials in some of these early works have not been surpassed in later publications. This is especially true for Latin American studies, which enjoyed a greater vogue among North American authors during the 1960s and 1970s than later.

A number of works on national character and to a lesser extent on managerial values, published during the 1970s (and earlier), remain classic statements. Later works are often mere duplications or footnotes to these "classics." Some of these works have been included, though I have been highly selective.   Often,   such   classics   were   authored   by anthropologists, sociologists, psychologists, and other non-business specialists. While some do not focus on business-related matters, later authors used these pioneers' insights within a more restricted business-related context.

A decade or two ago, a number of journalists and Asian studies specialists alerted others to the cultural uniqueness of Japanese society and Japanese work behavior. More recently, journalists and sinologists "discovered" China for the West. Such works are included in this collection when their contents help readers better understand a culture. In these instances, the information prepares future expatriates for living and working in specific cultures. These works have the potential to reduce the culture shock all expatriates experience to some extent when living and working in a foreign culture.

The first chapter deals with the problems of cross-cultural communication.   Unfortunately, Americans (those from the U.S.A.) tend to lack knowledge of foreign languages. Such knowledge is not seen as important nor is it rewarded by employers. Americans tend to be monolingual while most other global businesspersons are not.

Lack of linguistic skills is not the only problem experienced by Americans abroad.   National patterns of expression and communication styles often create barriers to understanding. The Japanese, for example, use an indirect communication style that is non-assertive and supportive. Americans familiar with only their own aggressive and frank communication style are in danger of misunderstanding when a Japanese means "no" when saying "yes" (45, 54, 59, and 60).

Koreans and Malaysians avoid delivering news that would distress the listener, even to the point of passing on misinformation.   Koreans often delay negative information until the end of the workday or week in order to not spoil the other person's day or week.   Americans who wish to receive complete information from Koreans or Japanese learn to listen carefully for what is not being said as well as what is being hinted at or suggested.

The second chapter deals with training persons to deal with those from different cultures. Many of the articles decry American's lack of knowledge of foreign cultures and customs. Most Americans dealing with foreigners lack the sensitivity to understand the behavior of foreigners, though some multinationals offer excellent cross-training facilities. IBM (101) maintains regional offices throughout the world that train employees to blend into local cultures. The Japanese (135) also carefully train future expatriates to develop a thorough knowledge of a client's culture.

The consensus of the literature is that American multinationals do not adequately prepare their employees for foreign duty.   On the other hand, some excellent cross-cultural programs exist, many of which involve all members of an employee's family (91, 106).

The third chapter deals with the problems of living and working abroad. Those working in foreign cultures (called expatriates) experience culture shock if unprepared, and have high early return and assignment failure rates. Cross-cultural training (157, 184) can reduce this failure rate (which is highest in American multinational firms).

While proper training and preparation are important issues, also of concern is how to select employees for foreign assignment. What are the personal and educational qualities needed for successful foreign posting? These qualities, usually defined as "factor X," are primarily psychological, such as a willingness to want to work abroad and a tolerance of ambiguity (179, 196, 211, 213, 287).

Expatriates face other problems. Compensation is a complex issue that is difficult to treat to all parties' satisfaction (165, 188, 212, 217). Another problem not generally recognized is related to reentry and return. Expatriates often find that they have been forgotten by their home country supervisors, and that the company no longer has a place for them when they return (153, 222, 225-6). After being away for several or more years, they find that they must rebuild their contacts and resume their place in the company's career ladder (244).

Other expatriates experience a decrease in their standard of living after returning from a foreign post. Living in a foreign country can be very pleasant for some. They enjoy the foreign life styles and tax advantages, and return can result in culture shock (214, 226, 279).

The fourth chapter deals with national negotiation differences. Each culture exhibits unique patterns of negotiation. The literature is dominated by John L. Graham and associates, who have conducted negotiation experiments throughout the world. They have found that bargaining strategies are highly culture-specific. The U.S. negotiating style is (322) aggressive, impersonal, and combative. By contrast, the Japanese negotiating style stresses cooperation, personal relations, and an avoidance of overt conflict (319, 332, 341, 365).

In recent years, Americans have found Chinese-style negotiation to be extremely difficult (353, 358, 364). The Asian style of negotiation in general is unfamiliar to foreigners, and behavior is often guided by unique cultural values. A number of works in this chapter detail how the negotiation process should be conducted with Japanese, Koreans, and Chinese.

The fifth chapter, "Multicultural Studies," contains many of the model publications in international business research. This chapter consists of studies which deal with three or more cultures or societies. The field is dominated by Geert Hofstede, who has developed a theoretical framework to compare behavior from one culture to another. Hofstede (420) studied work-related attitudes of employees working for the same corporation in forty different countries. He later added ten other national samples to his study. Some have extended his findings while others have criticized them.

Nevertheless, Hofstede's four dimensions of culture offers one of the few truly comparative theoretical frameworks in use today (445). There has been other (396, 404, 455, 461) excellent multi-cultural research, such as done by Haire and co-researchers (411), and those associated with the Aston Programme (430). The latter, however, published most of their works before 1980, and therefore fall outside our time range. In addition, an effort of the Aston Programme was to test the "bold hypothesis": that universal factors (especially size) influence organizational structural changes more than do cultural factors. The purpose of this collection, however, is to indicate the importance of cultural factors rather than the opposite.

In spite of research by Hofstede and his associates, most international research is atheoretical, or else does not build on earlier work. As a result, there is little cumulation of knowledge, and little truly comparative analysis. Roberts (476) evaluated pre-1970 cross-cultural research, and also found little cumulation of findings, weak sampling and methodology, and little theoretical and practical relevancy. These conclusions remain partly valid for research published during the 1980s.

While exceptions exist (479, 492) few researchers have utilized standardized theoretical frameworks or sampling procedures for truly global comparison. Most studies in the "Multicultural Studies" chapter deal with three or four national samples. Most use haphazard sampling and selection methods, and the findings are seldom comparative in terms of previous works. The field's great obstacles, such as translation problems and travel, have retarded the maturity of the field as a whole.

In spite of the above criticisms, the 1980s produced excellent research whose findings improved our knowledge of international business behavior. Poon et al., (472) contrast managerial policies of four national groups of multinationals (MNCs). Negandhi (461) studied related issues over a ten-year period using over 200 MCNs. The works of Harari, Gomez-Mejia, Keeley et al., Luthans, (406,

413, 439, 449) and many others are truly comparative and well-done.

The sixth chapter, "The Americas," deals with material from North and South America and from the Caribbean. Many citations discuss the Japanese influence, actual or potential, on U.S.-style management. Others offer advice to North Americans when doing business in Latin America.

The selections dealing with Latin America contain major omissions. Many of the best studies included in this bibliography were published before 1980 and it is obvious that researchers have neglected Latin America in favor of Japan and China, and recently Eastern Europe.

The selections dealing with U.S. topics indicate a certain loss of nerve in the face of a presumed superiority vis-a-vis Japanese-style management. This sense of inferiority is more pronounced in the "Japan" chapter. Nevertheless, there are a number of excellent selections on American national character (I am referring here to the United States for convenience. I realize that the term "America" properly includes Canada and Latin America).

The seventh chapter, "Europe," consists of publications dealing with Great Britain and Continental Europe, including what was formerly the U.S.S.R. Much of the research on Russian management behavior will remain valid for some time, since they emerge out of the Russian national character as much as from a Communist context.

The selections dealing with France and Britain tend to be pessimistic and generally include a sense of crisis. Commentators feel that managers in both countries are undergoing change, and that they are unprepared for future demands (641, 667, 711). European studies do properly point out that their expatriates are generally well-informed and prepared for working in foreign countries, but a sense of uncertainty permeates the literature.

There are nevertheless excellent organizational studies using material from European countries. There are surveys using carefully-matched samples comparing German and British factories and managers (675, 686-7, 701) or European and non-European managerial practices (636, 664, 670, 698, 699).

Chapter eight introduces studies using material from the Middle East and Africa. Many deal with the values of Saudi managers. Often, these are more analyses of Arab and Moslem national character than of business practices per se. Many studies are excellent in content.

Chapter nine, "Japan," is the largest. Studies of Japanese management techniques were in vogue during the

1980s and they remain popular.   While a large number of publications deal with whether Japanese-style management can be transferred to other cultural contexts, there are also excellent research reports on Japanese managerial and workers' activities.   Others are of lesser quality and are often simple restatements of previous publications.   There is a large number of analyses of national character (871, 908, 948, 978, 991, 999), societal features (883, 901, 904), and work behavior (909, 927, 1002).   The reader can note that there are in recent years more studies on Japanese employers working outside Japan (917, 1001).

This chapter also contains the largest number of "how-to" publications.   These deal with how to conduct business with the Japanese and in Japan.   These practical guides are often more journalistic than academic in style and content; yet they often offer valuable insights on Japanese national character and business protocols.   Many of these guides relate specific Japanese business behavior to their cultural origins and societal contexts.   Rather than just listing Japanese protocols, these publications explain why these practices exist.

Unfortunately, this search for cultural coherence is generally lacking when authors discuss U.S. business customs.   There is less introspection -- and therefore cogent analysis -- among those discussing U.S. customs, as if they exist in a cultural vacuum.   Readers therefore learn much more about Japanese culture and national character in chapter nine ("Japan") than they learn about U.S. cultural traits in chapter six ("The Americas").

Chapter ten, "China and Related Areas," deals with material from the People's Republic of China and other Chinese-influenced areas, such as Hong Kong, Taiwan, and Singapore.   The opening of China during the 1980s to foreign researchers and analysts produced a number of excellent studies of modern China's national character and business/management behavior and values.   Especially well-done are studies of pre- and post-Mao management and forms of organization (1080, 1092, 1115, 1180).

The West's business-related interest in China has resulted in a large number of recently-published guides on doing business in China.   The consensus of this "how-to" literature is that conducting business in China is extremely difficult, and that knowledge of Chinese culture and protocol is necessary to achieve commercial success.

The eleventh chapter deals with material from the remaining nations in the Pacific Rim, South East Asia, and India.   I have included Australian studies in this chapter as well.   The material on India and South Korea is plentiful, especially on the topics of managers' values and attitudes.   There is also emerging an impressive scholarship on Thailand and the Philippines.

Readers will find that there exist serious gaps in research and knowledge. Much research follows various fads; Korean material is on the rise and resembles in character the earlier studies and reports on Japan and China. Although excellent work is plentiful, there are nevertheless lacunae.   Latin American and African topics have generally been neglected. Often, recent international research is not comparative or cumulative enough.   Relatively few research endeavors are using previously published measurements and theoretical frameworks. The result is too much atheoretical research of uncertain quality, with too little accumulation of much dependable empirical and theoretical knowledge. Nevertheless, the 1,326 citations in this work include impeccable research and highly informative analyses of national character, culture, and national business behavior and protocols.   The field is achieving maturity, and the 1980-1991 period exhibits improvements in both the quality and the quantity of material on the cultural dimensions of international business.

The Social Dimensions
of International Business

1

Cross-Cultural Communication

0001   Allen, Gray (1990) "Every Market Needs a Different
        Message," <u>Communication World</u> 7 (April): 16-8.

Saatchi and Saatchi developed a series of award-winning
commercials for the Blue Diamond Growers. These ads cannot
be used in other countries, because different communication
campaigns are needed in each country.

0002   Aviel, David (1990) "Cultural Barriers to
        International Transactions," <u>Journal of General
        Management</u> 15 (Summer): 5-20.

Cultural insensitivity has been responsible for many cross-
cultural business failures. Each culture exhibits unique
motivational structures which often will not be effective in
other cultural settings. The author discusses the elements
of culture (status, time, space, priorities, etc.) and
analyzes a number of international blunders. An example is
packaging golfballs in groups of four for the Japanese
market, where four is considered an unlucky number.

0003   Barnlund, Dean C. and Miho Yoshioka (1990)
        "Apologies: Japanese and American Styles,"
        <u>International Journal of Intercultural
        Relations</u> 14 (2): 193-206.

Japanese and Americans differed in their manner of coping
with situations in which one person harmed another. The
Japanese preferred to apologize directly, used a wider range
of apologies, and reacted more to the status of the other
party. Americans also apologized directly but offered more
explanations to justify their acts. The apology styles of
each culture would not communicate adequate regret to the
other party.

0004   Barraclough, Robert A., Diane M. Christophel, and
        James C. McCroskey (1988) "Willingness to
        Communicate: A Cross-Cultural Investigation,"
        Communication Research Reports 5 (December): 187-92.

Australians and Americans differ in terms of willingness to
communicate. Australians were significantly less willing to
communicate irrespective of the setting, such as meetings,
dyads, with strangers or friends, etc.

0005   Barrett, John F. and Martha B. Sherwood (1988)
        "Enhancing Human Resource Role by Improving
        Communication," Journal of Compensation and
        Benefits 4 (July/August): 37-8.

U.S. human resource managers can improve employee
performance in six communication areas (rewards, planning,
etc.) by adopting selected Asian communication practices.

0006   Becker, Carl B. (1986) "Reasons for the Lack of
        Argumentation and Debate in the Far East,"
        International Journal of Intercultural Relations
        10 (1): 75-92.

Communicative and rhetorical styles differ from the East to
the West. East Asians avoid argumentation and find its use
distasteful. The structure of the Chinese language makes
concrete, logical references difficult while it encourages
ambiguity. There are social reasons why Asian discussion
styles are unique, including the values of person-
centeredness and stress on interpersonal harmony. The
Western understanding of Pacific Rim communicative styles
demands a sensitivity to Asian speech patterns.

0007   Berger, Michael (1987) "Building Bridges over the
        Cultural Rivers," International Management 42
        (July/August): 61-2.

A major problem in cross-cultural settings is non-
communication. Inter-cultural training programs help reduce
business failures due to communicative failures and early
return of expatriates.

0008   Berrington, Robin A. (1985) "Bridging the Gap:
        International Communication Problems," Speaking of
        Japan 5 (Feb.): 23-7.

There are four basic problems in communication. Japanese-
U.S. communication is beset by cultural misunderstandings.
Japanese and English are both extremely difficult languages.
Different styles in non-verbal communication also cause
misinterpretation, including gestures and different
definitions of personal space.

0009   Brabant, Sarah, C. Eddie Palmer, and Robert Grambling
        (1990) "Returning Home: An Empirical Investigation
        of Cross-Cultural Reentry," International Journal
        of Intercultural Relations 14 (4): 387-404.

Culture shock for returning expatriates may not be as great
a problem as some authors have indicated. Return is more
problematic for females than males. The sample was based on
96 international university students. Intermittent home
visits reduced "returning shock."

0010   Chorafas, Dimitris (1969) The Communication Barrier
        in International Management (AMA Research Study 100).
        New York: American Management Association, Inc.

This report is based on 143 interviews in 17 countries
dealing with the errors U.S. business personnel make when
dealing with foreigners. Multinational firms tend to over-
manage their foreign subsidiaries and insist on procedures
not suited to their foreign cultural context. The work
contains illustrations of typical communicators and
communication channels, as well as causes of communication
problems. One chapter gives examples on how U.S. enterprises
structure their international communications. Though dated,
the material is practical and remains useful.

0011   Cline, Rebecca J. and Carol A. Puhl (1984) "Gender,
        Culture and Geography: A Comparison of Seating
        Arrangements in the United States and Taiwan,"
        International Journal of Intercultural Relations
        8 (2): 199-219.

The use of space varies from culture to culture and is based
on cultural values and messages a person wishes to give off.
Taiwanese and U.S. respondents indicated different preferred
seating arrangements. The Taiwanese preferred side-by-side
seating. Seating separated same-sex American respondents but
not for the Taiwanese sample. The Taiwanese seating
preferences reflected a greater value for harmony and non-
aggressivenes.

0012   Cohen, Raymond (1987) "Problems of Intercultural
        Communications in Egyptian Diplomatic Relations,"
        International Journal of Intercultural Relations
        11 (1): 29-48.

Intercultural factors are crucial in cross-cultural
communication. Languages are divided into high/low contexts
and communicative styles (directedness vs. indirectedness,
exaggeration vs. understatement, etc.). These dimensions
complicate understanding cross-cultural messages.

0013   Coveney, John and Julian Amey (1978) <u>Glossary of</u>
         <u>Spanish and English Management Terms</u>. London: Longman
         Group Limited.

This pocket-sized (137 pages) work contains English-to-
Spanish and the reverse business terms drawn from all
aspects of business (management, finance, personnel. etc.).

0014   Coveney, James and Christina Degens (1977) <u>Glossary</u>
         <u>of German and English Management Terms</u>. London:
         Longman Group Limited.

Business terms are listed in German-to-English format and
the reverse in a pocket-sized (160 pages) booklet.

0015   Cramer, Bernice A. (1990) "Developing Competitive
         Skills: How American Businesspeople Learn
         Japanese," <u>The Annals of the American Academy of</u>
         <u>Political and Social Science</u> 511 (September): 85-96.

American businesspeople in Japan find that learning the
Japanese language while employed full-time is difficult and
is regarded negatively by those at the home office (for
"going native"). Extended foreign tours harm corporate
career paths. Knowledge of Japanese is seldom appreciated in
U.S. companies and is more encouraged by Japanese-owned
firms located in the U.S.

0016   Dean, Ozzie and Gary L. Popp (1990) "Intercultural
         Communication Effectiveness as Perceived by American
         Managers in Saudi Arabia and French Managers in the
         U.S.," <u>International Journal of Intercultural</u>
         <u>Relations</u> 14 (4): 405-24.

Respondents selected and ranked five abilities that
facilitate intercultural interactions. The U.S. Managers'
rankings (in descending order) are: ability to work with
other people, ability to deal with unfamiliar situations,
ability to handle stress, ability to communicate, and
ability to change life styles. For French managers, the
rankings were: ability to deal with unfamiliar situations,
ability to deal with changes in life styles, ability to
enter meaningful dialogues with others, ability to work with
other people, and having communication skills.

0017   Diggs, Nancy (1991) "Japanese Adjustment to American
         Communities: The Case of the Japanese in the Dayton
         Area," <u>International Journal of Intercultural</u>
         <u>Relations</u> 15 (1): 103-16.

A survey of 66 Japanese in Dayton, Ohio indicated that
language, social and school adjustments and transportation
(due to the women's inability to drive) were the major
sources of perceived problems with living in the United
States. Most (83%) were satisfied with their American
experiences. Positive aspects were the slower pace of life,
friendliness, and a spacious environment.

0018   Dodd, Carley H. (1987) <u>Dynamics of Intercultural</u>
        <u>Communication</u> (second edition). Dubuque, Iowa:
        William C. Brown Publishers.

The author places intercultural communication patterns
within a number of theoretical approaches, defines the major
concepts in the discipline, and offers pragmatic advice to
increase intercultural effectiveness. There is a good
sensitizing overview of the field, and a large bibliography.

0019   Dulek, Ronald E., John S. Fielden and John S. Hill
        (1991) "International Communication: An Executive
        Primer," <u>Business Horizons</u> 34 (Jan/Feb): 20-5.

U.S. businesspersons have the lowest foreign language
proficiency of any major trading nation in the world. There
are some generalizations that can be made concerning
international communications. Countries can be divided
according to their placement on a high-context and low-
context continuum. Placement on this continuum gives hints
how conversations and messages should be presented. The U.S.
"business English" is inappropriate when communicating with
many foreigners.

0020   Dupecher, Martha (1990) "Wait a Minute...Do
        These People Speak English?" <u>Communication World</u>
        7 (August): 24-7.

Using a capable interpreter is necessary when Americans
conduct business abroad. The current rate for freelance
conference interpreters is roughly $375 a day. The author
offers five strategies to use one's interpreter effectively.

0021   Eure, Jack D., Jr. (1976) "Applicability of American
        Written Business Communication Principles Across
        Cultural Boundaries in Mexico," <u>The Journal of</u>
        <u>Business Communication</u> 14 (Fall): 51-64.

A sample of Mexican college students evaluated some business
letters written using American principles of communication
and some letters that did not. The letters written using
established U.S. principles were more positively evaluated.
The findings suggest that "correct" U.S.-style business
communications have universal applications.

0022   Fixman, Carol S. (1990) "The Foreign Language Needs of
        U.S.-Based Corporations," <u>The Annals of the American</u>
        <u>Political and Social Science</u> 511 (September): 25-46.

32 interviews conducted in nine companies indicated that
while cross-cultural understanding was viewed as important
for doing business on a global basis, foreign language
skills were rarely considered as significant. Language
problems were seen as easily solved through the use of
foreign nationals, interpreters, or translators. Smaller
companies were more sensitive to the value of foreign
language skills than larger firms.

0023   Forrest, Anne B. (1988) "The Continental Divide:
        Coping with Cultural Gaps," Communication World
        5 (June): 20-3.

Cross-cultural communications in Hong Kong are made
difficult because, although English is the major business
language, speakers from China, the U.S., England, Hong Kong,
and China often misunderstand each other. Consultants who
recognize these communication problems are needed in Hong
Kong.

0024   Frymier, Ann Bainbridge, Donald W. Klopf, and
        Satoshi Ishii (1990) "Affect Orientation: Japanese
        Compared to Americans," Communication Research
        Reports 7 (June): 63-6.

364 Japanese and American students completed the Affect
Orientation Scale, which measures the propensity to use
affect as information. Affect message content includes
emotional appeals rather than logical, factual reasoning.
American males scored higher in affect than Japanese males;
U.S. females scored higher than U.S. males.

0025   Glenn, Edmund S. and Christine G. Glenn (1981)
        Man and Mankind: Conflict and Communication
        Between Cultures. Norwood, NJ: Ablex Publishing
        Company.

Members in each culture collect and organize information in
unique ways, based in part on their social and geographic
environments. The authors stress the cognitive processes of
gathering information. This allows for the development of a
communication model from which one can make predictions on
how people will behave in new situations. The book contains
chapters that deal with classifying cultures, cognitive
pathology, and political and social movement analyses.

0026   Gould, John W., P. Thomas McGuire and Chan Tsang Sing
        (1983) "Adequacy of Hong Kong-California Business
        Communication Methods," The Journal of Business
        Communication 20 (Winter): 33-40.

Interviews with 43 managers in Hong Kong and California
indicate the most common channels of international business
communication and the advantages/disadvantages of each. The
telex method is most commonly used, but users tend to
develop a telegraphic style which leads to ambiguity and
incompletely understood messages. The authors indicate how
to avoid the disadvantages of each trans-Pacific method
used.

0027   Gudykunst, William B., G.E. Gao, Tsukasa Nishida,
        Michael H. Bond, Kwok Leung, Georgette Wand, and
        Robert A. Barraclough (1989) "A Cross-Cultural
        Comparison of Self-Monitoring," Communication
        Research Report 6 (June): 9-14.

Self-monitoring persons are those who are sensitive to the
expressions and self-presentation of others and use verbal
and non-verbal cues as guidelines for changing their own
behavior to suit the other persons. One theory predicts that
self-monitoring behavior is more likely in individualistic
than in collectivistic cultures. Samples from the U.S. and
Australia (which are individualistic cultures) and from
Japan, Hong Kong, and Taiwan (collectivistic cultures)
supported this theoretical model.

0028   Gudykunst, William B., Lori L. Sodetani, and
        Kevin T. Sonoda (1987) "Uncertainty Reduction
        in Japanese-American/Caucasian Relationships in
        Hawaii," Western Journal of Speech Communication
        53 (Summer): 256-78.

Caucasians are more assertive and verbally expressive than
Japanese Americans. Japanese and Americans exhibit different
types of communication and verbal reactions to strangers.

0029   Gudykunst, William B. and Young Yun Kim (1984)
        Communicating with Strangers: An Approach to
        Intercultural Communication. Reading, Mass.:
        Addison-Wesley Publishing Company.

The authors of this textbook present a model of
intercultural communication using a feedback system with
cultural, sociocultural and psychocultural dimensions.
Intercultural communication involves universalities of
communication in general. Communications with strangers and
sub-cultural and other culture members are all part of the
same phenomenon. The ability to communicate interculturally
involves sensitivity, knowledge of other cultures, and
personal growth. The 34-page bibliography is complete and
inter-disciplinary.

0030   Halpern, Jeanne W. (1983) "Business Communication in
        China: A Second Perspective," The Journal of Business
        Communication 20 (Fall): 43-55.

Continuing the account of business communication in China by
Zong and Hildebrandt (0076), Halpern suggests that those
communicating with Chinese need to better understand the
political and educational contexts of Chinese business
personnel.

0031   Haneda, Saburo and Hirosuke Shima (1982) "Japanese
        Communication Behavior as Reflected in Letter
        Writing," The Journal of Business Communication
        19 (Winter): 19-32.

Business communications entail a variety of purposes. Yet
Japanese writers maintain a "Japanese" style throughout. The
authors present five examples of translated business
letters, each of which denotes a different mood or purpose
(a humble attitude, a traditional style, a direct style,
indirectedness, and a successful sales letter).

0032   Haworth, Dwight A. and Grant T. Savage (1989) "A
        Channel-Ratio Model of Intercultural Communication:
        The Trains won't Sell, Fix Them Please," Journal of
        Business Communication 26 (Summer): 231-54.

A method is proposed that measures the ratio of implicit and
explicit information in a message. The resulting high/low
context measure can be used in cross-cultural communication.
The method can help prepare businesspersons for intercultural interaction.

0033   Hawkins, Steve (1983) "How to Understand Your
        Partner's Cultural Baggage," International
        Management 38 (September): 48-51.

The article presents a list of cultural errors in etiquette
and protocol throughout the world, based partly on an
interview with Robert T. Moran. Scratching one's head
indicates anger in Japan. Westerners are obsessed with time
schedules. Africans, Arabs, and Latin Americans view time
differently, nor do they view "being on time" in the same
way as Europeans and North Americans.

0034   Held, Jeff (1989) "A Manager's Perspective on
        International Communications: No More Ugly
        Americans," Network World 5 (September): 33-8.

U.S. managers need to be aware of the different economic and
social customs in other countries. Pricing policies vary by
nation. There is a slower pace of doing business in Europe.

0035   Hildebrandt, Herbert W. (1975) "Cultural
        Communication Problems of Foreign Business
        Personnel in the United States," The Journal of
        Business Communication 13 (Fall): 13-24.

German expatriate workers and wives living in the U.S. are
more highly technically than culturally competent, resulting
in verbal and non-verbal communication problems with
Americans. The Germans were ambivalent about American
informality, found authority divisions ambiguous, and felt
that too many Americans were monolingual.

0036   Hildebrandt, Herbert W. (1978) "Business
         Communication Consulting and Research in
         Multinational Companies," The Journal of
         Business Communication 15 (Spring): 19-26.

Communication problems are more complex in cross-cultural
settings because parties may hold different views on home-
work separation, use of time, use of titles, and written
communications.

0037   Hilderbrandt, Herbert W. (1990) "Ethnographic
         Variables Affecting Concepts of Chinese Business
         Communication," World Communication 19 (Spring):
         21-6.

1005 managers in the People's Republic of China indicated
that communication skills had little significance in
advancing their careers, in contrast to the beliefs of U.S.
and other Asian respondents. The reasons for denying the
importance of communication skills include the existence of
"democratic centralism," in which the minority accepts the
majority's views, the importance of interpersonal influence,
and the peculiar structure of the economy.

0038   Hofmann, Mark A. (1988) "Loss Control can be Lost
         in Translation," Business Insurance 22 (November):
         11-2.

Insurance coverage and claims are different in foreign
countries. Insurance activities defined as normal in the
U.S. may be defined in foreign countries as against national
compensation practices or even contrary to local religious
beliefs. Language translation problems will increase
misunderstandings.

0039   Johnson, Jean (1980) "Business Communication in
         Japan," The Journal of Business Communication 17
         (Spring): 65-70.

The Japanese language is ambiguous compared to English.
Japanese speakers prefer to suggest or hint rather than be
direct. Business communications in Japan begin with set
phrases for greetings (usually including a reference to the
season) in order to not seem rude or abrupt. Bad news and
demands are couched indirectly.

0040   Kale, Sudhir H. (1991) "Culture-Specific
         Marketing Communications: An Analytic Approach,"
         International Marketing Review 8 (2): 18-30

The author presents a general framework to assess the
effectiveness of cross-cultural communication, using tourism
(India's attraction to Americans) as a test. The concepts
are based on Hofstede's work on the four dimensions of
culture. The persons' positions on the dimensions of the
cultures of the buyer and seller should match in order to
avoid cross-cultural communication barriers.

0041   Kedia, Ben L. and Rabi S. Bhagat (1988) "Cultural
        Constraints on Transfer of Technology Across Nations:
        Implications for Research in International and
        Comparative Management," The Academy of Management
        Review 13 (October): 559-71.

The authors present a conceptual model for the understanding
of the cultural constraints on the transfer of technology
and managerial knowledge from the U.S. to other countries,
based in part on Hofstede's four dimensions of culture.
Major "paths" are (1) between developed nations, (2) between
industrialized to moderately industrialized nations, and (3)
from industrialized to developing economies.

0042   Keen, Peter G.W. (1990) "Sorry, Wrong Number,"
        Business Month 135 (January): 62-7.

Many American managers do not know enough about global
communications technology to be able to successfully compete
internationally. European managers feel U.S. managers are
ignorant and naive in terms of communications. The best way
to become global is to be assigned to several areas of the
world.

0043   Keen, Peter G.W. and David S. Hooper editors (1972)
        Readings in Intercultural Communication volumes 1
        and 2. Pittsburgh, PA: Regional Council for
        International Education.

These works contain five articles on the theory of culture
conflict   and   culture   shock,   four   perspectives   on
intercultural   communications   workshop   programs,   and
seventeen course syllabi on intercultural communications.
The publication is a definitive statement on the field of
intercultural communication and training for the pre-1970
era. The volumes are available through the ERIC Document
Reproduction Service.

0044   Kilpatrick, Retha H. (1984) "International Business
        Communication Practices," The Journal of Business
        Communication 21 (Fall): 33-44.

A survey of 66 U.S. corporations indicated that Spanish,
French, German, and Japanese were the most commonly used
languages   in   letters   received   from   foreign   countries.
Letters received tended to vary in style from those letters
sent by Americans to overseas business associates. Letters
by foreigners used exaggerated courtesy and compliments.
American letter style stressed the use of the personal tone
(use of personal pronoun). Students need to be aware of
different writing styles in foreign countries.

0045   Klopf, Donald W. (1991) "Japanese Communication
        Practices: Recent Comparative Research,"
        Communication Quarterly 39 (Spring): 130-43.

The findings from seven comparative studies, and other
reports, of Japanese and American speech patterns indicate
major national differences. The Japanese are less inclined
to argue or rely on emotional appeals, feel more lonely in
relational situations, and are less assertive. The Americans
feel more comfortable than Japanese when talking to
strangers and they talk more in general. The four-page
bibliography is definitive.

0046   Knotts, Rose (1989) "Cross-Cultural
        Management: Transformations and Adaptations,"
        Business Horizons 32 (Jan/Feb): 29-33.

Successes in international business environments demand a
knowledge of local communication patterns. Each culture
differs in terms of its definitions of religion, family
relationships, and worker-to-worker relationships.

0047   Kobayashi, Yasuhiko (1980) "Differences in
        Advertising Between the U.S. and Japan: A Cultural
        Point of View," The Journal of Business Communication
        17 (Winter): 23-31.

The deep cultural differences separating Japan and the U.S.
include communicating ideas in advertising messages.
Comparative advertising is not allowed in Japan because of
that culture's negative view of direct competition. American
advertisements focus more on regional themes while Japanese
audiences are more eager to learn about their society's
center, Tokyo.

0048   Koike, Hiroko, William B. Gudykunst, Lea P. Stewart,
        Stella Ting-Toomey, and Tsukasa Nishida (1988)
        "Communication Openness, Satisfaction, and Length of
        Employment in Japanese Organizations," Communication
        Research Reports 5 (December): 97-102.

Japanese working in organizations located in the Tokyo area
indicated that upward, downward, and lateral communication
were positively associated with both relational and
organizational satisfaction. Those who had been with the
same employer longer exhibited more communication openness,
though this relationship was moderated by size of firms.

0049   Lambert, Richard D. (1990) "Foreign Language Use
        Among International Business Students," The
        Annals of the American Academy of Political and
        Social Science 511 (September): 47-59.

A report on 600 graduates of three of the best-known
international business programs indicates that foreign
language skills are underutilized and relatively
unappreciated in U.S. corporations. Fourteen percent of

those being sent abroad received extra pay for foreign language competence. The respondents felt language skills were important in their work, but only 48% of those in foreign posts said such skills were significant factors in promotion.

0050   Limaye, Mohan R. and David A. Victor (1991)
        "Cross-CulturalBusiness Communication Research:
        State of the Art and Hypotheses for the 1990s,"
        The Journal of Business Communication 28 (Summer):
        277-99.

Employers increasingly need cross-cultural communication skills and knowledge. However, the traditional paradigm of intercultural communication--that communication styles and management contain universals--is inadequate. The authors criticize existing research (usually based on anecdotal information) and offer a series of hypotheses based on an awareness of cultural variations. There is an excellent bibliography.

0051   Maddox, Robert C. and Douglas Short (1988)
        "The Cultural Integrator," Business
        Horizons 31 (Nov/Dec): 57-9.

All societies have unique business practices and business-related behavior patterns. Multinational corporations can facilitate successful international dealings is by establishing in each country a "cultural integrator." This person is familiar with the customs of home and host countries and can guide other personnel and family members toward better cross-cultural communication.

0052   Masterson, John T., Norman H. Watson, and Elaine
        J. Cichion (1991) "Cultural Differences in
        Public Speaking," World Communication 20
        (July): 39-47.

344 students from different nations or regions (North America, Latin America, Bahamas) indicated different cultural expectations in terms of public speaking. N.A. Anglos perceived speakers as less credible than did Bahamians in terms of trustworthiness, competence, and objectivity.

0053   Marshall, Terry (1990) The Whole World Guide to
        Language Learning. Yarmouth, Maine: Intercultural
        Press, Inc.

Written for adults living in foreign countries, this work offers advice on how to develop a "survival" knowledge level of a foreign language. Techniques discussed include working with a mentor and beginning with problems faced in daily life.

0054   Nomura, Naoki and Dean Barnlund (1983) "Patterns of
        Interpersonal Criticisms in Japan and the United
        States," International Journal of Intercultural
        Relations 7 (1): 1-18.

Japanese and U.S. college students were administered an
Interpersonal Criticism Questionnaire. The Japanese employed
passive forms of criticism by using third persons or
criticizing ambiguously or humorously. The status of the
other person was a significant variable. Americans chose
more active forms of criticism by being more overtly angry,
more direct, or by making constructive suggestions.

0055   Oches, Norman (1989) "Cross-Cultural Presentations-
        How to Make Them More Effective," Sales and
        Marketing Management 141 (September): 84-4.

Cross-cultural presentations demand unique communication
skills. Useful techniques include speaking slowly,
repetition, and restating a question when confusion exists.
Cultural areas have their own communicative characteristics.

0056   Pascale, Richard Tanner (1973) "Communication and
        Decision-Making Across Cultures: Japanese and
        American Comparisons," Administrative Science
        Quarterly 23 (March): 91-110.

There are great similarities in communication and decision-
making styles in Japanese and American firms. The forms,
volumes, and styles of communication were similar. Japanese
and U.S. managers were equally likely to use a consultative
decision-making process.

0057   Prosser, Michael H. editor (1973)
        Intercommunication Among Nations and People.
        New York: Harper and Row, Publishers.

Beginning with articles on the theories of cross-cultural
communication and political rhetoric, this collection
includes specific case studies of national communication
styles (the Islamic sermon form and communication in Indian
villages and Latin America). There are also sections on
propaganda and censorship.

0058   Prosser, Michael H. (1978) The Cultural Dialogue:
        An Introduction to Intercultural Communication.
        Boston: Houghton Mifflin.

Communication and culture are tightly inter-linked and are
in turn related to social conflict, stability and control.
This work presents the basic elements of communication
theory from the intercultural and linguistic viewpoints.
There are detailed comparisons between U.S.-Philippino and
U.S.-Japan national characters and communicative patterns.
The twenty-seven page reference section contains classic
citations on language, communication, semantics and national
character.

0059   Prunty, Allicia M., Donald W. Klopf, and
        Satoshi Ishii (1990) "Argumentativenes:
        Japanese and American Tendencies to Approach
        and Avoid Conflict," Communication Research
        Reports 7 (June): 75-9.

Japanese are found to be less willing to argue than North
American university students. The former are weaker in
argumentative skills. These differences cause cross-cultural
communication problems between the two nationalities.

0060   Rosch, Martin and Kay G. Segler (1987) "Communication
        with Japanese," Management International Review 27
        (4): 56-67.

Success in the Japanese market depends on knowing specific
Japanese communicative styles and understanding Japanese
culture. Successful joint ventures with Japanese partners
demand knowledge of Japanese communication patterns, such as
understanding the non-verbal context of a message, proper
social relations, and how the Japanese view time.

0061   Ruch, William V. (1989) International Handbook of
        Corporate Communication. Jefferson, NC: McFarland
        & Company, Inc.

The work contains a comprehensive and impressive survey of
non-socialist countries in terms of geography, economic
facts, ethnic diversity, language, etc. For most countries,
there are summaries of personal communication styles
(gestures, facial expressions, eye contacts) and corporate
communication channels (upward, downward, and horizontal).
There are tips on business protocol (business cards) and
cultural patterns (use of time, context of language, shaking
hands). There are case studies of corporate communication
patterns for selected countries.

0062   Ruhly, Sharon (1976) Orientations to Intercultural
        Communication. Chicago: Science Research Associates,
        Inc.

After a general introduction on the concepts of culture, the
nature of communication, ethnocentrism, and prejudice, this
work presents a large number of examples of intercultural
communication problems--usually in a humorous manner--to
illustrate the basic elements of verbal and non-verbal
cross-cultural communication. Each section contains a series
of exercises to sensitize students to intercultural
communication problems.

0063   Samovar, Larry A. and Richard E. Porter editors
        (1988) <u>Intercultural Communication: A Reader</u>
        Fifth Edition. Belmont, CA: Wadsworth Publishing
        Company.

This collection deals with the social and psychological
factors of intercultural communication. The topics covered
include verbal and non-verbal communication patterns in the
U.S, Saudi Arabia, Mexico, China, and Japan. There are
presentations   on   international   negotiation   styles,
prejudice, and face-to-face communication differences from
one culture to another.

0064   Samovar, Larry A., Richard E. Porter, and
        Nemi C. Jain (1981) <u>Understanding Intercultural</u>
        <u>Communication</u>. Belmont, CA: Wadsworth
        Publishing Company.

Intercultural communication necessitates cultural self-
awareness as well as knowledge of other cultures in all of
their diversity. This textbook discusses the nature of
culture and its dimensions (time, definitions of human
nature, activity orientation, etc.). The emphasis throughout
is placed on the characteristics of multi-cultural forms of
communication. Each chapter contains a list of additional
readings and relevant exercises to develop inter-cultural
communication skills and sensitivity.

0065   Sarbaugh, L.E. (1979) <u>Intercultural Communication</u>.
        Rochelle Park, NJ: Hayden Book Company, Inc.

Intercultural communication involves participants that are
culturally heterogeneous. This lack of cultural overlap can
be overcome through an awareness of cultural differences.
Though guided by theoretical principles, this work contains
examples of communication problems from different cultures.
The discussions are more theoretical than concrete.

0066   Sitaram, K.S. and Roy T. Cogdell (1976)
        <u>Foundations of Intercultural Communication</u>.
        Columbus, Ohio: C.E. Merrill Publishing Co.

There is a general introduction of the field of
intercultural communication using fundamental principles and
concepts. Several chapters deal with verbal styles, non-
verbal communication, the relationships between speaker and
audience, word order, and retention of information.

0067   Skapinker, Michael (1986) "Why Speaking English is
        No Longer Enough," <u>International Management</u> 41
        (November): 39-42.

Learning a client's or business associate's language offers
a person a competitive edge, reduces a dangerous reliance on
interpreters, and allows for better communication/relations
with staff. Speaking the local language may be a necessity

(as in France) and indicates a willingness to understand and respect the local culture.

0068   Stewart, Edward C.P. (1986) "Western Dreams and
        Japanese Decisions: The Cross-Cultural Communication
        Gap," Speaking of Japan 7 (April): 14-21.

A major source of misunderstanding between Japan and the U.S. originates in each country's different communication and decision-making styles. Japanese culture emphasizes harmony, cooperation, and group consensus.

0069   Stull, James B. (1986) "Demonstrating Empathy for
        Foreign-Born Employees Through Openness and
        Acceptance: A Quasi-Experimental Field Study,"
        The Journal of Business Communication 23 (Spring):
        31-40.

Foreign-born employees respond to openness in communication by perceiving such messages as positive responses to their own openness. These employees also responded more favorably to statements showing a commitment to action.

0070   Sullivan, Jeremiah and Naoki Kameda (1982) "The
        Concept of Profit and Japanese-American Business
        Communication," The Journal of Business Communication
        19 (Winter): 33-39.

Communication problems exist between Americans and Japanese when business issues are involved. One problem is that each culture defines certain concepts differently. The Japanese define the term "profit" as related primarily to rewards to businessmen for taking risks to produce innovations needed by society. Americans define "profit" multidimensionally. Responses were based on a sample of 278 Japanese and American business students in Tokyo and Seattle.

0071   Sullivan, Jerry, Naoki Kameda, and Tatsuo Nobu (1991)
        "Bypassing in Managerial Communication," Business
        Horizons 34 (Jan/Feb): 71-90.

"Bypassing" occurs when participants define the same words differently. This happens often during cross-cultural encounters. Often, people do not know bypassing is occurring because communication is more difficult than is realized. The authors provide a list of words that are vague or easily misunderstood in cross-cultural communication, such as could, should, normal, and help.

0072   Tung, Rosalie L. (1990) "Language Training and
        Beyond: The Case of Japanese Multinationals,"
        The Annals of the American Academy of Political
        and Social Science 511 (September): 97-108.

A review of cross-cultural programs in 18 Japanese multinationals illustrates one reason for Japanese global economic success. Japanese firms expend more effort and resources on human development than U.S. firms. Japanese programs include extensive language training, field experience, education abroad, and in-house training.

0073   Varner, Iris I. (1988) "A Comparison of American and French Business Correspondence," The Journal of Business Communication 25 (Fall): 55-65.

French letters tend to be more formal than American letters. The French discuss price more openly and present negative news without qualification. The format of letters is different in each country. The French use conditional and subjunctive tenses, which allows them to be more polite and more ambiguous.

0074   Weissman, Diane and Adrian Furnham (1987) "The Expectations and Experiences of a Sojourning Temporary Resident Abroad: A Preliminary Study," Human Relations 40 (5): 313-26.

Nearly 60 Americans were interviewed at the beginning and end of their stay in England, some staying six months. The mental health of these expatriates was heavily influenced by their expectations and their levels of confidence in being able to avoid culture shock. The authors conclude by suggesting how future expatriates can avoid culture shock and negative evaluations of their host countries.

0075   Wolniansky, Natasha (1989) "We Do (Do Not) Accept Your Offer," Management Review 78 (December): 54-5.

Ignorance of foreign languages results in lost sales and opportunities. In addition, American businesspersons abroad do not respect translators, nor understand how to use them effectively. The author offers guidelines and provides the address of the Translation Services Directory, which lists competent translators. This directory is published by the American Translator's Association.

0076   Zong, Baolin and H.W. Hildebrandt (1983) "Business Communication in the People's Republic of China," The Journal of Business Communication 20 (Winter): 25-32.

The Beijing Institute of Foreign Trade requires students to take three courses in foreign business communication. The courses focus on practical knowledge of protocol, business phrases, and terms rather than theories of communication. Translation techniques are presented to the students, resulting in a very concrete and practical training.

2

Cross-Cultural Training

0077   AlRomaithy, Abdulhamied (1981) "Take the ACHE out of
      International Training," <u>Training</u> 18 (June): 34-37.

International assignments demand comprehensive preparations
training. Expatriate failures can be reduced through an ACHE
program: Area, Culture, Humanism and Expertise. This program
prepares future expatriates by exposing them to general
information about host cultures.

0078   Ballard, Lynne and Brian H. Kleiner (1988)
      "Understanding and Managing Foreign-Born and Minority
      Employees," <u>Leadership & Organization Development
      Journal</u> 9 (4): 22-4.

During 1987, American firms brought approximately 85,000
foreign personnel for training in American-style management.
American managers must learn foreign workways or else they
will misunderstand many of their foreign workers. Cross-
cultural misunderstandings include ignoring differences in
levels of individualism and uncertainty avoidance, and
differences in languages. Training programs should be
tailored to the cultural backgrounds of the trainees.

0079   Berger, Michael (1987) "Building Bridges over
      Cultural Rivers," <u>International Management</u> 42
      (July/August): 61-2.

Cross-cultural training in communication includes learning
how to listen, interrupt, how to praise, and how to scold.
Such techniques are more important than learning a language.
European firms have lagged behind the U.S. in terms of
providing intercultural training.

0080   Bird, Allan and May Mukuda (1989) "Expatriates
        in Their Own Home: A New Twist in the
        Human Resource Management Strategies of Japanese
        MNCs," Human Resource Management 28 (Winter):
        437-53.

The authors present the advantages and disadvantages to
Japanese firms located in foreign countries in hiring host
nationals as managers. One policy is hiring foreigners,
retaining them in Japan for three or four years, then
assigning them back to their own countries as "expatriates."
The article compares traditional and new staffing approaches
of U.S.-European and Japanese multinationals.

0081   Black, J. Stewart and Mark Mendenhall (1989)
        "A Practical but Theory-Based Framework for
        Selecting Cross-Cultural Training Methods,"
        Human Resource Management 28 (Winter): 511-39.

The authors present a framework for cross-cultural training.
The dimensions of this training program include degree of
interaction expected with host nationals, degree of job, and
cultural novelty expected, and the degree of training rigor
or amount of effort wanted. Two case studies are used as
illustrations.

0082   Black, J. Stewart and Mark Mendenhall
        (1990) "Cross Cultural Training Effectiveness:
        A Review and a Theoretical Framework for Future
        Research," The Academy of Management Review 15
        (January): 113-36.

The authors evaluate the literature on cross-cultural
training since U.S. managers and expatriates are so poor in
cross-cultural contacts. Cross-cultural training programs
are in fact effective. The article ends with a model based
on learning theory. One useful technique used in cross-
cultural training programs is for participants to assume
national identities.

0083   Black, J. Stewart, Mark Mendenhall, and Gary
        Oddou (1991) "Toward a Comprehensive Model of
        International Adjustment: An Integration of Multiple
        Theoretical Perspectives," Academy of Management
        Review 16 (April): 291-317.

The authors review the literature on adjustment during
foreign assignments on the part of expatriates. They then
develop a theoretical framework to integrate theory with
empirical work, a union that has been lacking. The authors
also point out the gaps in research on cross-cultural
training needs.

0084   Black, J. Stewart and Lyman W. Porter (1991)
        "Managerial Behaviors and Job Performance: A
        Successful Manager in Los Angeles May Not Succeed
        in Hong Kong," Journal of International Business
        Studies 22 (1): 99-113.

This study compares the self-reported behavior of American
expatriate managers in Hong Kong to samples of U.S. managers
working in the U.S. and Chinese managers in Hong Kong. The
expatriate managers behaved in a very similar fashion to
managers in the U.S. These patterns of management were not
as effective in Hong Kong as in the U.S. This paper tests
the propositions that (1) U.S. managerial practices can be
exported when Americans work abroad (and hence need no pre-
assignment training) versus (2) the effectiveness of a
managerial practice is dependent on adapting it to its local
cultural context. The second model is supported.

0085   Bolt, James F. (1988) "Global Competition: Some
        Criteria for Success," Business Horizons 31
        (Jan/Feb): 34-41.

A review of companies that have achieved multinational
successes indicates a number of common features. These
features include acting from a multinational perspective,
having managers who are comfortable with world-wide
activities, interest in local political changes, and having
an international management team.

0086   Brewster, C.J. (1980) "IR Training for Expatriate
        Managers: Part 1," Human Resource Development 4
        (6): 7-10.

Training for foreign assignments generally assumes a British
manager will go abroad. There is also a need to train
expatriates who work in the United Kingdom. Foreigners from
cultures radically different from the UK culture (China,
Japan, Arabia) need to be trained in British customs in
order to "fit in." Expatriates from former colonies also
exhibit special needs.

0087   Brewster, C.J. (1980) "IR Training for Expatriates
        Managers: Part 2," Human Resource Development 4
        (7): 2-5.

Problems faced by expatriate managers living in the United
Kingdom include not understanding the roles that the
government and labor unions have in relation to business and
the roles of managers within a British cultural context.
Each problem area demands unique training approaches, based
on the national origins of the participants.

0088   Carson, William M. (1989) "Prepare Them to Thrive
        in Foreign Countries," Journal of Management
        Consulting 5 (4): 30-2.

Preparing an employee for foreign assignment often demands
the use of a consultant. Pre-departure training includes (1)
giving employee and spouse information about terms of
employment, (2) concise information about the host country,
and (3) building an overseas self-help group among a
company's expatriates.

0089   Casse, Pierre (1982) Training for the
        Multicultural Manager. Wash., D.C.: The
        Society for Intercultural Education,
        Training and Research.

Intercultural sensitivity is best developed through role
playing, self-assessment exercises, and group interaction.
This work offers a series of exercises, divided into five
workshops, to sensitize participants for cross-cultural
interaction.

0090   Chorafas, Dimitris N. (1967) Developing the
        International Executive. New York: American
        Management Association.

Based on a survey of more than 200 executives throughout the
world, the author discusses international managerial
development practices, how to select the best person for a
foreign post, and managerial roles in an international
context. There is a focus on executive training in three
European countries and in the U.S. The findings are still
valid.

0091   Cleveland, Harlan and Gerard J. Mangone
        editors (1957) The Art of Overseasmanship:
        Americans at Work Abroad. Syracuse, New York:
        Syracuse University Press.

Writers with a variety of backgrounds discuss the problems
and issues related to Americans working abroad. John W.
Masland discusses "Factor X" as the determining
characteristics of successful U.S. expatriates. This factor
is (1) being technically competent, (2) patience, (3)
empathy, (4) some language skills, and (5) knowledge of self
and U.S. culture.

0092   Copeland, Lennie (1988) "Learning to
        Manage a Multicultural Work Force,"
        Training 25 (May): 48-56.

As the labor force of American corporations becomes more
culturally diverse, good personnel relations include an
awareness of these differences rather than treating all
workers in a culturally-blind "one best way." Cultural
differences should be recognized but not emphasized.

0093   Cushner, Kenneth (1989) "Assessing the
        Impact of a Culture-General Assimilator,"
        International Journal of Intercultural
        Relations 13 (2): 125-46.

A culture-general assimilator is a collection of short
stories and incidents that focus on the interaction of two
or more persons from different cultures. Each case ends in a
conflict in which the characters involved cannot complete an
activity due to intercultural misunderstanding. Trainees
read, discuss, and react to these "problems" to learn a
culture's values and roles. The use of a culture-general
assimilator had a significant effect in adjustment among
international exchange students living in New Zealand.

0094   Cyr, Robert (1990) "Client Relations
        in Japan," Training and Development
        Journal 44 (September): 83-5.

The author defines the stages of a training program to
prepare expatriates for assignment in Japan.

0095   Dillon, Linda S. (1990) "The Occidental Tourist,"
        Training and Development Journal 44 (May): 72-80.

Thirty Japanese and Americans who had completed pre-
departure training were interviewed. The Americans
recognized potential cross-cultural problems but stressed
the importance of cross-cultural learning. The Japanese
refused to acknowledge that cultural differences could be
problematic. In a study of seven Japanese firms located in
the U.S., there were a number of cross-cultural problems.
Japanese stress other values than competence and have
different work values. Training can avoid these and other
cross-cultural misunderstandings.

0096   Distefano, Joseph (1983) "Managing in Other Cultures:
        Some Do's and Some Don'ts," pp 484-97 in Herman O.J.
        Overgaard et al. (eds.), International Business: The
        Canadian Way. Dubuque, Iowa: Kendal/Hunt Publishing
        Company.

There are a number of problems faced by persons who are
involved in intercultural meetings and interactions. These
problems, including culture shock, are listed. There is also
a discussion of which elements should be included in a
useful intercultural program.

0097   Dunbar, Edward and Allan Katcher (1990)
        "Preparing Managers for Foreign Assignments,"
        Training and Development Journal 44 (September):
        45-7.

Only one-third of U.S. multinationals provide cross-cultural
training for their expatriates, according to a survey of
Fortune 500 international personnel managers. There is also
little thought about developing cultural sensitivity. The

authors list the five components involved in preparing future expatriates.

0098   Earley, P. Christopher (1987) "Intercultural
        Training for Managers: A Comparison of Documentary
        and Interpersonal Methods," The Academy of Management
        Journal 30 (December): 685-98.

A useful technique to develop cross-cultural skills and sensitivity is for some participants in a training program to "assume" a national identity. The other participants learn to recognize and react to foreign national cultural patterns.

0099   Foxman, Loretta W. and Walter L. Polsky
        (1989) "Cross-Cultural Understanding,"
        Personnel Journal 68 (November): 12-4.

Cross-cultural training can include the buddy system and support groups. All members of a work force should be involved in cross-cultural training.

0100   Frankenstein, John and Hassan Hosseini (1989)
        "Advice from the Field: Essentials Training
        for Japanese Duty," Management Review 77 (July):
        40-43.

North American and Japanese nationals working in Japan were asked what was necessary for expatriate managers in Japan to succeed. Knowing the Japanese language was cited as the most important item. Other "essential" characteristics were the knowledge of Japanese social practices and culture. "Important" items included knowledge of the Japanese economy, negotiation styles, and the sociology of Japanese business. Living in Japan changed foreign residents' values and attitudes. Cross-cultural training and cultural shock training were important preparations.

0101   Geber, Beverly (1989) "A Global Approach to
        Training," Training 26 (May): 42-7.

Many multinational corporations use standard training procedures throughout the world in order to develop unified corporate cultures and standardized work patterns. This approach ignores the cultural differences from one nation to another. An ideal solution is, like IBM, to maintain an education department in each location, though this is an expensive option. IBM tries to blend its corporate culture into the local cultures. The article discusses other options of personnel training that cross international borders.

0102   Gemmel, Art (1986) "Fujitsu's Cross-Cultural
        Style," Management Review 75 (June): 7-8.

Fujitsu America Inc. sponsors an extensive training program for its U.S. managers. American managers are sent to Japan for a ten-day orientation program. They learn Fujitsu's corporate culture as well as Japanese-style management.

0103   Guptaza, Pralihu (1986) "How to Find the Training
        Your Globetrotters Will Need," International
        Management 41 (October): 80-2.

Orientation courses to prepare future expatriates can be done by outside consultants. Such training programs vary in length. However, training programs should include self-knowledge information, stress management, and culture shock preparation.

0104   Harris, Philip R. and Dorothy Harris (1986)
        "Decision Making for a New Work Culture,"
        Management Decision 26 (5): 5-8.

Global managers must become culturally sensitive. Managers need to develop a win-win attitude and learn how cultural background affects managerial goals and behavior.

0105   Harvey, Michael G. (1983) "The Multinational
        Corporation's Expatriate Problem: An Application
        of Murphy's Law," Business Horizons 26 (Jan/Feb):
        71-8.

There is a shortage of qualified and willing executives ready for foreign assignments. This article outlines a plan for a training program to prepare executives for foreign duty. Included in the program are such elements as family in-company counseling, meetings with returned expatriates, informative and detailed (where laundries are located, etc.) handbooks of an expatriate's destination, and cross-cultural sensitivity training.

0106   Hogan, Gary W. and Jane R. Goodson (1990)
        "The Key to Expatriate Success," Training and
        Development Journal 44 (January): 50-2.

Expatriate selection and training should be integrated. The expatriate's family should be involved in this training. Training should involve the development of a host culture's communication, leadership and conflict management skills.

0107   Howard, Cecil (1970) "International Executives: A
        Look into the 21st Century," Management of Personnel
        Quarterly 9 (Spring): 11-17.

The era of "foreign executivism" (foreign-owned enterprises managed by expatriates) is coming to an end. The response is to train and promote host country managers as quickly as possible. Foreign-owned enterprises must also become "good citizens" if they are to avoid expropriation and harassment of personnel through special tax levies, visa quotas, etc.

0108   Howe, Irene Chew Keng, Anthony Tsai-Pen Tseng,
        and Adrian Teo Kim Hong (1990) "The Role of
        Culture in Training in a Multinational Context,"
        Journal of Management Development 9 (5): 51-7.

Cross-cultural training develops insight into the customs
and work-related behavior of host country nationals. One
technique to develop cross-cultural empathy is "action
learning."

0109   Ibe, Masanobu and Noriko Sato (1989)
        "Educating Japanese Leaders for a Global Age:
        The Role of the International Education Center,"
        Journal of Management Development 8 (4): 41-7.

After World War II, the Japanese expended a large amount of
resources to train future leaders in English. Programs were
developed in cross-cultural communication, translating, and
international studies. Class resources included resident
foreigners who can provide cross-cultural, face-to-face
interaction experiences.

0110   Illman, Paul E. (1980) Developing Overseas
        Managers-and Managers Overseas. New York:
        American Management Association.

All aspects of the overseas assignment and the selection and
training of personnel are discussed in this work. While many
of the sections are short, abstract, or utopian in their
discussions, the work also contains useful practical advice.

0111   Katz, Jan Hack (1988) "Cultural Issues in
        International Business," Section 2 in Ingo Water
        and Tracy Murray (eds.) Handbook of International
        Business Second edition. New York: John Wiley & Sons.

A number of different types of cross-cultural training
programs are available for those expecting to be sent on
foreign assignments. The chapter also reviews the elements
of culture in relation to international business. Training
programs must take into account the type of society a person
is being sent to. Some societies encourage less aggressive
and confrontational behavior. People from such cultures will
not explain when they feel offended by a foreigner's
behavior and they will withdraw from the expatriate rather
than say anything.

0112   Kobrin, Stephen J. (1984) International
        Expertise in American Business. How to Learn
        to play with the Kids on the Street. New York:
        Institute of International Education.

This small (59 pp.) brochure reports on the responses of 333
mailed questionnaires and interviews. Managers involved in
international operations were asked what types of
international expertise were important and how these talents
were acquired. Tables and extensive quotes indicate managers

believe adaptability, cultural empathy, and work-related
expertise to be highly important. Specific cultural
knowledge of a country was secondary. Knowledge of a foreign
language was defined as very important, after one's
technical/business skills. Most respondents belittled formal
educational and training programs which prepared employees
for their expatriate experiences.

0113   Kuzela, Lad (1986) "The Rise of the Mega
        Managers," Industry Week 231 (November):
        37-42.

Tomorrow's corporations will need managers who have a global
view. The trends of increased international trade, mergers,
joint ventures, and worldwide consumption demand managers
who are cosmopolitan. Cross-cultural training programs must
be developed.

0114   Layne, Benjamin H., Karla W. Stein, Michael
        Jedel Jay, and Charles A. Burden (1986) "An
        International Business Study Program for
        Managers," Advanced Management Journal 51 (2):
        41-6.

The Georgia State University European Study Program sponsors
trips allowing U.S. students to study European management
styles. The students respected German managers and workers
more than those in other countries. The course teaches
students to become more international, adaptable, and
confident in non-U.S. business environments.

0115   Lee, Chris (1983) "Cross-Cultural Training: Don't
        Leave Home Without It," Training 20 (July): 20-5.

Culture shock is inevitable for expatriates unless they are
carefully prepared for foreign assignments. Such intercultural training avoids the costs of early returns. Aramco
offers its employees extensive publications to acquaint
future expatriates with foreign cultures as well as training
programs. Attendance in these programs includes spouses and
children as well as employees. The article lists several
ways culture shock can be reduced.

0116   Lopez, Joe T. (1989) "Communicating Outside Our
        Borders" Communication World 8 (July/August): 60-61.

American firms no longer have the foreign advantages they
enjoyed after the Second World War. Competition in global
markets demands cultural awareness and sensitivity. The
Global Public Affairs Institute at New York University
offers training in international topics.

0117   Lowe, Judy (1980) "Training for International
        Operations," Human Resource Development 4 (1): 23-25.

Future international managers are likely to experience
shorter foreign assignments and more time in their home

countries than has been the custom. Expatriates should consider their major responsibility to be training nationals to achieve all ranks in a foreign subsidiary. Those going abroad need especially to be aware of cultural differences in terms of (1) power and responsibility, (2) role of family members in terms of business, (3) concepts of time, and (4) the degree to which the work ethic is accepted.

0118   Machan, Dyan (1988) "Ici on Parle Bottom-Line Responsibility," Forbes 141 (February 8): 138, 140.

Knowing a foreign language is given a low priority in most U.S. firms. There exist crash courses that teach foreign languages and customs, especially those in Asian countries. Foreign language skills will be needed in the future.

0119   Masterson, Bob and Bob Murphy (1988) "Internal Cross-Cultural Management," Training and Development Journal 40 (April): 56-60.

Due to the increased numbers of foreign workers in the U.S. labor force, managers and supervisors must increase their cross-cultural sensitivity and knowledge. Foreign employees will need training courses in language, company culture, and career development paths.

0120   Mortellaro, James S. (1989) "Business Across a Cultural Void: Japan's Management Imperialism," Business Marketing 74 (February): 62, 64-6.

Some Japanese managers in American subsidiaries do not understand U.S. authority and communication patterns, or work habits. Cultural misunderstandings can be reduced by the Japanese attending training programs on U.S. values and behaviors.

0121   Murray, F.T. and Alice Haller Murray (1986) "Global Managers for Global Business-SMR Forum," Sloan Management Review 27 (Winter): 75-80.

A major problem in international business is how to reduce the high rate of Americans who do not complete their foreign assignments. Basing their suggestions for reform on Japanese business practices, the authors list the elements to be included in training programs, within the contexts of three types of expatriates: long-term, short-term, and expatriates working in the United States.

0122   Nigh, Douglas and Philip L. Cochran (1987) "Issues Management and the Multinational Enterprise," Management International Review 27 (1): 4-12.

Multinational firms face unique problems, including cross-cultural communication and their prestige levels in foreign countries. However, transnational firms also have a number of advantages.

0123   Osborn, T. Noel and Diana Bergerhouse
        Osborn (1986) "Leadership Training in a Latin
        Context," Issues and Observations 6 (2): 7-10.

The Center for Creative Leadership offers international
training programs. The authors have found that Mexican
trainees differ from U.S. trainees in terms of their
leadership style and decision-making process. Latin American
managers are likely to be more Extroverted, Sensing,
Feelers, and Judgers. They enjoy longer discussions on
philosophical points and were not detail-oriented. U.S.
managers were more likely to be Thinkers rather than Feelers
and to use their intuition. Latin Americans want more
control over subordinates. U.S. managers were more
participative. These cultural differences were significant;
cross-cultural interactions and training programs must take
these differences into consideration.

0124   Parkin, Ernest J., Jr. (1982) "How to Set Up a
        Language Training Department," Training 19 (July):
        56-7.

Multinational corporations cannot avoid the necessity of
making available language training to employees being sent
abroad. One solution is a company-based language training
program, though there are other alternatives. This article
offers some guidelines for staffing, scheduling, class size,
etc.

0125   Patterson, Timothy D. (1990) "The Global Manager,"
        World 24 (2): 10-17.

Pre-departure training programs for U.S. expatriates tend to
be inadequate. Some firms do offer comprehensive pre- and
post-departure and re-entry programs. Some of these programs
include video cassettes of experienced expatriates giving
advice.

0126   Schwind, Hermann F. (1989) "Staffing and Personnel
        Problems in Multinational Corporations in the Asia-
        Pacific Region," pp 145-79 in Erdener Kaynak and
        Kam-Hon Lee (eds.), Global Business: Asia-Pacific
        Dimensions. London and New York: Routledge.

The author offers a survey of the literature dealing with
the criteria for selection of personnel for foreign
assignments, desirable traits of candidates and the contents
of cross-cultural training programs. Included is specific
information for those going to Pacific Rim nations on the
roles of labor unions, government intervention policies, and
national wage policies. The most complete and detailed
sections deal with China and Japan.

0127   Sutton, David C. (1987) "Models for Developing
        Managers," R and D Management 17 (April): 127-36.

Management training should include a number of perspectives,
including the development of a world view.

0128   Syrett, Michel (1990) "Have the British Employers
        Responded to the Training Challenge?" Industrial
        Society (September): 16-8.

The Price Waterhouse Cranfield survey of 5,000 workers in
five European countries found that European employers
recognized the importance of training programs. Firms are
devoting more resources to train workers, though monitoring
procedures are inadequate. Training is not always linked to
business needs.

0129   Teague, Burton W. (1976) Selecting and Orienting
        Staff for Service Overseas. New York: The Conference
        Board.

This sixty-page brochure presents information on the ways
future expatriates can be trained to avoid culture shock,
what their personal characteristics should be, and how to
select the right persons. There are examples of different
types of programs, compensation issues, the issue of
returning expatriates, and how to host foreign nationals.

0130   Temporal, Paul and Ken Burnett (1990)
        "Strategic Corporate Assignments and
        International Management," Journal of
        Management Development 9 (5): 58-64.

Multinational firms will increasingly need managers who can
be assigned to various cultural areas. "Hands on" experience
is the best training method. But the expatriate must be
carefully prepared before leaving.

0131   Thiagarajan, Sivasailam and Barbara
        Steinwachs (1989) BARNGA: A Simulation
        Game on Cultural Clashes. Yarmouth, Maine:
        Intercultural Press, Inc.

BARNGA is a card game with different sets of rules for sub-
groups of players. Verbal communication is forbidden and
participants learn to interact with each other when the
rules of interaction are ill-understood. The game simulates
culture-shock and the problems in cross-cultural relations.

0132   Trafford, Vernon (1977) "Developing Appraisal Skills:
        An Indian Experience," Journal of European Industrial
        Training 1 (3): 17-20.

A ten-day conference was established to facilitate the
introduction of planned change and faculty development among
36 Indian principals of engineering colleges. There was
great resistance among attenders until the program was

legitimated. The conference was shortened to six days due to the occurrences of Hindu and Moslem religious festivals. Management education in India must take into account religious backgrounds and the perceived needs of those involved, as well as skill levels.

0133   Tung, Rosalie L. (1982) "Selection and Training
        Procedures of U.S., European, and Japanese
        Multinationals," California Management Review 24
        (Fall): 57-71.

A survey of 144 Japanese, European, and U.S. multinationals indicates large differences in their policies for personnel selection and staffing for foreign assignment. U.S. companies were less rigorous in selection and training. They also experienced a much higher rate of failure in foreign placements as measured by early and involuntary returns.

0134   Tung, Rosalie L. (1984) Key to Japan's Economic
        Strength: Human Power. Lexington, Mass.: D.C. Heath.

A careful analysis of personnel practices in Japanese and U.S. international enterprises indicates that the Japanese carefully prepare their personnel for foreign assignments. On the other hand, relatively few U.S. firms support any cross-cultural programs for their personnel. The result is that the Japanese enterprises have a very low rate of expatriate failure, and their workers are more effective when in foreign countries.

0135   Tung, Rosalie L. (1988) The New Expatriates:
        Managing Human Resources Abroad. Cambridge, Mass:
        Ballinger Publishing Company.

The author presents the results of a survey dealing with human resource policies for expatriate workers in British, Italian, Swiss, German, and U.S. multinationals. U.S. training programs are relatively few and inadequate, causing the highest rate of early return and expatriate failure of any national group. The author reviews training programs among specific multinationals and international training institutes in Japan and England. European multinationals give much importance to foreign assignments and they become part of the promotion process. European and Japanese firms offer extensive training programs for potential expatriates.

0136   Tung, Rosalie L. (1990) "Language Training
        and Beyond: The Case of Japanese Multinationals,"
        Annals of the American Academy of Political and
        Social Science 511 (September): 97-108.

The author describes the cross-cultural training programs of 18 Japanese firms.

0137   Tung, Rosalie L. and Edwin L. Miller (1990)
        "Managing in the Twenty-First Century: The
        Need for Global Orientation," Management
        International Review 30 (1): 5-18

As the U.S. economy becomes more international, there is a
greater need to develop human resource management programs
with strong international components. Training programs
should include some international content, how to adjust to
foreign assignments, and re-entry counseling.

0138   Van Pelt, Peter and Natalia Wolniansky (1990) "The
        High Cost of Expatriation," Management Review
        79 (July): 40-1.

The cost of maintaining a worker in a foreign assignment is
between two and three times the base salary. Reduction of
costly early returns can be achieved by increased cross-
cultural training and better selection of person and family.
Financial and legal counseling of home and host country
practices are beneficial.

0139   Veiga, John F. and John N. Yanouzas (1989)
        "An Approach to Assessing the Transferability of
        Management Training Techniques Across Cultural
        Boundaries," International Journal of Management
        6 (June): 196-205.

The Lego Man Exercise requires small teams to compete in
replicating a model of a 48-brick man. Some of the values
embodied in this exercise reflect Hofstede's four cultural
dimensions. Members from different cultures will allot
different amount of time to each phase of the exercise.
Greek participants, who score high on uncertainty avoidance,
will consume all pre-assembling time to planning. The
article describes the results of the Lego Man exercises
using Afrikaan South African and American respondents.

0140   Weeks, William H., Paul B. Petersen, and Richard W.
        Brislin editors. (1985), A Manual of Structured
        Experiences for Cross-Cultural Learning. Yarmouth,
        Maine: Intercultural Press.

This work presents a large number of exercises to increase
intercultural sensitivity among those who expect to deal
with persons from different cultural backgrounds. Many of
the exercises were developed by the Peace Corps to reduce
culture shock among volunteers. Some exercises teach
participants how to interact in a group where members have
multi-cultural backgrounds. Other exercises encourage
participants to review their own and other's values.

0141   **Weiss, Joseph W. and Stanley Bloom (1990)
        "Managing in China: Expatriate Experiences and
        Training Recommendations," Business Horizons 66
        (May/June): 23-9.**

Expatriates working in China face a very different culture
and third-world facilities. There is a lack of privacy and
activities. Pre-assignment training should use all methods
of instruction, including case studies, vignettes, and role
playing, to prepare those going to China.

0142   **Wittenberg-Cox, Avivah (1991) "Delivering
        Global Leaders," International Management
        46 (February): 52-5.**

The Global Leadership Programme includes a five-week
executive training course. This course includes rafting in
Maine, U.S.A., seminars at the University of Michigan, and
two-week visits in Brazil, China, India, and the Soviet
Union. The program teaches members how different cultures
view time and how cultures develop responses to problems,
and how to avoid multi-cultural communication problems.

0143   **Woods, Robert H. (1990) "Lessons from Bafa
        Bafa," Cornell Hotel and Restaurant Administration
        Quarterly 31 (August): 115-18.**

Bafa Bafa is a game that teaches players cross-cultural
sensitivity. One team become alphans, who are easy going,
value intimacy, and are sexist and patriarchal. Betans are
money-oriented and formal. Each team is to learn about the
other's culture and then the opposing members meet. They are
then debriefed and members find that stressing only cultural
differences is a limited way of learning a foreign culture.

0144   **Wurzel, Jaime editor (1991) Toward Multiculturalism.
        Yarmouth, Maine: Intercultural Press.**

This work consists of a collection of readings which are
meant to develop among students a sensitivity toward persons
from other cultures. Their feelings of ethnocentrism and
intolerance are reduced by exposing readers to descriptions
of a variety of different cultural environments.

0145   **Zeira, Yoram and Moshe Banai (1981) "Attitudes of
        Host-Country Organizations Toward MNCs' Staffing
        Policies: A Cross-Country and Cross-Industry
        Analysis," Management International Review 21
        (2): 38-47.**

A survey of 111 employees of multinationals from England,
Holland, Belgium, France, and Germany indicates a need to
better train expatriates and their home country superiors.
French home country officers were the most ethnocentric,
followed by Germans. Those from Belgium were the least
ethnocentric.

3

The Expatriate Experience

0146   Adler, Nancy J. (1984) "Women in International
       Management: Where are They?" <u>California Management
       Review</u> 26 (Summer): 78-89.

Although more and more domestic managers are women, most
(97%) U.S. corporate expatriate managers are men. Women,
when sent abroad, are given shorter assignments lasting less
than thirty days. Based on a survey of 686 U.S. and Canadian
companies, larger companies and banks send more female
managers on foreign assignments.

0147   Adler, Nancy J. (1987) "Pacific Basin Managers: A
       Gaijin, Not a Woman," <u>Human Resource Management</u>
       25 (Summer): 169-91.

52 female successful expatriates who had returned from Asian
assignments said their experiences were positive. The
greatest problem was their relationships with males within
their own companies. Foreign women in the Orient are defined
as foreigners rather than as females.

0148   Adler, Nancy J. and Dafna N. Izraeli editors (1988)
       <u>Women in Management Worldwide</u>. Armonk, New York:
       M.E. Sharpe.

The first chapters deal with how women managers are viewed
in various countries within the context of seven commonly
found themes. Other chapters analyze national attitudes of
women in relation to work (management) and family.

0149   Ali, Abbas and Robert Masters (1988)
        "Management Perceptions of Qualities for National
        Success: an Empirical Study," International Journal
        of Management 5 (September): 287-95.

195 Multinational executives ranked 16 statements according
to their importance for managing in multinational
environments. The highest ranked items, in descending order,
were: (1) managerial competence and experience, (2)
technical competence, and (3) ability to make decisions in
an atmosphere of risk and uncertainty. The least ranked
items were (15) spouse and family willingness to move to
foreign countries and (16) ability of spouse to adapt

0150   Allen, Keith R. (1987) "An Umbrella Plan for
        Expatriates," Benefits and Compensation International
        17 (July): 3-6.

Union Carbide Europe has a pension benefit plan for
expatriates which allows an employee to change countries to
retire if wanted. The plan uses a "home country" base but
can be adapted to the retirement country of one's choice.

0151   Alteny, David (1989) "Europe 1992: Culture Clash,"
        Industry Week 238 (October 2): 13-20.

American businesspersons need to learn to adapt to European
cultures and business-related ways of behaving. The body
languages are different, as are negotiating styles, work vs.
non-work issues, and friendship patterns. It is a mistake to
assume all European cultures are the same, since there are
great differences from one nation to another.

0152   Anderson, Jack B. "Compensating Your Overseas
        Executives, Part 2: Europe 1992," (1990)
        Compensation and Benefits Review 22
        (July/August): 25-35.

Home-based international compensation policies may not be
effective under a more unified Europe. What is needed are
pay programs that combine home and host country elements.
There is also a need to develop longer-term benefits and
tax-deferred foreign service allowances.

0153   Austin, Clyde N. (1983) Cross-Cultural Reentry:
        An Annotated Bibliography. Abilene, Texas: Christian
        University Press.

This 128 page bibliography is the first of its kind. It is
comprehensive while it omits general-interest magazine
sources. This is a valuable reference for locating material
on reentry published during the 1970s and early 1980s. Some
items are not annotated.

0154   Axtell, Roger E. (1990) Do's and Taboos of Hosting
        International Visitors. New York: John Wiley & Sons.

The author provides suggestions on how to correctly
entertain foreign visitors. He compares American customs
(eating, tipping, toasting, drinking, conversational taboos,
etc.) with those from other countries. The bulk of the book
deals with business customs throughout the world with an
emphasis on Canadian, British, and Japanese customs. This is
a very useful and comprehensive guide to cross-cultural
social and business protocols.

0155   Baines, Alison (1987) "Home Thoughts of a Broad,"
        Women in Management Review 6 (2): 78-84.

A sample of United Kingdom female expatriates gave
"increased incomes" as the most important reason for working
abroad. If money is the major reason, potential expatriates
should investigate tax benefits and establish non-resident
exemptions. Women also should learn whether support systems
exist. They should also learn about the host country before
leaving.

0156   Ballard, Lynne and Brian H. Kleiner (1988)
        "Understanding and Managing Foreign-Born and
        Minority Employees," Leadership and Organizational
        Development 9 (4): 22-4.

The increase of foreign-born and minority employees in the
U.S. labor force has created a need for greater cross-
cultural sensitivity among managers. Cultural differences
include ways of thinking, verbal and non-verbal
communication, and employees' expectations. Cross-cultural
management training programs are needed to prepare managers.

0157   Bashleigh, Cline (1986) "Confessions of
        a Far-Flung Communicator," Communication
        World 3 (October): 11-5.

The author has lived abroad for about 30 years. He offers
advice on how to successfully live in foreign cultures.
Preparation is a key to adjustment.

0158   Beckmann, David M., Timothy J. Mitchell, and Linda
        L. Powers (1985) The Overseas List: Opportunities
        for Living and Working in Developing Countries
        revised edition. Minneapolis: Augsburg Publishing
        House.

The book contains lists of organizations, private and public
as well as profit and non-profit, which offer short and
long-term employment throughout the third world. There are
sections on living in developing countries, tax and travel
information, internships, and study abroad opportunities.

Christian and humanitarian mission work opportunities are emphasized.

0159   Beeman, Don R., Thomas W. Sharkey,
        and Sharon L. Magill (1988) "Will You
        Return from Your Next Business Trip?"
        Business Horizons 31 (July/August): 58-63.

Various forms of terrorism (high-jacking, kidnapping, bombings, etc.) are possibilities during foreign assignments. The authors present distributions of terrorist acts by region for 1985. The article concludes with advice on how to behave in order to reduce the risks of being a terrorist target.

0160   Berger, Michael (1987) "A Japanese Psychiatrist's
        answer to Executive Stress," International Management
        42 (March): 49-50.

Overseas assignments are creating psychological stress for an increasing number of Japanese expatriates. There is a computer program called Life Track which identifies sources of stress. The program is also being used in Japan to sensitize and prepare prospective expatriates.

0161   Berlitz, Charles (1991) Around the World with 80
        Words. New York: G.P. Putnam's Sons.

The author presents basis phrases and words in twenty-five languages. The vocabulary lists consist of useful "survival" and etiquette terms.

0162   Bertrand, Kate (1987) "Real-Life Risky
        Business," Business Marketing 72 (January): 48-54.

Americans working abroad face political risks and harassments. The author offers examples of business turmoil throughout the world. She discusses the experiences of American Motors Corp. in China and presents a qualitative approach to the measuring of political risks for the world's nations or regions.

0163   Bickerstaffe, George (1982) "Have Spouse,
        Will Travel (if You Find Us Both a Job),"
        International Management 37 (March): 21-26.

A major problem in foreign transfers is the spouse's reluctance to interrupt his/her career. Relocation of two-career families can reduce family income as well as cause the loss of a desired job. One solution is for a company to locate a position for the spouse, which is called a policy of "transplacement."

0164   Bird, Allan and Roger Dunbar (1991) "Getting
        the Job Done Over There: Improving Expatriate
        Productivity," National Productivity Review 10
        (Spring): 145-56.

U.S. expatriate personnel have very high (25-50%) failure
rates. This is due in part to the inability of the
expatriate and family members to adjust to living in a new
culture. Cross-cultural training to increase inter-cultural
sensitivity is necessary. There is also a need for pre- and
post-departure and reentry counseling.

0165   Bishko, Michael J. (1990) "Compensating Your
        Overseas Executives, Part I: Strategies for the
        1990s," Compensation and Benefits Review 22
        (May/June): 33-43.

Many compensation policies of U.S. corporations are being
exported to their foreign subsidiaries and divisions. Doing
so demands knowledge of national conditions and compensation
issues such as the tax rates for employer and employees, and
foreign currency control laws.

0166   Black, J. Stewart (1988) "Workrole Transitions: A
        Study of American Expatriate Managers in Japan,"
        Journal of International Business Studies 19
        (Summer): 277-94.

American expatriates in Japan evaluated their adjustment to
working and living in Japan and the causes for adequate or
lack of adjustment. The degree of family members' adjustment
was a significant factor, as were pre-departure knowledge
and association with Japanese nationals. Role ambiguity and
conflict had negative effects on adjustment and morale.

0167   Black, J. Stewart (1990) "The Relationship of
        Personal Characteristics with the Adjustment of
        Japanese Expatriate Managers," Management
        International Review 30 (2): 119-34.

A sample of 250 Japanese expatriates in the U.S. were tested
for their degree of psychological adjustment. The findings
support earlier findings.   Among the findings was that
ethnocentrism was negatively correlated with the degree of
interaction adjustment.

0168   Black, J. Stewart and Hal B. Gregersen (1990)
        "Expectations, Satisfaction, and Intention to Leave
        of American Expatriate Managers in Japan,"
        International Journal of Intercultural Relations 14
        (4): 485-506.

General dissatisfaction was the strongest predictor of
intent to leave an assignment early among 51 U.S. males

working in Japan. Satisfaction was related to findings that adjustment problems were less than expected. Higher satisfaction with being in Japan was also related to finding "no surprises" in terms of work issues.

0169   Black, J. Stewart and Hal B. Gregersen (1991)
        "Antecedents to Cross-Cultural Adjustment for
        Expatriates in Pacific Rim Assingments," Human
        Relations 44 (May): 497-515.

The authors investigate the factors associated with successful adjustment of expatriates in the Pacific Rim.

0170   Black, J. Stewart and Mark Mendenhall (1991) "The
        U-Curve adjustment Hypothesis Revisited: A Review
        and Theoretical Framework," Journal of International
        Business Studies 22 (2): 225-47.

The process of adjustment to a foreign culture has been assumed to take a U-curve shape, although the evidence for this hypothesis is scant. The authors review the relevant literature and develop a series of testable propositions to form a research agenda on the U-curve hypothesis that is theory-driven.

0171   Black, J. Stewart and Gregory K. Stephens (1989)
        "The Influence of the Spouse of American
        Expatriate Adjustment and Intent to Stay
        in Pacific Rim Overseas Assignments,"
        Journal of Management 15 (December): 529-44.

Past studies have indicated that (1) U.S. firms experience a high rate of failure in overseas assignments and that (2) spouses' attitudes and feeling are central to U.S. expatriates' success in a foreign assignment. This study measures the effect of spouses' attitudes on expatriate adjustment and morale. The spouses' adjustments and intent to stay are highly correlated with expatriate managers' attitudes and intent to stay overseas.

0172   Bock, Philip K. (1971) Culture Shock: A
        Reader in Modern Cultural Anthropology.
        New York: Alfred A. Knopf, Inc.

Examples of culture shock are found in literature and personal experiences. The editor includes accounts of anthropologists conducting fieldwork in foreign cultures, a black American in the Alps, and a description of an American staying in a Japanese inn.

0173   **Boddewyn, J.J. (1970) "The Top Management Job in
        International Business," Economic and Business
        Bulletin 23 (Fall): 1-5.**

The author summarizes a number of studies related to the
qualities needed for those going on foreign assignments. All
managers need technical, human relations, and conceptual
skills. International business skills form another dimension
of needed aptitudes.

0174   **Brooks, Brenda (1987) "Exporting: Abroad
        is Different," Industrial Marketing Digest 12
        (2): 75- 80.**

A survey indicated that 7 out of 10 expatriates in one
British firm returned early. The major reason for these
failures was the inability to adjust to a new culture.
Selection procedures and training must be improved.
Learning the language of the host country is necessary.

0175   **Brooks, Brian J. (1987) "Trends in International
        Executive Compensation," Personnel 64 (May): 67-70.**

Pay systems for multinational executives are becoming more
complex and are being revised. Companies are equalizing pay
to their executives in different countries. They are also
giving executives more choices in compensation types.

0176   **Brown, Michael B. (1989) "International Assistance
        Aid Travelling Executives," Broker World 9 (March):
        62-4, 86.**

Roughly one million U.S. citizens travelling or working
abroad will need medical treatment during the year. Foreign
hospitals and medical personnel have different payment
policies, such as payments in advance. They may not accept
U.S. group medical plans. There are many International
Assistance Programs (IAP) that can help U.S. citizens with
their medical emergencies. IAPs can notify family members,
recommend physicians, provide translators, etc.

0177   **Carty, Peter and Jerome Chanmugan (1990)
        "Opportunity Abroad: Work Hard Play Hard,"
        Accountancy 106 (November): 66-8.**

Those with accountancy qualifications can work throughout
the world. Developed countries offer career advancement
opportunities. Less developed countries offer excitement and
experience.

0178   Chumir, Leonard H. and Nancy T. Frontczak (1990)
        "International Management Opportunities for
        Women: Women and Men Paint Different Pictures,"
        International Journal of Management 7 (September):
        295-301.

222 American upper-level managers were asked to evaluate the
opportunities for women in international management. The
women respondents were much more pessimistic than were men
about such opportunities. Women also were more likely to
state that larger numbers of qualified women were available
for foreign assignments than are being sent. Both genders
agreed foreigners were strongly prejudiced against women in
business.

0179   Cleveland, Harlan and Gerard J. Mangone eds. (1957)
        The Art of Overseasmanship. Syracuse, New York:
        Syracuse University Press.

This work is a classic statement of the problems faced by
expatriates. There is a discussion of the characteristics
making up "Factor X:" the ideal features of someone to be
sent on a foreign assignment. Later studies have supported
the findings in this book.

0180   Cooke, Alan (1990) "International Employees:
        Multinational Pension Plan Practices," Benefits and
        Compensation International 20 (October): 8-11.

A survey of ten multinationals in Europe, the U.S., Canada
and Bermuda indicates that pension plans often include
enrolling employees in a plan in the host country when other
options are exhausted. Funded offshore pension plans were
another option, among others.

0181   Crandall, Lin P. and Mark I. Phelps (1991) "Pay for
        a Global Work Force," Personnel 70 (February): 28-
        33.

Most compensation systems for expatriates are based on home
or host country practices. These create confusion and high
personnel costs. One solution is to pay expatriates the same
as host co-workers.

0182   Dakin, Juile Ann (1989) "The ABCs of Going to
        School in China," China Business Review 16
        (Nov/Dec): 44-7.

The three major cities of China now have excellent schools
for English-speaking children. They follow an American-style
curriculum. They are accredited, have small classes, and
offer cross-cultural perspectives.

0183   Davies, Michael (1989) "Measurement of Hardship
        in Expatriate Postings," Benefits and Compensation
        Benefits 19 (October): 19-21.

The U.S. Department of State (DOS) has established a
classification to provide hardship allowances for American
expatriates. The system, however, was developed for the DOS
staff, whose life styles and locations may not reflect those
on foreign assignments for business purposes. The author
lists the required elements for a hardship classification
for multinational business personnel.

0184   Dowling, Peter J. (1987) "Human Resources Issues in
        National Business," Syracuse Journal of
        International Law and Commerce 13 (Winter): 255-71.

Expatriate failure is a recurring problem. The Japanese
multinationals train all levels of their personnel for
foreign assignments. U.S. and European firms train only
higher level personnel. This allows the Japanese to use
their international human resources more efficiently.

0185   Dowling, Peter J. (1989) "Hot Issues Overseas,"
        Personnel Administrator 34 (January): 66-72.

34 international human resource managers listed the major
problems associated with expatriate behavior. Two of the
major problems most commonly cited were the lack of the
consistency of managerial practices from one country to
another and career development. Living and working in a
foreign cultural environment and selection of expatriates
were also commonly cited as major concerns.

0186   Farr, Michael (1990) "Tokyo on the Rhine,"
        International Management 45 (August): 42-3.

The most important Japanese expatriate center outside of New
York is Dusseldorf, Germany. It has become the decision
center for Japanese European activities. The expatriate
community is large and offers support groups, training, and
advice for Japanese newcomers. The large school for Japanese
children is a major attraction.

0187   Fenning, R. Offord (1990) "UK Non-approved Plans-
        Domestic and National Aspects," Benefits and
        Compensation International 20 (November): 10-4.

The United Kingdom offers its expatriates tax incentives for
deferring payments until retirement. UK citizens abroad are
not taxed for most types of incomes. By contrast, U.S.
expatriates bear a heavier U.S. tax burden on worldwide
income.

0188   Fergus, Mike (1990) "Employees on the Move," HR
        Magazine 35 (May): 44-6.

Sending an employee on a foreign assignment for one or two
years costs the employer from $200,000 to $250,000. Yet most
companies do not provide expatriates adequate pre- and post-
departure information concerning foreign cultures, language,
and customs. Allied Van Lines has developed the Strategies
Customer Advisory Network (SCAN), a database on countries
and thousands of cities for resident expatriates, not
tourists. This information includes data on business
practices, customs and etiquette.

0189   Frith, Stan W. (1981) The Expatriate Dilemma: How
        to Relocate and Compensate U.S. Employees Assigned
        Overseas. Chicago: Nelson-Hall.

Foreign assignments involve unique problems of compensation,
taxation, moving, residence and vacation needs. The author
details methods of compensation used in a number of
corporation and points out the various complexities and
issues that need to be recognized before an employee and
family leave on a foreign assignment.

0190   Furnham, Adrian and Stephen Bochner (1986)
        Culture Shock: Psychological Reactions to
        Unfamiliar Environments. London: Methnen.

The authors analyze the reactions of persons in unfamiliar
environments, including foreign cultures and new settings
such as hospitals and educational institutions. The
variables, degrees, and dimensions leading to culture shock
are discussed, as well as situation-appropriate coping
mechanisms. The authors define culture shock as the result
of a person's lack of social skills rather than as a refusal
to adjust. This approach leads to specific training needs
and procedures.

0191   Gajek, Marion and Monica M. Sabo (1986) "The
        Bottom Line: What HR Managers Need to Know
        About the New Expatriate Regulations,"
        Personnel Administrator 31 (February): 87-92.

New tax regulations offer U.S. expatriates some economic
advantages. There are housing and tax exclusions that can
reduce the expenses of foreign assignments.

0192   Gibson, Virginia L. and Edward D. Burmeister
        (1990) "American-Based ESOPs Get a Worldwide
        Look," Pension World 26 (July): 22-3.

Global companies are increasingly developing international
pension plans. Many foreign employees of U.S. firms would
rather have equity in the form of corporate stock than other
types of pension benefits.

0193   Gomez-Mejia, Luis and David B. Balkin
        (1987) "The Determinants of Managerial
        Satisfaction with the Expatriation and
        Repatriation Process," Journal of Management
        Development 5 (1): 7-17.

Of 89 returned U.S. expatriates, 82% were highly satisfied
with their foreign assignments. Only 35% were satisfied with
the re-entry process. The reasons for this dissatisfaction
include difficulty in re-adjustment into the U.S. culture
and career limitations. Solutions to the problems of
repatriation are listed.

0194   Gonzales, Richard F. and Anant R. Negandhi (1966)
        The United States Overseas Executive: His
        Orientations and Career Patterns. East Lansing,
        Michigan: Institute for International Business
        and Economic Development Studies.

A survey of 1,161 directors of international operations was
conducted to describe the career advantages, needs, and
paths of expatriates. Data include spouse and parental data,
career mobility patterns (age at first foreign assignment,
etc), socioeconomic background data, attitudinal measures of
the perceived advantages and disadvantages of foreign
assignments, etc. This work is a classic study of "Factor
X:" what are the ideal qualities of expatriates, including
the degree of adaptability of spouse/family.

0195   Gray, Andrew (1982) "Repatriation at the Burr
        Hamilton Bank," Business Horizons 25 (March/April):
        13-14.

This article is a fictional and humorous account of a
returning expatriate's adjustment problems after having
stayed in a foreign country too long. It also illustrates
some of the problems faced by returning expatriates.

0196   Gregersen, Hal B. and J. Stewart Black (1990) "A
        Multifaceted Approach to Expatriate Retention in
        International Assignments," Group and Organization
        Studies 15 (December): 461-85.

Responses from 301 expatriates in seven countries indicate
that commitment/loyalty to the parent company was a major

factor in the intent to complete a foreign assignment. Adjustment to the local culture was also an important variable in the intent to stay.

0197   Gregory, Ann (1984) "The ASEAN Challenge to
        Ethnocentric Management: A Comparison of American
        and Japanese Personnel Policies," Proceedings
        of the Academy of International Business: 706-22.

The author compares the selection and training of expatriate managers in Japanese and U.S. firms. Greater care is taken by Japanese executives in the selection of their future expatriates. The Japanese are more likely to use different criteria for the selection of personnel for domestic vs. international assignments. Selection and training of American expatriates were more informal and unstructured.

0198   Grove, Cornelius (1990) "An Ounce of Prevention:
        Supporting International Job Transitions,"
        Employment Relations Today 17 (Summer): 111-19.

There are a number of policies that can reduce expatriate failures and early returns. Using self-selection is a first step. The length of assignments should be increased, and the host office should provide support for the expatriate and family. Cultural training should also be provided both before and after departure.

0199   Grove, Daniel A. (1989) "Before its too Late,
        Evacuate," Security Management 33 (November): 47.

The author provides advice on evacuation of American expatriates based on his experiences in the Philippines and from those who had been in China during the Beijing Tiananmen Square events. The advice includes (1) when you are certain you should evacuate, it's probably too late; (2) take the first flight to any safe location; (3) any evacuation plan is better than no plan; (4) expatriates should not expect to be able to take servants or friends; and (5) establish an emergency center with one designated spokesperson.

0200   Guptara, Prabhu (1986) "Searching the Organization
        for the Cross-Cultural Operators," International
        Management 41 (August): 40-2.

Some employees are better candidates than others for foreign assignments. The author lists the sources of extra expenses (housing, higher salaries and bonuses, costs-of-living adjustments, etc.) which make correct personnel selection important. There are a number of ways the effectiveness of expatriates can be increased.

0201   Hamil, Jim (1989) "Expatriate Policies in British
         Nationals," Journal of General Management 14
         (Summer): 18-33.

The author discusses the policies of British multinationals
in terms of staffing, performances, and policies of
expatriates. The failure rate of British expatriates is very
low (5%). The reasons for this success are that (1) British
expatriates are more internationally mobile than their U.S.
counterparts, and (2) policies dealing with expatriates are
more developed.

0202   Harrick, Philip J. (1989) "Dangerous Waters,"
         Security Management 33 (November): 44-50.

A large amount of resources has been expended by various
U.S. government agencies and multinational firms to reduce
the threat of terrorist kidnapping of U.S. expatriate
executives. The author offers guidelines for establishing a
risk-reduction program.

0203   Harris, Philip R. (1979) "The Unhappy World of the
         Expatriate," International Management 34 (July):
         49-50.

U.S. companies experience between 45%-85% failure rate among
their expatriates, costing companies up to $150,000 per
early returnee. Ways to reduce this high failure rate (lower
for European and Japanese companies) are better cross-
cultural training and careful preparation before being sent
on a foreign assignment.

0204   Harris, Philip R. (1986) "Employees Abroad:
         Maintain the Corporate Connection," Personnel 66
         (August): 107-10.

Potential expatriates should enroll in a company-sponsored
cultural sensitivity and training program before leaving.
Foreign assignments should be part of regular career paths
for all managers. On-site supervision can reduce culture
shock.

0205   Harris, Philip R. and Dorothy L. Harris (1987)
         "Women Managers and Professionals Abroad,"
         Journal of Managerial Psychology 2 (3): 1-11.

Preparing women expatriates for foreign assignments should
include (1) counseling together with their husbands, (2)
establishing a support network, and (3) providing services
with regard to the care of dependents.

0206   Harvey, Michael (1985) "A New Corporate Weapon
        Against Terrorism," Business Horizons 28 (Jan/Feb):
        42-7.

Multinational corporations can reduce the threat of
terrorism by joining together and forming anti-terrorist
organizations. The author outlines the ways the three phases
of a terrorist crisis should be handled, including media
relations, the organizing of a crisis management team, and
family counseling activities.

0207   Hayden, Spencer (1990) "Our Foreign Legions are
        Faltering," Personnel 67 (August): 40-4.

A majority of 116 executives of companies in the Forbes 500
found that the selection and training of expatriates were
major problems. It was easier to hire host country
nationals. The training and motivating of host managers were
also problems. Most respondents stressed the advantages of
local managers knowing the local cultures and languages.

0208   Heitzman, Robert E., Jr. (1990) "International
        Employees: Are They Losing Out on Retirement?"
        Financial Executive 6 (Sept/Oct): 44-50.

Designing retirement programs for expatriates and host and
third country nationals is a very complicated matter, since
there are no single solutions for tax systems and various
local retirement practices. All-encompassing umbrella plans
work to the financial disadvantage of global employees of
multinational firms.

0209   Hill, Roy (1977) "East is Still East,"
        International Management 32 (May): 15-18.

An overview of the training program at Japan's International
Studies and Training School indicates how future expatriates
are prepared for foreign assignments. They are taught
foreign languages and cultures in a one-year program,
including one month spent overseas. There is also a survey
of the students' attitudes toward business practices and
work-leisure conflicts.

0210   Hixon, Allen L. (1986) "Why Corporations Make
        Haphazard Overseas Staffing Decisions," Personnel
        Administrator 31 (March): 91-3.

Roughly 25% of U.S. expatriates fail to complete their
foreign assignments. There are eight reasons for this high
failure rate, including lack of training and proper
selection/evaluation procedures.

0211   Hogan, Gary W. and Jane R. Goodson (1990) "The Key
        to Expatriate Success," Training and Development
        Journal 44 (January): 50-2.

Expatriate managers living in Japan and working in ten
different firms identified the key factors contributing to
expatriate success. Key factors include being able to adjust
to a foreign culture and use that knowledge within the
company. Unlike U.S. firms, Japanese companies emphasize
pre-departure training for future expatriates. Foreign
assignments are announced over a year ahead of time so that
training is possible.

0212   Hourihan, Gary C. (1990) "Crafting the Global Pay
        Package," Directors and Boards 14 (Summer): 48-51.

Many U.S. multinationals are replacing U.S. expatriates with
host country nationals. This is due to the high costs of
maintaining expatriates. The result is a need to develop pay
packages based on local customs, local inflation rates, and
local tax systems. World-wide compensation strategies are
needed that reflect both local employee needs and the goals
of the enterprises.

0213   Howard, Cecil G. (1972) "Why Executives Fail Abroad,"
        Human Resource Management 11 (Spring): 32-6.

U.S. executives' failures abroad are caused by three general
problems, some of which are beyond the expatriates' control,
such as changes in company ownership and political changes
in the host country. Other problems are inherent in the
executives, such as poor health, separation-anxiety, and
lack of cultural adaptability, etc.

0214   Howard, Cecil G. (1974) "The Returning Overseas
        Executive: Cultural Shock in Reverse," Human
        Resource Management 13 (Summer): 22-6.

While some executives attend cultural sensitivity and
orientation programs prior to going on foreign assignments,
few go through formal de-sensitivity programs after they
return. Problems experienced include (1) reduced income, (2)
loss of prestige, (3) job qualifications and duty issues,
and (4) disenchantment with their home cultures. The
expatriate's family and employer also face "returning
cultural shock."

0215   Howard, Cecil G. (1987) "Out of Sight--Not Out of
        Mind," Personnel Administrator 32 (June): 82-90.

The evaluation of expatriates is done badly if done at all.
There are six areas of problems involved in performance
evaluation, including the host culture and the reward

systems. There are six strategies to use in overseas performance evaluation.

0216   Hubbard, Ghislaine (1986) "How to Combat Culture
        Shock," Management Today (September): 62-65.

Working abroad was more difficult than most expatriates had expected. One in seven Europeans and one in three Americans sent overseas return home early. The spouse is frequently the major cause of early returns. Royal Dutch Shell has developed a program to ease cultural shock among its expatriates. This method is described in the article.

0217   Hume-Rothery, Richard (1989) "Fringe Benefits,"
        National Journal of Manpower 10 (9): 16-17.

International transfers involve fringe benefits. The most common are housing, transportation, medical coverage, and schooling. Such payments reduce expatriates' taxes as well as increase their status and living standards. The host governments generally do not like such fringe benefits for expatriates, because they are difficult to tax.

0218   Ivancevich, John M. (1969) "Perceived Need
        Satisfaction of Domestic versus Overseas
        Managers," Journal of Applied Psychology
        53 (August): 274-78.

Overseas managers had lower levels of need fulfillment for security and social needs. They had higher perceived fulfillment needs than domestic managers in terms of esteem.

0219   Izraeli, Dafna N., Moshe Banai, and
        Yoram Zeira (1980) "Women Executives in
        MNC Subsidiaries," California Management
        Review 23 (Fall): 53:63.

Women expatriates of U.S. foreign subsidiaries face problems when they are sent to countries which do not encourage women in the higher business ranks. From surveys of officials in MNCs, the authors present a list of strategies to reduce the possible handicap of gender. The advice includes: make certain clients know an employee is a woman; entertain in first-class restaurants that are well-lit (to avoid misunderstandings), and to stress a woman's formal qualifications during a preview or introduction.

0220   Janssen, Gretchen (1989) Women Overseas:
        A Christian Perspective on Cross-Cultural
        Adaptation. Yarmouth, Maine: Intercultural Press.

The author offers advice on how to adapt to a foreign cultural environment from a Christian perspective. The work provides useful guideline for all potential expatriates.

0221   Jelinek, Mariann and Nancy J. Adler (1988)
         "Women: World-Class Managers for Global
         Competition," The Academy of Management
         Executive 2 (February): 11-9.

Conducting business abroad demands skills of relationship
development of personal relationships, communication, and
social sensitivity. American women have traditionally been
strong in those skills. Even in sexist cultures, American
female expatriates are succeeding because of, not in spite
of, their gender.

0222   Kandall, D.W. (1981) "Repatriation: An Ending and a
         Beginning," Business Horizons 24 (Nov/Dec): 21-5.

Returning expatriates experience five major problems. These
are (1) changing lifestyles, (2) educational continuity for
their children, (3) family cash flow, (4) housing, and (5)
new job shock. The author offers possible solutions.

0223   Kirk, William Q. and Robert C. Maddox (1988)
         "International Management: The New Frontier for
         Women," Personnel 85 (March): 46-8.

More women are now seeking international work. There is
prejudice against women expatriates in top-level jobs.
Superior performance can reduce this discrimination. Larger
companies are more receptive to promoting women.

0224   Klein, Robert B. (1991) "Compensating Your
         Overseas Executives, Part 3: Exporting U.S. Stock
         Option Plans to Expatriates," Compensation and
         Benefits Review 23 (Jan/Feb): 27-38.

Many local incentive plans are inadequate for those going on
foreign assignments. Taxation policies vary greatly from one
country to another, while expatriates and host country
employees are often taxed differently. There are guidelines
for deciding which type of stock options is the best.

0225   Koco, Linda (1989) "Expatriates Need Advice, Over
         There and on Return," National Underwriter 93
         (April): 7, 10-11.

Those going on foreign assignments need financial advice and
planning that are seldom provided by employers. Part of the
financial burden of expatriates involves potentially paying
two sets of taxes and household/moving expenses. Financial
planning should be done before as well as after a person
leaves on a foreign assignment.

0226   Kohls, L. Robert (1984) <u>Survival Kit for Overseas
        Living</u>. Second Edition. Yarmouth, Maine:
        Intercultural Press, Inc.

This book offers advice on how to live in a foreign country,
avoid culture shock, and how to be able to fit in foreign
daily life situations. There is an extended chapter on
resources available to expatriates. One chapter deals with
the issues of re-entry.

0227   Kobrin, Stephen J. (1988) "Expatriates Reduction
        and Strategic Control in American Multinational
        Corporations," <u>Human Resource Management</u> 27
        (Spring): 63-75.

There has been a large reduction in the numbers of
expatriates working in U.S. corporations. U.S. MNCs need to
train and promote more host country and third country
nationals as employees.

0228   Kobrin, Stephen J. (1989) "Expatriate Reduction
        in American Multinationals: Have We Gone Too Far?"
        <u>ILR Report</u> 27 (Fall): 22-9.

The number of U.S. Expatriates has decreased in recent
years. This is due to the high cost of relocation and the
relatively high failure rate and early returns. This trend
has gone too far and contains a number of disadvantages for
U.S. firms, including a lack of internationalization among
employees.

0229   Krupp, Neil B. (1990) "Overseas Staffing for the
        New Europe," <u>Personnel</u> 67 (July): 20-5.

In order to effectively manage in a unified Europe, foreign
multinationals will need three types of workers. Local
nationals will almost always cost less than home country and
third country expatriates. Conditions influence which type
of worker is preferable or available.

0230   Lance, Charles E. and Deborah R. Richardson (1988)
        "Correlates of Work and Non-Work Stress and
        Satisfaction Among American Insulated Sojourners,"
        <u>Human Relations</u> 41 (10): 725-38.

"Insulated sojourners" are persons who live in foreign
countries for a short time and who are relatively insulated
from that culture. They refuse to integrate into the local
culture by spending all free time with persons of their own
nationality. The study is based on 97 sojourners working in
Japan, South Korea and Thailand. Most were U.S. military
personnel. The findings in part found that non-work stress
levels and work satisfaction were inversely correlated.

0231   Lank, Alden G. (1988) "Designing Policies
        for the International Transfer of Managers,"
        Canadian Manager 11 (March): 23-5.

There are three types of personnel in a multinational
venture: home country nationals, host country nationals, and
third-country nationals. International success depends on a
firm's correct handling of issues dealing with transfers for
each type of employee.

0232   Lansing, Paul and Kathryn Ready (1988) "Hiring Women
        Managers in Japan: An Alternative for Foreign
        Employers," California Management Review 30
        (Spring): 112-27.

Larger numbers of well-educated Japanese women are now
available as managers. Legal as well as social changes
encourage women to enter careers. The resistance of Japanese
males to work for foreign-owned enterprises can be offset by
an untapped source of local managerial talent: Japanese
women.

0233   Lee, Yosup and Laurie Larwood (1983) "The
        Socialization of Expatriate Managers in
        Multinational Firms," Academy of Management
        Journal 26 (December): 657-65.

American expatriates in Korea, Korean managers, and U.S.
trainees were compared in terms of their management-related
attitudes. Korean and U.S. managers differed in terms of ten
attitudes (materialism, achievement, reflectiveness, etc.).
The values of U.S. expatriates fell between the two other
groups, indicating a socialization process.

0234   Littlewood, Roland (1985) "Jungle Madness: Some
        Observations on Expatriate Psychopathology," The
        International Journal of Social Psychiatry
        31 (Autumn): 194-7.

Early medical theories dealing with adjustment problems of
expatriates supported the concept of avoiding foreigners and
making a "home away from home" to avoid what the British
called "jungle madness." Expatriates face the opposing poles
of being away from home and living in a foreign culture.

0235   Maddox, Robert C. (1991) "Terrorism: The Current
        Corporate Response," Advanced Management Journal
        56 (Summer): 18-21.

The chances of international terrorism have increased, and
will continue to do so in the near future. This will
increase the risks for multinationals. In a survey of
seventeen firms, the author finds a relatively low level of
preparedness. Although 12 firms did have contingency plans,

most (40%) of the sample had decentralized the authority for dealing with terrorist issues, reducing the level of interest and expertise in preparing for terrorist attacks.

0236   **Maguire, Fiach, Don McClune, and Geoffrey Kelso (1989) "The Rise to Globalization: Human Resource Policy," Benefits and Compensation International 19 (January): 11-14.**

Multinational firms experience equity problems in terms of compensation and benefits for their multi-national employees. There are large international variations in reward levels and types of benefits, including pay levels, longer-term incentives, and cost-of-living differentials. In most countries except Japan, benefits are increasingly tied to performance. Cultural differences increase the complexity of global compensation packages.

0237   **March, Robert M. (1980) "Manpower and Control Issues," pp 166-92 in Bob Garratt and John Stopford (eds.), Breaking Down Barriers: Practice and Priorities for International Management Selection. Westmead, England: Gower Publishing Company Limited.**

Expatriate executives face the problem of adjusting to foreign cultures. It is necessary to provide proper pre-departure briefing in order to avoid occupational and personal problems during foreign assignments. A sample of workers in multinational subsidiaries in Australia, Indonesia, the Philippines, Malaysia, and Japan exhibited different levels of adjustment, based on national origins, destination, etc. Japan is defined as the most difficult nation for expatriates to get to know and understand.

0238   **McEnery, Jean and Gaston DesHarnais (1990) "Culture Shock," Training and Development Journal 44 (April): 43-7.**

Expatriates face unique problems due to their being sent to unfamiliar cultural environments. Family members may also find it difficult to adjust to living in a new culture. In addition to technical competence, an expatriate needs to be familiar with the host culture. Training and preparation programs are needed.

0239   **McFee, Wendy E. (1986) "Expatriates and Third Country Nationals," International Insurance Monitor 10 (December): 1-6.**

There are four alternatives to consider in a compensation plan for an expatriate. There are ten considerations for payment in a host country, including national tax systems, labor laws, and social security payments.

0240   Mendenhall, Mark and Gary Oddou (1986)
         "Acculturation Profiles of Expatriate
         Managers: Implications for Cross Cultural
         Training Programs," Columbia Journal of World
         Business 21 (Winter): 73-9.

The training of potential expatriates should be based on
their being classified according to four categories. Each
type responds best to a different acculturation and training
program.

0241   Mendenhall, Mark E. and Gary Oddou (1988) "The
         Overseas Assignment: A Practical Look,"
         Business Horizons 31 (Sept/Oct): 78-84.

Foreign assignment have unique problems, disadvantages, and
advantages. The authors list the cross-cultural adaptation
skills needs for successful assignments. There are also
discussions of organizational characteristics to observe for
those considering accepting a foreign post.

0242   Miller, Edwin L. and Raymond E. Hill
         (1978) "A Comparative Study of the Job Change
         Decision for Managers Selecting Domestic and
         Overseas Assignments," Academy of Management
         Proceedings: 287-91.

The decision structures of managers choosing new domestic
positions or overseas assignments are the same. Both samples
were concerned for their career potentials and both scored
equally high on professional competence items. Foreign
assignments should be presented to candidates in terms of
career enhancement, closeness to the person's professional
competence, and location factors. The influence of family
members has to be recognized and respected.

0243   Miller, Edwin L. and R. Julian Cattaneo
         (1982) "Some Leadership Attitudes of
         West German Expatriate Managerial Personnel,"
         Journal of International Business Studies 14
         (Summer): 39-65.

This investigation provides data about West German
expatriate managers' leadership attitudes. The results
indicate that the managers' perceptions about their
subordinates' qualifications form an important variable
influencing their leadership styles. There are regional and
other variables which influence leadership behavior.

0244   **Moran, Robert T.** (1988) **"Corporations
         Tragically Waste Overseas Experience,"**
         International Management 13 (January): 74.

Returned expatriates experience two problems. Their foreign
experience is seldom appreciated or used, and they face re-
entry problems that are ignored by their firms.

0245   **Nirenberg, John** (1986) **"Reducing Culture Shock for
         the Expatriate Manager,"** pp 391-98 in Subhash C. Jain
         and Lewis R. Tucker (eds.) International Marketing:
         Managerial Perspectives revised edition. Boston:
         Kent Publishing Company.

Foreigners define U.S. business persons as insensitive to
foreign cultural patterns. The authors develop a matrix
using six dimensions (planning, organization, supervision,
etc.) to guide U.S. expatriates in their dealings with host
country nationals. The matrix uses Malay cultural traits as
examples. Other cultural anecdotes are presented.

0246   **Nishida, Hiroko** (1985) **"Japanese Intercultural
         Communication Competence and Cross-Cultural
         Adjustment,"** International Journal of Intercultural
         Relations 9 (3): 247-70.

Japanese students visiting the U.S. were measured in terms
of their language skills and personality traits to discover
which variables increased cross-cultural adjustment and
decreased culture shock. Tolerance of ambiguity was found to
be the most significant factor. The speaking and listening
skills were related to interaction effectiveness.

0247   **Nunez, German** (1990) **"Managing the Foreign
         Service Employee,"** Advanced Management Journal
         55 (Summer): 25-9.

Expatriates are vital elements in technology transfer, and
it is important that they are motivated and effective.
Motivational policies can include bonuses for foreign
service. Problems include the inability of adjusting to new
cultural environments. One suggestion is sending a potential
expatriate to the destination for a short while before a
formal assignment is made.

0248   **Nye, David** (1988) **"The Female Expat's Promise,"**
         Across the Board 25 (February): 38-43.

U.S. women sent on overseas assignments to the Pacific Rim
countries are highly productive. The author lists ways
female expatriates can become even more effective.

0249   Oddou, Gary R. and Mark E. Mendenhall (1991)
        "Succession Planning for the 21st Century: How Well
        Are We Grooming Our Future Business Leaders?"
        Business Horizons 34 (Jan/Feb): 26-34.

One in five expatriates leaves the firm after returning from
a foreign assignment. A survey indicates that returned
expatriates are not valued highly by their employers, nor
are their special talents and experiences used extensively.

0250   Okazaki-Luff, Kazuko (1991) "On the Adjustment of
        Japanese Sojourners: Beliefs, Contentions, and
        Empirical Relations," International Journal of
        Intercultural Relations 15 (1): 85-102.

Japanese sojourners find living in foreign countries
difficult, partly because of language problems. This results
in their staying within their own national social networks
and avoiding host nationals. Communication with foreigners
is difficult because the Japanese language uses context more
than words to communicate messages. Group limits are rigid
and do not encourage full interaction outside the primary
group's ties. The article contains a bibliography on
Japanese culture shock and interaction with foreigners.

0251   Ondrack, Daniel A. (1985) "International Transfers
        of Managers in North American and European MNEs,"
        Journal of International Business Studies 16 (Fall):
        1-19.

Four European and U.S. multinational firms were studied in
terms of their international transfer policies. All four
firms used regional or polycentric decentralization
procedures for personnel coordination. Personnel policies
varied by country. The focus was on regional integration
rather than world-wide integration.

0252   Orr, David (1987) "Plus Ca Change--Plus
        C'est La Meme Chose," Benefits and Compensation
        International 17 (September): 7-10.

The compensation of expatriates remains a major problem.
Expatriates must consider home country expenses as well as
those in the host country. Another complication is whether
to link compensation to averages at home.

0253   Palsen, Peter C. and Arthur L. Fisher (1990)
        "Reducing the Burden Abroad," World 24 (2): 20-1.

One way of reducing the high costs of expatriate support is
through careful tax planning. Tax reimbursement plans can
reduce U.S. and foreign taxes for both company and employee.

0254   Parker, Barbara and Donald W. Hendon (1989) "The
        Voluntary Expatriate Female in Three Countries:
        An Underutilized Resource," International Journal
        of Management 6 (September): 254-9.

There are many female Americans who live abroad and could
work for multinational companies. These females compare
favorably with those with jobs. Voluntary expatriates are an
underutilized resource, though the authors list a number of
problems in terms of compensation, work permits, etc.

0255   Parsons, Kenneth O. (1983) Strategies for Getting
        an Overseas Job. Babylon, New York: Pilot Industries,
        Inc.

The work offers advice on resume-making, proper interview
behavior and how to find an overseas job. There is a list of
the addresses of fifty U.S. firms with overseas projects.

0256   Pazy, Asya and Yoram Zeira (1985) "Compatibility
        Expectations in Training Parent-Country
        Managers and Professionals in Host-Country
        Organizations," International Studies of Management
        and Organization 15 (Spring): 75-93.

A question in the training of personnel is whether or not
foreign candidates should be trained in the home countries
of multinational corporations. The results of a three-year
study suggests that such a training program can be a very
useful policy.

0257   Piontek, Stephen (1984) "American Expatriate
        Outlines Differences Between U.S., European Markets,"
        The National Underwriter (Life, Health Insurance
        Edition) 88 (May 19): 6, 8.

This article summarizes the interview with an American
director of a U.S. subsidiary in Europe who has lived in
Vienna for 13 years. Europeans tend to be tolerant of the
Americans' lack of languages and knowledge of proper
etiquette. Austrians have a different set of values in terms
of investment and business behavior.

0258   Reynolds, Calvin (1976) "Managing Human
        Resources on a Global Scale," Business Horizons
        19 (December): 51-56.

International business contains unique problems in terms of
human resource development. Many qualified employees do not
want foreign assignments, or else need special training.
Foreign tours are often shorter than other assignments and
disrupt normal career paths. Many assignments have the
purpose of training host nationals, a task that many
technical experts find unpleasant.

0259   Reynolds, Calvin (1989) "Cost-Effective Compensation
        of Expatriates," Topics in Total Compensation 4
        (Summer): 319-26.

There are a number of plans for compensation of expatriates,
including benefits based on host country standards. The
costs and complexity of rewards encourage reductions in the
numbers of expatriates.

0260   Richardson, Leon D. (1982) "Executive Kidnap:
        How one Man Kept his Wits and Survived,"
        International Management 37 (November): 32-7.

Executive expatriates in many countries are in danger of
being kidnapped for political or financial reasons. This
article provides an autobiographical account of a 100-day
kidnapping in Mexico. The article ends with ten rules on how
to avoid, prepare for, and survive a kidnapping.

0261   Samuel, James (1990) "Living Through the
        Business Trip," Sales and Marketing Management
        142 (March): 72-74.

The author offers practical advice on national as well as
international travel, both for personal and business
purposes.

0262   Savich, Richard S. and Waymond Rodgers (1988)
        "Assignment Overseas: Easing the Transition
        Before and After," Personnel 65 (August): 44-8.

Managers working in foreign countries need to be culturally
sensitive and able to adjust to a new environment. There is
a training program called TIDE which helps to prepare future
expatriates.

0263   Schrier, Chris (1990) "The European Community
        and the Movement of Expatriates," Benefits and
        Compensation International 20 (November): 15-9.

Although Europe is moving toward a single market,
compensation of employees and expatriates will remain a
complex problem. The economics, pay levels, and tax policies
of European countries will continue to vary. There will be
pension differences, among others.

0264   Scotti, Anthony J. (1986) Executive Safety and
        International Terrorism: A Guide for Travellers.
        Englewood Cliffs, NJ: Prentice-Hall, Inc.

This book contains comprehensive discussions related to
international terrorism when businesspersons and foreign
facilities are threatened. There are case studies, advice to
potential targets, and how to protect overseas personnel,

facilities and residences. When all else fails, there is advice on how to react to and survive hostage events. There are checklists of items to watch and a discussion of the responsibilities of U.S. agencies.

0265   Shearer, John C. (1960) High-Level Manpower in
        Overseas Subsidiaries: Experiences in Brazil and
        Mexico. Princeton: Industrial Relations Section,
        Princeton University.

Based on interviews with top-level managers in 77 U.S. corporations and subsidiaries in Mexico and Brazil, the findings provide still-valid comparisons of employment characteristics, expatriate-national personnel ratios, etc. The discussions of expatriate selection, training needs, recruitment, maintenance costs and home office relations have been supported by later studies, making this work a "classic." The work contains an early analysis of "Factor X:" the characteristics leading to success in the selection of expatriates. The relevant factors of adjustment include adaptability, willingness of the spouse to live in a foreign country, friendliness, and cultural empathy.

0266   Shenkar, Oded and Yoram Zeira (1990) "International
        Joint Ventures: A Tough Test for HR," Personnel 67
        (January): 26-31.

International joint ventures have unique human resource problems, including conflicts among employees, compensation differences and communication errors. Prior planning can avoid or limit most problems. Joint ventures with dominant parent firms do better than those with other types of ownership arrangements.

0267   Sherman, Michael J., Philip G. Huntley, and Brian
        Rockett (1989) "A Cause for Alarms," Security 33
        (November): 52-9.

The most common threat to U.S. expatriates in less developed countries is residential crime. The authors offer a number of guidelines for a comprehensive residential security system. They also discuss the four basic issues to consider when installing an alarm system in a foreign country.

0268   Skapinker, Michael (1986) "Businessmen Behind Bars:
        The Growing Hazards of Flouting the Law in Foreign
        Lands," International Management 41 (October): 20-9.

More and more countries are willing to enforce their laws by arresting, and even jailing, foreign business persons. A thorough briefing of a nation's laws and legal behavior is necessary before being transferred to a foreign post. Muslim countries are now less tolerant of foreigners' dress and drinking habits. A list of dos and don'ts is presented, including the proper reaction after being involved in an auto accident, selection of literature to bring into certain countries and how to behave while in a foreign prison.

0269   Smetanka, John A. (1985) "International Cooperation and the Expatriate Manager: A Study of the Japanese Executive in Canada," International Journal of Intercultural Relations 9 (1): 79-100.

Support for Japanese-Canadian interaction and cooperation was based on economic interests, and the latter influenced business behavior. Japanese expatriates have a clear view of their company's interests and these interests are more important than personal or ideological interests.

0270   Suptara, Prabhu (1986) "Searching the Organization for the Cross-Cultural Operators," International Management 41 (August): 10-2.

The author lists the reasons international assignments are costlier than local ones. There are many ways of determining which employees are best in terms of being sent on foreign assignments.

0271   Torbiorn, Ingemar (1982) Living Abroad: Personal Adjustment and Personnel Policy in Overseas Setting. New York: John Wiley & Sons.

This work presents all facets of working and living abroad, generally using descriptive and theoretical perspectives. There are chapters on culture shock and the U-shaped adjustment curve, the psychology of being an expatriate, adjustment of family members, determinants of expatriate satisfaction, cultural barriers to adjustment, etc. The field has added little information since the publication of this work.

0272   Toyne, Brian and Robert J. Kuhne (1983) "The Management of the International Executive Compensation and Benefit Process," Journal of International Business Studies 14 (Winter): 37-50.

Respondents from 83 companies in international commerce indicated compensation and benefits programs for expatriates were centralized. The funding for these programs, however, was more decentralized.

0273   Tung, Rosalie L. (1984) Key To Japan's Economic Strength: Human Power. Lexington, Mass: Lexington Books.

In contrast to U.S. enterprises, Japanese MNCs train future expatriate extensively to prepare them for foreign assignments. This training can greatly reduce the failure rates of those sent on overseas assignments. By contrast, U.S. enterprises sponsor relatively little preparation, resulting in a high rate of early returns of expatriates.

0274   Tung, Rosalie L. (1984) "Human Resource Planning in Japanese Multinationals: A Model for U.S. Firms?" <u>Journal of International Business Studies</u> 15 (Fall): 139-50.

U.S. failure rates for foreign assignments are higher than for Japanese multinationals. 76% of U.S. firms had failure rates ranging from 10% to 40%. U.S. firms should adopt human resource development programs similar to those developed in Japan.

0275   Tung, Rosalie L. (1986) "Corporate Executives and Their Families in China: Their Need for Cross-Cultural Understanding in Business," <u>Columbia Journal of World Business</u> 21 (Spring): 21-5.

Expatriates living in China encounter a large number of adjustment problems. There are few facilities, the language is completely different, and lifestyles differ. Business behaviors are also very different.

0276   Tung, Rosalie L. (1987) "Expatriate Assignments: Enhancing Success and Minimizing Failure," <u>Academy of Management Executive</u> 1 (May): 117-26.

Eighty-one respondents working in Japanese or European multinationals were surveyed and/or interviewed. Their answers were compared to U.S. respondents. Common factors defined as successful global strategies include having (1) a long-term perspective, (2) an international orientation, and (3) a foreign language capability.

0277   Tung, Rosalie L. (1988) "Career Issues in International Assignments," <u>Academy of Management Executive</u> 2 (August): 241-4.

The author compares U.S. and foreign multinationals in terms of their attitude toward and support of expatriate employees. There are recommendations for building successful repatriation programs.

0278   Volard, Sam V., Dennis M. Francis, and Frank W. Wagner III (1988) "Underperforming U.S. Expatriate Managers: A Study of Problems and Solutions," <u>Practising Manager</u> 8 (April): 33-7.

U.S. expatriates have the highest failure rates in the world. There are five reasons why early returns are so frequent, including a lack of understanding of non-U.S. ways of doing business and failure of families to adjust to living in a foreign environment. In addition, U.S. expatriates experience re-entry problems as well as difficulties being re-integrated into their former jobs.

0279   Wakeford, Tony (1989) "Accommodation Issues:
        Coming and Going," International Journal of
        Manpower 10 (6): 37-42.

Expatriates' compensation packages include assistance for living accommodations. Such benefits have tax and social security implications. For short assignments, expatriates may wish to keep their homes. Doing so necessitates careful tax and other financial preparations.

0280   Ward, Colleen and Wendy Searle (1991)
        "The Impact of Value Discrepancies and
        Cultural identity on Psychological and
        Sociocultural Adjustment of Sojourners,"
        International Journal of Intercultural
        Relations 15 (2): 209-25.

155 student sojourners from 42 countries and residing in New Zealand were measured in terms of mood disturbance and social difficulties. Levels of cultural identity and cultural knowledge were significant predictors.

0281   Willis, Rod (1986) "Corporations vs. Terrorists,"
        Management Review 75 (November): 16-23, 26-7.

U.S. facilities and personnel overseas are prime targets for terrorists attacks. The author provides ways to increase safety of expatriates, residences, and office. There are also ways to reduce the likelihood of kidnapping.

0282   Winsbury, Rex (1989) "Diary of an Expat,"
        Management Today 64 (December): 64-9.

The author recounts the frustrations of an assignment in Kenya. While there were advantages, there were also many disappointments, including broken contracts and difficulties in leaving the country. There was also resentment on the part of host nationals toward expatriates.

0283   Wrinkler, Connie (1987) "Working Abroad is no
        Holiday," Computerworld 21 (June 22): 81.

An American preparing for a foreign assignment should assign monetary values to the advantages and disadvantages of going abroad. There is also the necessity of adjusting to a new culture when working in a foreign country.

**0284   Zeira, Yoram (1976) "Management Development in
Ethnocentric Multinational Corporations,"
California Management Review 18 (Summer): 34-42.**

Ethnocentric multinational corporations are those whose
personnel deny the validity of cultural differences and
training in cultural sensitivity and adaptation. Such MNCs
have a high expatriate failure rate. This article describes
the self-destructive policies of such MNCs and policies to
remedy these dysfunctional attitudes.

**0285   Zeira, Yoram (1979) "Ethnocentrism in Host-Country
Organizations," Business Horizons 22 (June): 66-75.**

A survey of expatriate executives and heads of international
divisions of European-owned foreign subsidiaries indicates a
high level of ethnocentric attitudes toward staffing in
foreign countries. This policy of not employing host-country
nationals causes personnel conflicts among nationals.

**0286   Zeira, Yoram and Moshe Banai (1985) "Selection of
Expatriate Managers in MNCs: The Host-Environment
Point of View," International Studies of Management
and Organization 15 (Spring): 35-51.**

This study is based on three surveys dealing with the
selection criteria for foreign assignments by European
multinational corporations. Current selection tools are
inadequate for identifying potentially successful
candidates. Generally, those responsible for assigning
personnel to foreign posts feel their ideal criteria are
impossible to meet. As a result, they use more informal,
intuitive guidelines.

**0287   Zeira, Yoram and Moshe Banai (1987) "Selecting
Managers for Foreign Assignments," Management
Decision 25 (4): 38-40.**

The supply of capable and willing persons willing to be sent
on foreign assignments is limited. Careful selection is
necessary to avoid assignment failure. The authors list why
expatriates are needed. Foreign language ability and
cultural sensitivity are necessary attributes of potential
expatriates.

**0288   Zeira, Yoram and Ehud Harari (1977)
"Managing Third-Country Nationals in
Multinational Corporations," Business
Horizons 20 (October): 83-88.**

There are nine major problems faced by third-country
nationals, including blocked promotions, transfer anxieties,
inappropriate leadership styles, and insufficient authority.

4

Negotiations

0289   Adler, Nancy J. and John L. Graham (1989) "Cross-
        Cultural Interaction: The International Comparison
        Fallacy?" International Journal of Business Studies
        20 (Fall): 515-37.

A sample of 462 Japanese, Canadian, and U.S. business people
in negotiation simulations indicates that negotiation
behavior differs when the context is cross-cultural rather
than intra-cultural. Americans remained the most obstinate
irrespective of cross-cultural setting, and they made fewest
adjustments. The Japanese were high on adjustment when the
negotiating partner was American.

0290   Adler, Nancy L., John L. Graham, and
        Theodore Schwarz Gehrke (1987) "Business
        Negotiations in Canada, Mexico, and the United
        States," Journal of Business Research 15
        (October): 411-29.

Two-person simulated negotiation games were conducted in
three countries (N=486). The negotiating styles of the
Mexican and French-speaking Canadians were different from
the Americans' and English-speaking Canadians'. There were
differences in levels of satisfaction after the completion
of the negotiation simulations and also in the use of
instrumental tactics.

0291   Banks, John C. (1987) "Negotiating International
        Mining Agreements: Win-Win vs Lose-Lose Bargaining,"
        Columbia Journal of World Business 22 (Winter):
        67-73.

Traditional negotiating styles between multinational firms
and governments of less developed countries have been of a
win-lose nature to the disadvantage of the third world
countries. The integrative negotiating style stresses the

achieving of mutually beneficial agreements, in which a symbiotic relationship among parties is assumed.

0292   Banthin, Joane and Leigh Steizer (1988/1989) ""Opening" China: Negotiation Strategies When East Meets West," Mid-Atlantic Journal of Business 25 (Dec/Jan): 1-14.

The Chinese see the first stage of negotiations as establishing personal relationships. They also prefer to negotiate with the head of the foreign company and seldom feel an urgency to complete negotiations quickly. Westerners and Chinese often misinterpret one another's messages and intentions.

0293   Barnum, Cynthia and Natasha Wolniansky (1989) "Avoid the Great Wall Syndrome," Management Review 78 (February): 59-60.

There are certain principles of negotiating styles that can be learned from the negotiating behavior in Russia, China, and Turkey. Each country has its own negotiating style and system of logic.

0294   Barnum, Cynthia and Natasha Wolniansky (1989) "Why Americans Fail at Overseas Negotiations," Management Review 78 (October): 55-57.

The American negotiation style is often self-defeating when Americans negotiate with non-Americans. Americans focus upon disagreements and gloss over agreements. Americans are also in too much of a hurry and make concessions too quickly. Eastern European negotiators have more time and will make concessions very slowly and in small steps.

0295   Beliaev, Edward, Thomas Mullen, and Betty Jane Punnett (1985) "Understanding the Cultural Environment: U.S.-U.S.S.R. Trade Negotiations," California Management Review 28 (Winter): 100-12.

The Soviet negotiating style reflects the Soviet national character. This article indicates how specific negotiating strategies are derived from Soviet personality and political characteristics.

0296   Binnendijk, Hans editor (1987) National Negotiating Styles. Washington, D.C.: U.S. Department of State, Foreign Service Institute.

This collected work includes chapters on the national cultures and negotiating styles of China, the Soviet Union, Japan, France, Egypt, and Mexico. While the emphasis lies in diplomatic negotiating styles, there are insights on national negotiation behavior for business-related purposes.

0297   Blaker, Michael (1977) <u>Japanese International</u>
        <u>Negotiating Style</u>. New York: Columbia University
        Press.

Japanese negotiating behavior exhibits a number of
consistencies from one case to another. The author
illustrates the Japanese approach to negotiating with 18
cases of international diplomacy.

0298   Bryan, Robert M. and Peter C. Buck (1989) "The
        Cultural Pitfalls in Cross-Border Negotiations,"
        <u>Mergers and Acquisitions</u> 24 (Sept/Oct): 61-3.

Cross-cultural negotiations should stress accommodation. The
use of intermediaries is also recommended. European and U.S.
business persons customarily use different types of persons
as mediators. A fictional case study is used to illustrate
cross-cultural negotiation styles.

0299   Campbell, Nigel C. G., John L. Graham,
        Alain Jolibert, and Hans Gunther Meissner
        (1988) "Marketing Negotiations in France,
        Germany, the United Kingdom, and the United
        States," <u>Journal of Marketing</u> 52 (April): 49-62.

136 two-person teams negotiated in simulated sessions. U.S.
negotiators were influenced by on-going events. The French
were influenced by the status of the other participants. The
Germans were concerned with a balance of profit vs. buyer
satisfaction. Status and roles were both significant for the
British negotiators.

0300   Carment, D.W. and J.E. Alcock (1984) "Indian and
        Canadian Behavior in Two-person Games," <u>Journal of</u>
        <u>Conflict Resolution</u> 28 (September): 507-21.

Canadian and Indian students took part in two-person games
consisting of negotiations and compromises. The Indians were
more likely to retaliate for aggressive behavior.

0301   Casse, Pierre and Surinder Deol (1985) <u>Managing</u>
        <u>Intercultural Negotiations: Guidelines for Trainers</u>
        <u>and Negotiators</u>. Washington, D.C.: SIETAR
        International.

A series of exercises measures the levels of the reader's
listening and negotiating skills, international negotiating
skills, etc. These exercises increase the readers'
intercultural awareness and sensitivity as well as their
personal negotiating styles. One chapter describes the
characteristics of a successful inter-cultural negotiator.
Another chapter offers advice on how to negotiate across
cultures.

0302   Cohen, Jerome Alan (1983) "Negotiating Complex
        Contracts in China," chapter 2 in Parviz Saney and
        Hans Smit (eds.) Business Transactions with China,
        Japan, and South Korea. New York: Matthew Bender.

Chinese negotiators have their own practices, rhythms, and
goals that are different from those of Western negotiators.
Horizontal and vertical relations effect negotiating goals
and processes. These are influenced by Chinese history,
basic attitudes, and their view of risk allocation.

0303   Coll, Joan H. (1989) "Sino-American Cultural
        Differences: The Key to Closing a Business Venture
        with the Chinese," Mid-Atlantic Journal of Business
        25 (December): 15-9.

The Chinese have culturally specific negotiation and closing
procedures. The general values and attitudes of Chinese and
Americans differ dramatically. Americans stress individual
goals while the Chinese emphasize group goals. The Chinese
strongly feel that foreigners wishing to do business in
China must show respect.

0304   Crump, Larry (989) "One Way Ahead: Bridging the
        Negotiation Gap," Speaking of Japan 10 (July): 11-6.

The author is a professional negotiator at the Japan
Institute of Negotiation. He offers suggestions on the
values underlying the Japanese and U.S. negotiation styles.
These styles differ in five important dimensions. There are
a number of ways American negotiators could become more
effective when dealing with the Japanese.

0305   Davidson, William H. (1987) "Creating and Managing
        Joint Ventures in China," California Management
        Review 29 (Summer): 77-94.

Establishing joint ventures is the most promising strategy
for doing business in Soviet Russia. The author summarizes
the experiences of 47 U.S. firms operating joint ventures in
Russia. There are also five recommendations for managing the
negotiating process when establishing a joint venture in
Russia.

0306   Dennett, Raymond editor (1951) Negotiating with the
        Russians. New York: World Peace Foundation.

This work presents analyses of case studies of U.S.-Russian
negotiating experiences. The cases deal with foreign affair
issues, but they still remain useful for business-oriented
negotiators.

0307   DePauw, John D. W. (1981) U.S.-Chinese Trade
        Negotiations. New York: Praeger.

Negotiations with the Chinese offer a large number of
difficulties for the Western negotiator. The character of

Chinese negotiation is presented, especially the crucial element of time. The author explains why negotiations move very slowly. There are discussions of selected aspects of Chinese culture and business practices, such as guanxi. An appendix reproduces a Chinese-French contract.

0308   Druckman, Daniel, Alan A. Benton, Faizunisa
        Ali, and J. Susana Bagur (1976) "Differences
        in Bargaining Behavior: India, Argentina,
        and the United States," Journal of Conflict
        Resolution 20 (September): 413-51.

The bargaining behaviors, under experimental conditions, of adolescents from India, Argentina, and the United States indicate Indian bargainers negotiated longer, were the most competitive, and were the least willing to compromise. The Americans were the most likely to compromise. There is an excellent review of the relevant literature.

0309   Dupont, Christophe (1991) "International Business
        Negotiations," pp 331-342 in Victor A. Kremenyuk
        (ed.) International Negotiation: Analysis,
        Approaches, Issues. San Francisco, CA: Jossey-Bass
        Publishers. A Publication of the Processes of
        International Negotiations (PIN) Project.

The general theoretical and practical features and factors involved in business international negotiation are discussed using a number of examples and models. Selected concerns include short vs. long term planning, the separation of business and political agendas and concerns, and the features of joint-venture negotiations.

0310   Fisher, Glen (1980) The Cross-Cultural Dimension
        in International Negotiation. Washington, D.C.:
        Foreign Service Institute, Department of State.

The author discusses the problems inherent in cross-cultural negotiations, focusing on the Japanese, Mexican, and French negotiating styles. One problem is the attribution of motives to decrease the chances of inter-culture misunderstandings. Americans stress technical competency and authority by position. The Japanese avoid direct confrontation and define seniority as the basis for authority. Mexican negotiators are more individualistic and authority is given to the member with the most connections. The French easily make their negotiating counterparts feel inadequate.

0311   Fisher, Glen (1980) International Negotiation: A
        Cross-Cultural Perspective. Chicago: Intercultural
        Press Inc.

Negotiators carry with them unique negotiating styles and professional self-images derived from their own cultures. Negotiation is partly role playing, as defined by cultural values. There are also culturally-derived styles of logic.

The author discusses the major cultural dimensions of negotiation using examples primarily from France, Mexico and the United States.

0312   Ghauri, Pervez N. (1986) "Guidelines for
        International Business Negotiations,"
        International Marketing Review 3 (Autumn): 72-82.

There are five stages in the negotiation process. There are two groups of factors which influence this process.

0313   Ghauri, Pervez N. (1988) "Negotiating with Firms
        in Developing Countries: Two Case Studies,"
        Industrial Marketing Management 17 (February): 49-53.

Case studies are presented of the negotiation of buyers (Indian, Swedish and Nigerian) and sellers (Swedish). There were differences in culture and in negotiation behavior among firms by nationality. Differences existed in terms of (1) definitions of time, (2) commitment to an agreement, (3) understanding the other party's position, and (4) concepts of power.

0314   Graham, John L. (1983) "Brazilian, Japanese and
        American Business Negotiations," Journal
        of International Business Studies 14
        (Spring/Summer): 47-61.

Three national business negotiating styles are observed and analyzed under experimental conditions. The three nations have distinctly different styles and approaches to business negotiations.

0315   Graham, John L. (1985) "Cross-Cultural Marketing
        Negotiations: A Laboratory Experiment," Marketing
        Science 4 (Spring): 130-46.

Japanese and Americans conducted intra- and inter-cultural sales negotiations. The cultural dimension was found to be less important than the process variables (strategies, impression formation, and interpersonal attraction). Parties use more instrumental bargaining strategies in cross-cultural negotiations. More time should be spent learning about negotiating opposites (and their economic preferences) in cross-cultural negotiating situations.

0316   Graham, John L. (1985) "The Influence of
        Culture on the Process of Business
        Negotiations: An Exploratory Study,"
        Journal of International Business Studies
        16 (Spring): 81-96.

Brazilians, Japanese, and Americans have very different business negotiating styles. The study observed buyer-seller dyad behavior under laboratory conditions. Both verbal and non-verbal behavior were analyzed and reported.

0317   Graham, John L. (1988) "Negotiating
        with the Japanese: A Guide to Persuasive
        Tactics (Part 1)," East Asian Executive
        Reports 10 (November): 6, 19-21.

Negotiations take place in four stages. The contents and
importance of each stage differ for each nation. For
Americans, the persuasion stage is the most important. The
Japanese stress the sounding and information-exchange
stages. The Japanese tend to make concessions at the end of
negotiations while American negotiators make concessions
continuously.

0318   Graham, John L. (1988) "Negotiating with the
        Japanese: A Guide to Persuasive Tactics (Part 2),"
        East Asian Executive Reports 10 (December): 8, 16-17.

The Japanese negotiation-style includes first establishing
personal relationships, and the developing of a long-term
relationship. The author offers guidelines for Americans who
expect to negotiate with Japanese.

0319   Graham, John L. and J. Douglas Andrews (1987) "A
        Holistic Analysis of Japanese and American Business
        Negotiations," The Journal of Business Communication
        24 (Fall): 63-77.

The authors describe the methods and strategies used in
simulated business negotiations among twelve pairs of
business persons. Some of the findings are highlighted
through extensive quotations of participants.

0320   Graham, John L. and Roy A. Herberger, Jr.
        (1983) "Negotiators Abroad-Don't Shoot
        from the Hip," Harvard Business Review 61
        (July/August): 160-8.

U.S. negotiators are often very ill-prepared to deal with
foreigners. Negotiators should become aware of national
differences in doing business, especially in terms of their
negotiation strategies.

0321   Graham, John L. and Yoshihiro Sano (1984) Smart
        Bargaining: Doing Business with the Japanese.
        Cambridge, Mass.: Ballinger.

The authors discuss Japanese social values and national
character in terms of their negotiating behavior. There are
sections offering practical advice on how to follow business
protocol and how to negotiate effectively with Japanese.

0322   Graham, John L. and Yoshihiro Sano (1986) "Across
the Negotiating Table from the Japanese," Marketing
Review 3 (Autumn): 58-71.

The authors contrast the Japanese and American negotiating
styles. There are four stages in business negotiations. The
Japanese spend more time on the non-task sounding stage,
make concessions at the end, and avoid overt confrontation.

0323   Griffin, Trenholme J. and W. Russell Daggart (1990)
The Global Negotiator: Building Strong Business
Relationships Anywhere in the World. New York:
HarperBusiness.

This very informative work offers advice on how to negotiate
internationally. There are many anecdotes which illustrate
various strategies, advice, and cross-cultural experiences
by the authors and others. While many national examples are
offered, the authors focus on general principles and traps
that are found in international negotiation situations in
general.

0324   Gulliver, P.H. (1979) Disputes and Negotiations: A
Cross-Cultural Perspective. New York: Academic Press.

Negotiations are a special case of joint decision-making
behavior. The author develops two general models of the
negotiation process, using both anthropological cases and
industrial disputes as examples. There are also detailed
descriptions of negotiations and the best choices of
behavior in terms of specific strategies and contexts.

0325   Haber, Kaj (1988) "Negotiating Joint Ventures
in the Soviet Union," International Financial
Law Review 7 (November): 34-8.

Negotiating joint ventures in the Soviet Union should
include special attention to a number of factors, including
the arbitration clauses. The author reviews the negotiation
process in the USSR.

0326   Hahn, Elliott J. (1982) "Negotiations with the
Japanese," California Lawyer 2 (March): 20-22, 57-9.

The American negotiation style does not work well in Japan.
There are many extra-legal values that must be respected,
including many that Americans would call "social." Before
negotiations, extra care should be taken with the initial
contact and introductions.

0327   Harnett, Donald L. and Larry L. Cumming (1980)
Bargaining Behavior: An International Study.
Houston: Dame Publications.

Negotiation behavior, seen here as a dimension of decision-
making, is influenced by structural, individual and cultural
factors. National character varies in terms of a number of

dimensions (conciliation-belligerence, risk aversion vs risk taking, etc.) which influence negotiating behavior. The authors summarize a great amount of research and place their findings within a negotiation context. U.S. executives scored high on trust while other nationalities did not. U.S. executives also scored highest in terms of risk-taking and self-determination. There are also detailed analyses of bargaining strategies within the context of a Personality Attitude Schedule (PAS).

0328   Hawrysh, Brian Mark, and Judith Lynne Zaichkowsky
        (1990) "Cultural approaches to Negotiations:
        Understanding the Japanese," International
        Marketing Review 7 (2): 28-42.

The authors review the major models used to describe the Japanese negotiating style. The ethnographic approach to the behavior involved in each step of the negotiation process offers the most understanding.

0329   Hendon, Donald W. and Rebecca Angeles Hendon (1990)
        World-Class Negotiating: Dealmaking in the Global
        Marketplace. New York: John Wiley & Sons.

This comprehensive work analyzes the preferred negotiating styles and behaviors in a large number of cultures. There are simulated sessions with various nationals and detailed analyses of what the proper responses should be. There are lists of proper tactics and countermeasures, body language information, etc. This is one of the most ambitious and sophisticated attempts to prepare global negotiators.

0330   Hofstede, Geert (1989) "Cultural Predictors of
        National Negotiation Styles," pp 193-201 in Frances
        Mautner-Markhof (ed.), Processes of International
        Negotiations. Boulder, CO: Westview Press.

National rank on Hofstede's four dimensions of culture can help predict national negotiation style and behavior. For example, negotiators from high uncertainty-avoidance cultures will prefer highly structured, ritualistic procedures during negotiations.

0331   Honkanen, Matti (1991) "Sealed with a Kiss:
        Negotiating Tips for the Soviet Union,"
        Moscow International Review (Spring): 38-9.

Russians are extremely tough negotiators who are carefully selected and trained. The key to negotiating with Russians is having patience. Keeping exact minutes is important, since the Russians remember every detail to their advantage. In Russia, minutes are drafted and signed by both parties.

0332   Jastram, Roy W. (1974) "The Nakodo Negotiator,"
        California Management Review 17 (Winter): 88-90.

The Japanese term "nakodo" refers to business brokers who
arrange joint ventures and introductions and begin mediation
procedures. The use of a Nakodo to establish and maintain
business negotiations is imperative at times. Such mediators
help ease tensions and negotiate points of conflict.

0333   Kapoor, Ashok (1970) International Business
        Negotiations: A Case Study in India. New York:
        New York University Press.

The reasons for a joint venture failure between an Indian
and U.S. company are given step-by-step. The failure was
caused by cultural misunderstandings and by the fact that
each party had a different goal.

0334   Kapoor, Ashok (1975) Planning for International
        Business Negotiation. Cambridge, Mass: Ballinger
        Publishing Company.

The   author   discusses   the   nature   of   cross-cultural
negotiations, then presents five in-depth case studies of
international negotiations, as well as an analysis of the
cases.

0335   Kennedy, Gavin (1985) Doing Business Abroad. New
        York: Simon and Schuster.

This excellent work offers practical advice on how to
negotiate with Russians, Japanese, Arabs, Latin Americans,
Chinese, Europeans, and other nationals. There also guides
on doing business abroad in terms of how to react to
corruption, government restrictions, etc.

0336   Kirkbride, Paul S. and Sara F.Y. Tang (1990)
        "Negotiation: Lessons from Behind the Bamboo
        Curtain," Journal of General Management 16
        (Autumn): 1-13.

The Chinese have unique negotiating procedures. They prefer
to first establish general agreements, which they can later
use to their advantage. Negotiations proceed at a very slow
pace because a large number of levels of bureaucracies are
always involved.

0337   Kremenyuk, Victor A. editor (1991) International
        Negotiation: Analysis, Approaches, Issues. San
        Francisco: Jossey-Bass Inc., Publishers.

Although focusing on diplomatic negotiations (only one
chapter deals directly with international business), a
number of chapters are extremely useful to those expecting
to negotiate across cultures, no matter the issue. A number
of chapters offer theoretical and practical advice for those
negotiating business ventures. There are practical guides

for preliminary activities, general rules of negotiation, stages of the negotiating process, establishing timetables, etc. The emphasis is on how to develop a win-win conclusion through the understanding of common values.

0338   Lall, Arthur (1966) Modern International Negotiation: Principles and Practice. New York: Columbia University Press.

Focusing on diplomatic negotiations, the author discusses the national negotiating styles and goals of a number of nations. There are discussions of how to achieve negotiation results and avoid blocks.

0339   Last, Dianne L. (1988) "The China Link: Advice from an Expert," IEEE Spectrum 25 (April): 51-55

Chinese and American negotiators view the goals and process of negotiation in very different ways. The profit motive is suspect in China, and the Chinese prefer dealing with "old friends." The Chinese are interested in the long term rather than the short term.

0340   Lee, Kam-Hon and Thamis Wing-Chun Lo (1988) "American Businesspeoples' Perception of Marketing and Negotiating in the People's Republic of China," International Marketing Review 5 (Summer): 41-51.

136 members of the U.S. Chamber of Commerce in Hong Kong were surveyed in terms of their negotiating experiences in China. The most frequently listed problem was that language differences caused communication barriers.

0341   March, Robert M. (1988) The Japanese Negotiator: Subtlety and Strategy Beyond Western Logic. Tokyo: Kodansha International.

This work is a comprehensive description and analysis on how to negotiate with the Japanese. It is one of the best works on the topic. The author covers Japanese strategy and goals when negotiating, and how to deal with each stage. Most chapters include a list of questions and illustrative case studies.

0342   March, Robert M. (1989) "No-No's in Negotiating with the Japanese," Across the Board 26 (April): 44-51

Negotiating with Japanese should involve a number of specific policies and practices. A large amount of detail is necessary, as well as a presentation of a comprehensive proposal to guide negotiations.

0343   Mautner-Markhof, Frances editor (1989) <u>Processes of International Negotiations</u>. Boulder, CO: Westview Press.

A number of selections in this work deal with the negotiation process in establishing joint ventures, written from the point of view of authors from Finland, Hungary, Austria, and the U.S. The excellent bibliography includes articles from European publications.

0344   McCreary, Don R. (1986) <u>Japanese-U.S. Business Negotiations: A Cross-Cultural Study</u>. New York: Praeger.

The negotiating styles of Japanese and American businessmen are examined using psycholinguistic and sociohistorical perspectives. The study is based on interviews with negotiators and a detailed analysis of a Japanese-American negotiation process that failed to reach an agreement. The two styles of negotiating are contrasted in terms of each nation's national character and culture.

0345   Mendonsa, Eugene L. (1988) "Be a Winner When You Bargain Abroad," <u>Automation</u> 35 (April): 44-46.

There are six guidelines which increase the likelihood of the negotiation success in cross-cultural contexts. Three of these guidelines are: (1) be courteous as defined by the foreigners' culture; (2) learn about the foreign country's culture, and (3) learn about the other company. The author also offers several strategies, including having patience and using deadlines for your own advantage. The author is a member of the International and Domestic Negotiating Institute.

0346   Moran, Robert T. (1985) <u>Getting Your Yen's Worth: How to Negotiate with Japan, Inc</u>. Houston: Gulf Publishing Company.

The book begins with specific descriptions of the elements of Japanese national character, social values, negotiation styles and expectations. The negotiation process is explained through all of its stages. There is also a detailed self-administered test to measure the readers' preparedness to negotiate with Japanese.

0347   Moran, Robert T. and William G. Stripp (1991) <u>Dynamics of Successful International Business Negotiations</u>. Houston, Texas: Gulf Publishing Company.

The authors describe the cultural elements involved in cross-cultural negotiations, such as national definitions of time, authority patterns, and decision-making patterns.

0348   Nigel, C.G., John L. Graham, Alain
         Jolibert, and Hans Gunther Meissner (1988)
         "Marketing Negotiations in France, Germany,
         The United Kingdom and the United States,"
         Journal of Marketing 52 (April): 49-52.

Forty business persons from four nations took part in
negotiating sessions. Status and context are important for
the French; context is significant for Americans; the
Germans took the "hard sell" approach and were dogmatic. The
British established the status of participants before
negotiations started. Status and role were crucial in how
they behaved and related to others.

0349   Paton, Scott M. (1988) "Negotiating Strategy and
         Tactics," Corporate Accounting 6 (Winter): 53-56.

Cross-cultural negotiations should adhere to a number of
general principles. Foreign negotiators often claim to have
limited authority to make decisions. The negotiator should
insist on dealing with the top authorities. There are a
number of pressure tactics that are commonly used to
intimidate American negotiators.

0350   Pettibone, Peter J. (1990) "Negotiating a Joint
         Venture in the Soviet Union: How to Protect Your
         Interest," The Journal of European Business 2
         (Nov/Dec): 5-12.

Negotiating a proposal in Soviet Russia takes from one to
two or more years. The are certain strategies that should
be taken into account when negotiating an agreement. In
Russia, you can only do what is expressly permitted; in the
West, you can do anything that is not prohibited. A contract
should contain a "no-shop" clause which prohibits the
Soviets from negotiating with others, and a "no-competition"
clause, or your Soviet partner may become your competitor.

0351   Princen, Thomas (1987) "International
         Mediation-The View from the Vatican,"
         Negotiation Journal 3 (October): 347-366.

Vatican officials have negotiated a number of international
treaties or have mediated disputes. The article offers
guidelines on the strategies and techniques used by Vatican
negotiators to settle an Argentina-Chile dispute.

0352   Pye, Lucian W. (1982) Chinese Commercial Negotiation
         Style. Cambridge, Mass: Oelgeschlager, Gunn & Hain.

The author discusses the elements of negotiating with
Chinese. Buyers and sellers are treated differently. There
is concrete advice on how to negotiate, how to form a team,
etc. There is a section on Chinese national character. The
principles of negotiating with Chinese are listed.

0353   Pye, Lucian W. (1986) "The China Trade: Making the
        Deal," Harvard Business Review 64 (July/August):
        74, 76-80.

The Chinese use different negotiating techniques than do
Americans. The Chinese prefer to establish agreements on
general principles and later use these arguments to obtain
advantages for specific items. The author then offers
descriptions of other Chinese negotiation behavior and aims.

0354   Rajan, Mahesh N. and John L. Graham (1991)
        "Nobody's Grandfather Was a Merchant:
        Understanding the Soviet Commercial
        Negotiation Process and Style," California
        Management Review 33 (Spring): 40-57.

The Soviet negotiation process is (1) lengthy, (2) based on
unique priorities, (3) secretive, (4) risk-adverse, (5)
uncompromising, and (6) very manipulative. The concepts of
"profit" and "market" are ill-understood by the Soviets.
Contractual details are often not protected by the local
authorities. An example of manipulation is the Soviet
practice of negotiating with a company's competitors at the
same time. Another example is the bringing in of a stranger
who flies into a rage for "treating Soviet negotiators with
disrespect and distrust," then demanding concessions as
apologies.

0355   Scott, Bill and Bertil Billing (1990) Negotiating
        Skills in Engineering and Construction: Winning in
        the International Arena. New York: Van Nostrand
        Reinhold.

Negotiation is always a step-by-step process. Each step is
discussed (preparation, bidding, settling, post-contract
negotiations, etc.). An appendix offers cultural differences
in negotiating styles. The emphasis is on presenting
"universal issues" to aid construction engineers in
negotiating. The usefulness of the work is greater than its
use for engineers.

0356   Shenkar, Oded and Simcha Ronen (1987)
        "The Cultural Context of Negotiations:
        The Implications of Chinese Interpersonal
        Norms," Journal of Applied Behavioral
        Science 23 (2): 263-75.

Negotiations in Asian countries are influenced by Confucian
values. These values stress harmony, hierarchy, and kinship
ties. Compared to U.S. values, Chinese norms/behavior are
guided by the principles of (1) leadership, (2) credibility,
(3) collectivism, and (4) indebtedness. The Chinese, in
addition, differentiate among levels of friendships.

0357   Sheth, Jagdish (1983) "Cross-Cultural Influences on
        the Buyer-Seller Interaction/Negotiation Process,"
        Asia Pacific Journal of Management 1 (September):
        46-55.

The author provides a conceptual framework to guide
empirical research on cross-cultural influences on the
buyer-seller process.

0358   Stewart, Sally and Charles F. Keown (1989)
        "Talking with the Dragon: Negotiating in
        the People's Republic of China," Columbia
        Journal of World Business 24 (Fall): 68-72.

50 Chinese managers in Hong Kong were interviewed in terms
of proper and successful negotiation techniques in China.
Maturing Chinese negotiators are relying less on personal
relations than in the past. Chinese negotiation teams are
twice as large as Western teams. One Chinese tactic is to
make sudden demands to place Westerners at a disadvantage.

0359   Stone, Ray (1988) "The Chinese Negotiating Game,"
        Practising Manager 9 (Spring): 27-30.

Conducting negotiations in China demands patience, hard
work, perseverance, and deal-making expertise. The author
claims Australians generally lack these characteristics.
Foreign negotiators wishing to do business in China should
bring their own interpreters and arrange appointments before
arriving. Chinese negotiation tactics include repetition,
delays, and slowness in decision-making.

0360   Stone, Ray (1989) "Negotiating in Asia,"
        Practising Manager 9 (Autumn): 36-39.

Asian negotiation practices are different from those in the
West. Australians value informality while Asians do not. The
article contains a nine-point guide on negotiation behavior
in Asia.

0361   Stone, Ray (1990) "Negotiating Tactics: Negotiating
        in the Philippines," Practising Manager 10 (Winter):
        25-73.

The author offers a list of basic negotiating principles
which must be adjusted to specific cultural contexts. In the
Philippines, negotiation is best done indirectly through
personal relationships, while recognizing the power and
corruption dimensions. Patience and sincerity are major
factors.

0362   Sunoo, Jan Jung-Min (1990) "Some Guidelines for
        Mediators of Intercultural Disputes," Negotiation
        Journal 6 (October): 383-9.

The author describes a case study of negotiations between a
foreign-owned firm and a U.S. labor union. The case study

illustrates intercultural misunderstandings. The article
contains seven perceptive rules of thumb for intercultural
mediations.

0363   Swierczek, Frederic William (1990) "Culture and
        Negotiation in the Asian Context: Key Issues in the
        Marketing of Technology," Journal of Managerial
        Psychology 5 (5): 17-24.

This article describes the results of a conference in which
21 Asian participants simulated negotiation behavior. The
results illustrated Asian negotiation tactics and which
characteristics of negotiation work best.

0364   Tung, Rosalie L. (1982) "U.S.-China Trade
        Negotiations: Practices, Procedures, and Outcomes,"
        Journal of International Business Studies 13
        (Fall): 25-38.

The author describes how to best negotiate with the Chinese.
Data from 138 U.S. firms which had negotiated with Chinese
indicate the strategies felt to lead to success. Items which
result in success include "attitude of U.S. firms," which is
made up of the variables of preparation, patience,
sincerity, and personal relationships. Wishing to establish
long-term relationships is an important factor.

0365   Tung, Rosalie L. (1984) Business Negotiations with
        the Japanese. Lexington, Mass: Lexington Books.

The author is an expert on Pacific Rim societies, especially
Japan and China. Part of the book is based on the responses
from 114 questionnaires of Americans who have experienced
business negotiations in Japan. Important reasons for
negotiation success were (1) having had experienced previous
negotiations with the Japanese and (2) having read books on
Japanese culture and business culture. The author discusses
Japanese national character, correct business protocols, and
the elements of Japanese negotiating style.

0366   Tung, Rosalie L. (1984) "How to Negotiate with the
        Japanese," California Management Review 26 (Summer):
        62-77.

The process of negotiating with the Japanese is illustrated
by data from 114 U.S. firms operating in Japan. The
conclusions describe the social and cultural factors
associated with success or failure when negotiating with the
Japanese.

0367   Tung, Rosalie L. (1991) "Handshakes Across the Sea:
        Cross-Cultural Negotiating for Business Success,"
        Organizational Dynamics 19 (Winter): 30-43.

There are five key elements which aid in successful
negotiation with Koreans. These are derived from interviews
with 18 senior executives who have formed U.S.-Korean joint

ventures. Decision-making in Korean firms is centralized and quicker than in Japan, though Korean negotiators are willing to stall and delay to increase their advantages. Personal considerations are often more convincing than logic. Americans are often criticized for being "too logical." Money and profit are not the only important motivators among Koreans.

0368   Unterman, Israel (1984) "Negotiation and Cross-
        Cultural Communication," pp 69-75 in Diane B.
        Bendahmane and John W. McDonald, Jr. (eds.)
        International Communication Washington, D.C.: Foreign
        Service Institute, U.S. Department of State.

Training in negotiating skills is necessary and extremely effective. Elements that need to be studied in cross-cultural settings include body language, gateways and barriers to communication, understanding emotions, and learning how people from different cultures reach decisions. The author discusses in detail a program to teach cross-cultural negotiation skills.

0369   Wagner, Cecilia L. (1990) "Influences on
        Sino-Western Joint Venture Negotiations,"
        Asia Pacific Journal of Management 7
        (October): 79-100.

The author summarizes areas of satisfaction and problems experienced by Western partners in their joint ventures in China. Negotiation concerns and patterns have unique features reflecting the social, cultural, and governmental contexts, and influence the negotiation process in China.

0370   Watts, R.E. (1983) "Briefing the American
        Negotiator in Japan," International Lawyer
        16 (Fall): 597-612.

The author presents a typical problem in negotiation. There are also discussions of the Japanese conception of contracts and conciliation in terms of national character and values. Seventeen guidelines are presented. The article is superior.

0371   Weiss, Julian (1988) "The Negotiating Style of the
        People's Republic of China: The Future of Hong Kong
        and Macao," The Journal of Social, Political and
        Economic Studies 13 (Summer): 175-94.

The Chinese negotiation style is different from those in other countries. One set of strategies of the Chinese is to present non-negotionable demands, set deadlines and negotiate concessions only at the last minute. This last stage makes the foreign parties more willing to offer concessions in turn.

0372   Willmer, W. A. P. and W. Holden (1987) "Anglo-
        Japanese Negotiations: A Computer Simulation,"
        Industrial and Commercial Training 19 (July/August):
        21-23.

A computer simulation was developed to describe the elements
and stages of the Japanese-style negotiation in relation to
British counterparts. The Japanese use silence to frustrate
the British. There are also many other characteristics of
the Japanese negotiation behavior to take into account.

0373   Yuann, James W. (1987) "Negotiating a
        Technology License," China Business Review
        14 (May/June): 50-52.

The author describes the steps leading to doing business in
China. Early steps include being invited to deliver a
presentation in China. Negotiations will also follow a
certain sequence of stages. There is advice on specific
items to consider and/or demand.

0374   Zartman, William (1975) "Negotiations: Theory and
        Reality," Journal of International Affairs 29
        (Spring): 69-77.

An outline of a theory of cross-cultural negotiation is
presented. Basic elements of negotiations are "referents:"
the basic philosophical principles of the participants.
Negotiations also include "turning points."

0375   Zartman, I. William editor (1976) The 50% Solution:
        How to Bargain Successfully with Highjackers,
        Strikers, Bosses, Oil Magnates, Arabs, Russians,
        and Other Worthy Opponents in this Modern World.
        Garden City, New York: Anchor/Doubleday.

Although this collection deals primarily with political
negotiations, there are selections that present models of
international negotiations as well as business-government
negotiations.

5

Multicultural Studies

0376   Adler, Nancy J. (1983) "Cross-Cultural
        Management Research: The Ostrich and the
        Trend," The Academy of Management Review
        8 (April): 226-32.

An analysis of articles dealing with cross-cultural
management in 24 journals published during 1971-80 indicates
that less than five percent of organizational behavior
articles focus on cross-cultural topics. This percentage
shows no increase over time.

0377   Adler, Nancy J. (1983) "A Typology of
        Management Studies Involving Culture,"
        Journal of International Business Studies
        14 (Fall): 29-47

There are six approaches used to research cross-cultural
management issues: parochial, ethnocentric, polycentric,
comparative, geocentric, and synergistic. Each approach
involves specific assumptions, methodologies and questions.

0378   Adler, Nancy J. (1986-87) "Women in Management
        Worldwide," International Studies of Management
        and Organization 16 (Fall/Winter): 3-32.

The author surveys the extent women work outside the home
and reach managerial levels throughout the world.

0379   Adler, Nancy J., Robert Doktor, and S. Gordon
        Redding (1986) "From the Atlantic to the
        Pacific: Cross-Cultural Management Reviewed,"
        Journal of Management 12 (Summer): 295-318.

There is a growing shift in business from the Atlantic to
the Pacific Rim. The authors review the cross-cultural
literature in business and in the social sciences. They find
that cultural diversity is a significant factor in work-

related attitudes and behavior and should be recognized as such.

0380   Agthe, Klaus E. and Kim J. Pendergast (1983)
        "Bhumiputra: What is it? And Why do I Need It?"
        Business Horizons 26 (Nov/Dec): 60-8.

The Malaysian term "bhumiputra" means "native to the soil" and reflects a nationalistic attitude increasingly found throughout the world. U.S. companies wishing to maintain an international presence must adopt a multi-local orientation. There are guidelines and examples on how to select a partner for a joint venture under a variety of specific socio-economic conditions.

0381   Ashton, David (1984) "Cultural Differences:
        Implications for Management Development,"
        Management Education and Development 15
        (Spring): 5-13.

Cultures differ in their position on the instrumental-social dimension. Authority, for example, may be invested in a role or function, or may be person-based. Cultures also differ in terms of Hofstede's four dimensions of culture. The author discusses different workers' attitudes from various cultures. Each national culture produces its own organizational culture.

0382   Austin, James E. and Thomas Kohn editors (1990)
        Strategic Management in Developing Countries. New
        York: Free Press.

31 case studies from 18 different countries based on material developed at the Harvard Graduate School of Business Administration are presented to illustrate various problems of international business. Included are cases describing problems due to cultural misunderstandings and culture conflict.

0383   Bijinen, Emanuel J. and Ype H. Poortinga
        (1988) "The Questionable Value of
        Cross-Cultural Comparisons with the Eysenck
        Personality Questionnaire," Journal of
        Cross-Cultural Psychology 19 (June): 193-202.

The authors criticize the methodology used by Eysenck. Eysenck has developed a questionnaire to compare values along several dimensions using cross-cultural samples. This controversy is relevant to the cross-cultural study of values. See entry 0470.

0384   Boulgarides, James D. and Moonsong David
        Oh (1984) "A Comparison of Japanese, Korean, and
        American Decision Styles," Proceedings of the
        Academy of International Business: 730-41.

Four decision styles exist (directive, analytic, conceptual,
and behavioral). The Japanese and Korean samples were more
alike compared to Americans. American managers were more
analytic and less conceptual.

0385   Boyacigiller, Nakiye Advan, and Nancy J.
        Adler (1991) "Parochial Dinosaur:
        Organizational Science in a Global Context,"
        Academy of Management Review 16 (April): 262-90.

Management research, education, and theory are analyzed from
three perspectives. The results indicate that academic
management is parochial and limited by U.S. cultural biases.
An organizational science is needed which is universal,
regiocentric, and intercultural.

0386   Child, John (1981) "International Management: The
        Challenge of Cross-National Inquiry," Leadership
        & Organization Development Journal 2 (2): 2-5.

An important goal of cross-national studies is to determine
which aspects of organization and management are sensitive
to their national contexts and which aspects can be more
easily borrowed to help reform weak organizations. Three
general models (contingency, cultural, and capitalism) are
discussed.

0387   Christina, Allard (1990) "Changing Times: Former
        Fast-Trackers Take to watching the Clock,"
        Canadian Business 63 (June): 163-7.

Managers from different countries ranked "more time with
family" ahead of "more money" as things that would make them
happier. More employees are turning down promotions in order
to stay in their communities.

0388   Cole, Robert E. (1989) Strategy for Learning:
        Small Group Activities in American,
        Japanese and Swedish Industry. Berkeley:
        University of California Press.

The author studies the evolution and activities of
autonomous work groups in three countries. Each country
adopted small-group policies for different reasons, based in
part on differing national policies and cultural values.

0389   Conway, Michael A. (1986) "Mergers and Acquisitions
        3: Ten Pitfalls of Joint Ventures," Personnel 63
        (September): 50-1.

U.S.-foreign joint ventures are less likely to fail if
certain policy precautions are taken. These include a long-

term approach, careful selection of expatriates, and placing culturally-sensitive persons in charge of foreign divisions.

0390   Cosmas, Stephen C. and Jagdish N. Sheth (1980) "Identification of Opinion Leaders Across Cultures: An Assessment for Use in the Diffusion of Innovations and Ideas," Journal of International Business Studies 11 (Spring): 66-73.

Based on respondents from five different cultural backgrounds, there exists a set of common dimensions by which opinion leaders are evaluated. However, different cultures assign different weights to each dimension.

0391   Darling, John R. (1986) "Managing Up in the Multinational Firm," Leadership & Organization Development Journal 7 (1): 21-6.

Differences in cultural backgrounds cause difficulties in multinational firms. There are four types of social styles (amiable, analytical, driver, and expressive), each of which is acceptable in selected cultural contexts.

0392   Doktor, Robert (1989) "A Cross-Cultural Study of Time-Use Behavior by Chief Executives," International Journal of Management 6 (September): 318-24.

The differences in time use for CEOs in Japan, South Korea, Hong Kong, and the United States were analyzed. No differences in the relative amounts of time spent alone or with others were found. However, the average duration of each work unit varied by national origin. The amount of time spent on tasks lasting an average of less than nine minutes ranged from 10% (South Korea), 14% (Japan), 37% (Hong Kong Chinese) to 49% (U.S.).

0393   Ebrahimi, Bahman and John B. Miner (1991) "The Cultural Dynamics of Managerial Motivation Among Students from Pan-Pacific Basin Countries," Journal of Global Business 2 (Spring): 87-98.

Managerial motivational levels are studied using samples of students whose origins were the U.S., Thailand, and seven other Asian countries. Religion was not found to be a significant variable. Managerial motivation as measured by the Miner Sentence Completion Scale is found in all national samples, though there are sub-cultural variations in the U.S. High MSCS scores were found in the Japanese, Korean, and Taiwanese samples.

0394   El-Namaki, M.S.S. (1988) "Encouraging Entrepreneurs
        in Developing Countries," Long Range Planning 21
        (August): 98-106.

Social factors play an important part in establishing small
firms in developing countries. These factors, however, vary
from culture to culture.

0395   Elashmawi, Farid (1991) "Multi-Cultural
        Management: New Skills for Global Success,"
        Tokyo Business Today 59 (February): 54-6.

Culture is defined in different ways according to cultural
background. American managers define culture as beliefs,
values and ways of thinking. Asians would first emphasize
history and tradition. Arabs first mention history,
tradition, and religion. The other aspects of culture to
study are degrees of competition allowed, group harmony, and
authority patterns.

0396   Elizur, Dov, Borg Ingwer, Raymond Hunt,
        and Istvan Magyari Beck (1991) "The Structure
        of Work Values: A Cross Cultural Comparison,"
        Journal of Organizational Behavior 12
        (January): 21-38.

2,280 respondents from eight countries completed Work Values
Questionnaires. Using Guttman's Smallest Space Analysis,
essentially the same values structure was found across the
eight national samples. In terms of rank orders of work
values, achievement was ranked highest by respondents in
China, Taiwan, Korea, and Israel. U.S. respondents ranked
achievement second, and Dutch and Hungarian samples ninth.
Instrumental values were ranked low by Chinese, Dutch, U.S.,
and Israeli samples, and high for Koreans and Hungarians.

0397   Engholm, Christopher (1991) When Business East
        Meets Business West: The Guide to Practice and
        Protocol in the Pacific Rim. New York: John
        Wiley & Sons, Inc.

The author summarizes the major business protocols found in
the Pacific Rim. Discussions include negotiating styles,
women expatriates, translation problems, communication
issues, and business entertaining.

0398   England, George W. (1973) "Personal Value
        Systems and Expected Behavior of Managers--A
        Comparative Study in Japan, Korea and the
        United States," pp 25-48 in Desmond Graves (ed.),
        Management Research: A Cross-Cultural Perspective.
        San Francisco: Jossey-Bass.

This chapter tests the author's theoretical model of the
relationship of values to behavior, using samples of
managers in the U.S. (1071), Japan (394), and Korea (223).
National cultural differences were measured on four

dimensions of personal value orientations: pragmatic, moralistic, effective, and mixed. Koreans valued organizational efficiency and profit maximization least. Japanese valued high productivity and organizational growth most. American managers valued employee welfare highest.

0399   England, George W. and William T. Whitely (1990) "Cross-National Meanings of Working," pp 65-106 in Arthur P. Brief and Walter R. Nord (eds.), **Meanings of Occupational Work: A Collection of Essays**. Lexington, Mass.: Lexington Books.

Samples of adults in six countries (Belgium, West Germany, Israel, Japan, Holland, and the United States) were asked for their multidimensional meanings of work and what constituted "work." These attitudes were correlated with other values and national economic levels. Workers were classified into eight general categories according to their value profiles (economic, alienated, techno-bureaucratic, duty-oriented, work-centered, etc.). Each category was compared in terms of its optimum organizational environment or "best fit" in terms of person-work interaction.

0400   Evans, W. A., K.C. Hau, and D. Sculli (1989) "A Cross-Cultural Comparison of Managerial styles," **Journal of Management Development** 8 (3): 5-13.

A review of the literature dealing with cross-cultural managerial styles results in two general models. One model assumes that managerial behavior is determined by its specific cultural context. The second model assumes that management style is determined by the technological or developmental level of each society. A meta-analysis of the literature suggests each model is partly correct.

0401   Everett, James E., Bruce Stening, and Peter A. Longton (1982) "Some Evidence for an International Managerial Culture," **Journal of Management Studies** 19 (April): 153-62.

365 expatriate and local managers working for Singaporean subsidiaries of British, Japanese, and American firms were surveyed using 18 adjectival antonym pairs in terms of their semantic content. The results suggest that a shared international managerial culture exists.

0402   Fayerweather, John (1981) "Four Winning Strategies for the International Corporation," **The Journal of Business Strategy** 2 (Fall): 25-36.

There are four strategy models that characterize international corporations. One aspect of these models is the determination of which managerial skills are appropriate for each host nation. Each model includes the question of how managerial skills relate to the host culture.

0412   Handy, Charles (1986) <u>Gods of Management: The Changing World of Organisation</u>. London: Souvenir Press.

Organizations and personalities can be classified in terms of four managing styles and their combinations, defined as the (1) Zeus, (2) Apollo, (3) Dionysius, and (4) Athena models. Each country tends to favor one type of work pattern. The Japanese have developed organizations that approach the Apollonian ideal; Indians and Filipinos follow the Zeus model; Anglo-Saxon organization are influenced by the values of Athena; and French organizational behavior are a combination of the Zeus and Apollo models.

0413   Harari, Ehud and Yoram Zeira (1977) "Attitudes of Japanese and Non Japanese Employees: A Cross-National Comparison in Uninational and Multinational Corporations," <u>International Journal of Comparative Sociology</u> 18 (Sept/Dec): 228-41.

The authors conducted attitude surveys in six subsidiaries of international firms in Japan, France, the U.S., and Israel. In general, the attitudes of employees were similar, showing a growing cross-cultural homogenization among employees of large organizations, irrespective of national origin. The attitudes of Japanese workers were similar to those of other nationals.

0414   Hayes, John, and Christopher W. Allinson (1988) "Cultural Differences in Learning Styles of Managers," <u>Management International Review</u> 28 (3): 75-80.

The Learning Style Questionnaire was administered to 195 managers in India, East Africa, and the UK. The learning style of each culture was different. The cultural samples also differed in terms of Hofstede's four dimensions of culture.

0415   Hegarty, W. Harvey and Richard C. Hoffman (1990) "Product/Market Innovations: A Study of Top Management Involvement Among Four Cultures," <u>The Journal of Product Innovation Management</u> 7 (September): 186-99.

Managerial decisions on new products and markets vary by national background. Germanic managers focused on longer-term planning procedures and social trends the most. Anglo managers studied technical trends more closely than other cultural groups.

0416   Herold, Karl G. and David D. Knoll (1987)
        "Negotiating Drafting International
        Distribution, Agency, and Representative
        Agreements: The United States Exporter's
        Perspective," The International Lawyer 21
        (Fall): 939-87.

An important relationship variable often ignored by
Americans for successfully doing business outside U.S.
boundaries is the establishment and maintenance of trust
among parties. The authors discuss how differently
representative agreements and contracts are defined in
various countries and foreign legal systems and courts.

0417   Hill, John S., Richard R. Still, and Unal
        I. Boya (1991) "Managing the Multinational
        Sales Force," International Marketing Review
        8 (1): 19-31.

Some American sales methods work well abroad. It is
difficult to maintain standardized compensation policies
when a firm has a multinational sales force. Preferred
reward systems also vary by culture. Japanese employees
prefer group-based commission systems and an emphasis on
seniority.

0418   Hinrichs, Karl, William Roche, and Carmen Sirianni
        editors (1991) Working Time in Transition: The
        Political Economy of Working Hours in Industrial
        Nations. Philadelphia: Temple University Press.

This collection of essays on the extent and use of working
time in seven countries offers a wide range analysis of the
use of working time in terms of quantity and quality within
a historical context, including such related topics as
desire for less work vs. higher incomes, overtime, leisure,
and unemployment. The collection offers a cross-cultural
description of attitudes toward working time in industrial
and post-industrial societies.

0419   Hisrich, Robert D. (1986) "The Woman Entrepreneur:
        A Comparative Analysis," Leadership & Organization
        Development Journal 7 (2): 8-16.

1,283 female entrepreneurs in Puerto Rico, the Republic of
Ireland, Northern Ireland, and the United States were
surveyed. The Irish and U.S. samples ranked the desires for
independence and achievement highest. For Puerto Ricans,
economic need and job satisfaction were ranked highest.

0420   Hofstede, Geert (1980) Culture's Consequences:
        International Differences in Work-Related Values.
        Beverly Hills, CA.: Sage Publications.

This work forms a major research direction and is one of the
most significant work in the area of comparative work-
related attitudes. Hofstede operationalizes culture as
forming four dimensions. These dimensions form the work-
related issues/problems faced by members of all cultures.
The findings are based on over 100,000 questionnaires of
workers employed in 40 divisions of IBM throughout the
world.

0421   Hofstede, Geert (1980) "Motivation, Leadership, and
        Organization: Do American Theories Apply Abroad?"
        Organizational Dynamics 9 (Summer): 42-63.

This is a summary of Hofstede's survey of workers in 40
countries. He presents his concept of culture, which can be
operationalized on a comparative basis. Commentaries of this
article follow in vol. 10 (Summer, 1981) of Organizational
Dynamics.

0422   Hofstede, Geert (1981) "Culture and
        Organizations," International Studies of
        Management and Organization 10 (Winter): 15-44.

This article is a revised version of the author's first
chapter of Culture's Consequences (1980). It extends his
discussion of the concept "culture" and establishes the
foundation for a science of organizational culture on a
comparative basis.

0423   Hofstede, Geert (1983) "National Cultures in
        Four Dimensions: A Research-Based Theory
        of Cultural Differences among Nations,"
        International Studies of Management and
        Organization 13 (Spring/Summer): 46-76.

This is a summary of findings from an international survey
of over 116,000 questionnaires in 50 countries at two points
in time. Scale scores on four dimensions (Power Distance,
Uncertainty avoidance, Individualism vs. Collectivism, and
Masculinity vs. femininity) are given for national samples,
compared with previous studies, and correlated with national
economic data (per capita GNP, etc.)

0424   Hofstede, Geert (1983) "The Cultural Relativity of
        Organizational Practices and Theories," Journal of
        International Business Studies 14 (Fall): 75-90.

The author summarizes his findings related to cross-cultural
differences in work-related values using samples from 50
countries. Managerial theories based on one country's
experiences are no longer relevant, since work-related
values have been shown to vary from culture to culture.

0425   Hofstede, Geert (1984) "Cultural Dimensions in
        Management and Planning," Asia Pacific Journal
        of Management 1 (January):81-99.

Hofstede reports on his 50-nation study of the culture of
work. Management behavior and skills are culture-specific.
The author defines the various areas of work-related
behavior (time, showing-hiding emotions, emotional needs,
planning, etc.) that vary according to their cultural
contexts.

0426   Hofstede, Geert (1984) "National Cultures Revisited,"
        Asia Pacific Journal of Management 2 (September):
        22-28.

The author explains his theoretical framework and research
on cultural values in 50 countries. Such "national cultures
approach" studies--derived from the "national character"
school of the 1950s--allow anthropologists to make a number
of valuable contributions in the areas of intercultural
negotiations, cross-cultural management, etc.

0427   Hofstede, Geert and Michael H. Bond (1984)
        "Hofstede's Culture Dimensions: An Independent
        Validation using Rokeach's Value Survey,"
        Journal of Cross-Cultural Psychology 15
        (December): 417-33.

The authors re-analyze data collected earlier in nine Asian
and Pacific nations. The results showed a correlation
between the data and those collected by Hofstede. Selected
cultural value dimensions of Hofstede are found in the
secondary analysis.

0428   Hofstede, Geert, Neuijen Bram, and Denise
        Daval (1990) "Measuring Organizational Cultures:
        A Qualitative and Quantitative Study Across
        Twenty Cases," Administrative Science Quarterly
        35 (June): 286-311.

Twenty organizations in Denmark and the Netherlands are
studied in terms of six dimensions of corporate cultures.
The views of corporate culture were determined by the socio-
economic characteristics of the respondents. The methodology
and usefulness of this approach are defended.

0429   Hortum, Mustafel and Lloyd H. Muller (1989)
        "Management and Culture," Supervision 50 (1): 14-7.

Management styles reflect their cultural origins and are
often difficult to change. Hofstede's framework of four
dimensions of culture provides a conceptual framework to
understand foreign work-related behavior and how to
introduce and adapt Western managerial patterns into other
cultural contexts.

0430   Horvath, Dezso, Koya Azumi, David J. Hickson,
        and Charles J. McMillan (1981) "Bureaucratic
        Structures in Cross-National Perspective:
        A Study of British, Japanese, and Swedish
        Firms," pp 537-63 in Gunter Dlugos and Klaus
        Weiermair (eds.), Managing Under Differing Value
        Systems: Political, Social, and Economic
        Perspectives in a Changing World. Berlin and
        New York: Walter de Gruyter.

Contextual factors (size, technology, and inter-organization
links) exert similar pressures in 36 factories in three
countries. But personal adjustment to bureaucracies varies
according to national culture. The article is part of the
Aston Programme. The bibliography is comprehensive.

0431   Inzerilli, Giorgio (1978) "Some Hypotheses
        on the Nature of Managerial Roles in Developing
        Countries," Academy of Management Proceedings:
        282-6.

Traditional and modern societies have very different ideal
characteristics. These differences are reflected in changing
managerial   roles   and   behavior   under   conditions   of
modernization. This results in managerial role conflicts
among managers in developing countries.

0432   Izraeli, Dafna N. and Todd D. Jick (1986)
        "The Art of Saying No: Linking Power to
        Culture," Organization Studies 7 (2): 171-92.

There are different dimensions of refusing requests or
saying no. The "refusal ritual" tactics among managers in
Israel, Canada, and the U.S. indicate large cultural
differences in behavior. U.S. managers were most likely to
use entitlement types of denials. Canadian and Israeli
managers were more likely (76% and 46%, respectively) to use
normative invocations.

0433   Jackofsky, Ellen F., John W. Slocum, Jr.,
        and Sara J. McQuaid (1988) "Cultural
        Values and the CEO: Alluring Companions?"
        The Academy of Management Executive 2
        (February): 39-49.

The   authors   review   Hofstede's   findings,   explain   the
consequences of rankings on four dimensions of culture, and
relate these to CEO roles. Cultural values are seen as
determining organizational structure and CEO behavior.

0434   Jaeger, Alfred M. (1984) "The Appropriateness
        of Organization Development Outside North
        America," International studies of Management
        and Organization 14 (Spring): 23-35.

The author compares values dealing with Organizational
Development using samples of respondents from 40 countries

as developed by Hofstede. OD values deal with the adaptation of McGregor's Theory-Y assumptions in terms of four dimensions (power distance, uncertainty avoidance, masculinity, and individualism). The first two dimensions are especially good guides to measure particular cultural values in relation to Organizational Development acceptance.

0435   Jurgens, Ulrich (1989) "The Transfer of Japanese
        Management Concepts in the International Automobile
        Industry," pp 204-18 in Stephen Wood (ed.) The
        Transformation of Work? Skill, Flexibility and The
        Labour Process. Boston: Unwin Hyman Ltd.

Western management experts have borrowed a number of elements of Japanese-style management and production. The core of this borrowing is the decentralization of production responsibility. These ideas have reinforced borrowings from U.S. and Swedish firms.

0436   Kanungo, Rabindra N. and Richard W. Wright (1983)
        "A Cross-Cultural Comparative Study of Managerial
        Job Attitudes," Journal of International Business
        Studies 14 (Fall): 115-30.

Research in Canada, France, Japan, and the UK indicates that job outcomes and rewards sought by managers differ by culture. British managers seek extrinsic rewards more than do the French. Japanese managers received satisfaction from self-sacrifice for the good of the organization.

0437   Kelley, Lane and Reginald Worthley (1981)
        "The Role of Culture in Comparative
        Management: A Cross-cultural Perspective,"
        Academy of Management Journal 24 (March):
        164-73.

A review of the literature indicates that cross-national studies can be classified into two general models. The authors discuss these two major models in the discipline and test a third using U.S. and Japanese samples. The results support the model which posits that culture (rather than contextual variables) influences managerial attitudes.

0438   Kelley, Lane, Arthur Whatley, and Reginald
        Worthley (1987) "Assessing the Effects of
        Culture on Managerial Attitude: A Three-Culture
        Test," Journal of International Business Studies
        18 (Summer): 17-31.

The study attempts to differentiate cultural from other environmental factors by using samples of Japanese, Chinese, and Mexican Managers and their ethnic-American counterparts. The results indicate the persistence of unique cultural characteristics when the sub-samples are compared.

0439   Kelley, Lane, Art Whatley, and Reginald
        Worthley (1990) "Self-Appraisal, Life Goals,
        and National Culture: An Asian-Western
        Comparison," Asia Pacific Journal of Management
        7 (October): 41-58.

Self-appraisal levels were measured among samples of
managers in Korea, U.S., Japan, Philippines, Taiwan, and
Mexico. Asians were more likely (71-78%) to evaluate
themselves as equal to peers as compared to the Mexican
(63%), Philippine (54%), and the U.S. (54%) samples. The
importance of work was ranked higher by Japanese than by
Americans.

0440   Kobayashi, Noritake (1982) "The Present and
        Future of Japanese Multinational Enterprises:
        A Comparative Analysis of Japanese and
        U.S.-European Management," International
        Studies of Management and Organization
        12 (Spring): 38-58.

This is a survey of the degree of internationalization of
Japanese, American, and European multinationals. Japanese
MNCs lag in their degrees of internationalization and global
activities (planning, research and development, marketing,
etc.).

0441   Kozan, M. Kamil (1989) "Cultural Influences
        on Styles of Handling Interpersonal Conflicts:
        Comparisons Among Jordanians, Turkish and U.S.
        Managers," Human Relations 42 (9): 787-99.

Managers from three countries indicated a preference for the
collaborative style in handling conflicts, though this
differed according to whether the conflict involved peers,
subordinates or superiors. Jordanian managers reflected
managerial behavior which did not fit the stereotypical
"Arab" model.

0442   Kramer, Hugh E. (1977) "Concepts of Competition in
        America, Europe and Japan," Business and Society
        18 (Fall): 20-5.

Europeans, Japanese and Americans differ in how they define
the concept of competition. Each culture also evaluates the
consequences of competition differently.

0443   Lammers, Cornelius J. (1990) "Sociology of
        Organizations around the Globe: Similarities and
        Differences Between American, British, French,
        German and Dutch Brands," Organization Studies
        11 (2): 179-206.

Sociological research on organizations generally deals with
the effects of three dimensions (traditional vs. modern,
hierarchical vs. democratic, and mechanical vs. organic) on

organizational forms and processes. There are national varieties of organizational sociology.

0444   Laurent, Andre (1983) "The Cultural Diversity of Western Conception and Management," International Studies of Management and Organization 13 (1-2): 75-96.

Responses from 12 national samples indicate that perceptions of managerial activities (planning, personnel, resource management, etc.) differ from one culture to another.

0445   Leung, Kwok and Michael Harris Bond (1989) "On the Empirical Identification of Dimensions for Cross-Cultural Comparisons," Journal of Cross-Cultural Psychology 20 (June): 133-51.

The cross-cultural analysis used by Hofstede, based on the ecological approach, is the most commonly-used theoretical system to identify the assumed dimensions of culture. The authors discuss the methodological weakness of this approach, propose their solutions, and then present a new procedure to identify individual dimensions. Chinese respondents are used to illustrate this framework's utility.

0446   Levine, Robert V. and Kathy Bartlett (1984) "Pace of Life, Punctuality, and Coronary Heart Disease in Six Countries," Journal of Cross-Cultural Psychology 15 (June): 233-55.

The concept of time varies in the six countries under study. Public clocks were most accurate in Japan and the U.S., and least accurate in Indonesia. Average walking speed was fastest in Japan and slowest in Indonesia. Work speed, as measured by the time taken to complete a postal request, was slowest in Italy.

0447   Lipscomb, Thomas J., Michael C. Budden, and Connie L. Budden (1991) "Strategic Implementations of Ethics in the Business Curriculum: a Global Concern," Journal of Global Business 2 (Spring): 81-5.

Business-related scandals have been recently publicized throughout the world. The authors offer several ways global ethics can be integrated into business school curricula.

0448   Locke, William W. (1986) "The Fatal Flaw: Hidden Cultural Differences," Business Marketing 71 (April): 65, 72, 74, 76.

The author takes the position that the concept "global marketing" is self-defeating. Cultural areas differ in terms of consumer values and behavior. Each nation or cultural area must be studied in isolation to determine local values.

0449   Luthans, Fred, Harriette S. McCaul, and
        Nancy G. Dodd (1985) "Organizational
        Commitment: A Comparison of American,
        Japanese, and Korean Employees," Academy
        of Management Journal 28 (March): 213-219

1,659 workers in three countries were measured in terms of
their commitment to their firms. The U.S. employees had
significantly higher average commitment levels than Japanese
or Korean employees. Country of origin accounted for only
seven percent of the model's variance. Age and tenure were
positively correlated with organizational commitment in all
countries.

0450   Lysonski, Steven and William Gaidis (1991)
        "A Cross-Cultural Comparison of the Ethics of
        Business Students," Journal of Business Ethics
        10 (February): 141-50.

Samples of students from Denmark, New Zealand and the U.S.
were shown to have similar ethical tendencies with one
another and with practicing managers. Different levels of
ethical scenarios in relation to decision-making were
tested.

0451   Margerison, Charles (1988) "The Ways American,
        Australian and British Managers make their
        Organizations succeed," Management Japan 21
        (Autumn): 4-10.

The processes of privatization and global competition have
made managers from the U.S., Australia, and Britain more
professional. There is now more consensus decision-making
and decentralization of authority.

0452   Maruyama, Magoroh (1984) "Alternative Concepts of
        Management: Insights from Asia and Africa,"
        Asia Pacific Journal of Management 1 (May): 100-11.

Asian and Africa thought systems and value patterns differ
radically from the European and North American cultural
traditions. Such Western practices as unity by homogeneity,
individualism, specialization, etc. differ from more Asian
and African values.

0453   Maruyama, Magoroh (1985) "Mindscapes: How to
        Understand Specific Situations in Multicultural
        Management," Asian Pacific Journal of Management
        2 (May): 125-49.

The author presents four mental patterns ("mindscapes")
which are universal categories. These offer a unified
framework to study various aspects of business on a cross-
cultural level.

0454   **Maruyama, Magoroh (1988) "The Inverse Practice Principle in Multicultural Management,"** The Academy of Management Executive **2 (February): 67-8.**

Many persons have claimed that national managerial practices may be transferred from one culture to another. However, this has neither been proved nor disproved. The author gives examples of where expatriates did not follow their own business customs when dealing with host nationals.

0455   **McClelland, David C. (1961)** The Achieving Society. **New York: The Free Press.**

This work is part of a major research effort by McClelland and associates. They hypothesize that national character is closely linked to economic behavior, taking risks, and entrepreneurship. These values, defined as need for achievement (N-Ach) on the economic level, are developed in childhood and should be encouraged.

0456   **Michalos, Alex C. (1991)** Global Report on Student Well-Being. Volume 1: Life Satisfaction and Happiness. **New York: Springer-Verlag.**

The author first reviews the literature dealing with general measures and data on quality of life and related theories. He then reports the findings and their correlations on life satisfaction in thirty-nine countries, using samples of undergraduates from each country.

0457   **Miller, George A. (1987) "Meta-Analysis and the Culture-Free Hypothesis,"** Organizational Studies **8 (4): 309-26.**

Meta-analysis is used to correlate the results of 27 published studies based on 1,066 organizations in eleven different countries. The purpose was to test the "culture-free" hypothesis: that the effects of certain contextual variables (the Aston Programme's "bold hypothesis") and organizational structures (especially size) are similar irrespective of the cultural context. The paper focuses on the influence of organizational size on structure (centralization, etc.). The results strongly support the "culture-free" hypothesis. The data are robust enough for reliable interpretation and hypotheses testing even though sampling procedures are not always ideal.

0458   Misra, Sasi, Rabindra N. Kanungo,
         Luts Von Rosensteil, and Elmar A. Stuhler (1985)
         "The Motivational Formation of Job and Work
         Involvement: A Cross-National Study,"
         Human Relations 38 (6): 501-18.

The degrees of job motivation and involvement for Indian and
German samples are measured to test the scales' usefulness
using a cross-national methodology.

0459   Multinational Executive, Inc. (1987) 1987
         Multinational Executive Travel Companion. Boston:
         Multinational Executive, Inc.

This comprehensive reference book contains information on
business conditions in most countries and capitals of the
world. There are short presentations on business etiquette,
addresses useful to tourists and businesspersons, lists of
business holidays, currency data, visa, customs and weather
information, etc. It is a very complete source of necessary
information for the international business traveller.

0460   Negandhi, Anant R. (1973) Management and Economic
         Development: The Case of Taiwan. The Hague, The
         Netherlands: Martinus Nijhoff.

This book reports on a study of management practices and
effectiveness of 26 locally-owned and foreign subsidiaries
located in Taiwan. A model of analysis of comparative
management, topics include management behavior (planning,
time, horizons, etc.), organization, personnel policies
(promotion, compensation, training), leadership styles), and
control techniques and standards and management and
enterprise effectiveness. Comparable data are included from
five developing countries.

0461   Negandhi, Anant (1984) "Interaction Between
         Multinational Corporations and Host Countries:
         Power, Conflict and Democratization in Decision-
         making," pp 87-113 in Bernhard Wilpert and Arndt
         Sorge (eds.), International Perspectives on
         Organizational Democracy Volume II. New York:
         John Wiley & Sons.

The research of this chapter is based on the author's 1972-
82 work with 244 multinational companies operating in six
developing and in seven industrialized countries. The open-
system approach is utilized to investigate the impact of
the internal structures of large organizations on external
relationships. One trend is toward increased centralization
in decision-making among U.S., European, and Japanese
multinationals vis-a-vis their foreign subsidiaries.

0462   Negandhi, Anant R. (1989) "Management Strategies
        and Policies of American, German and Japanese
        Multinational Corporations," pp 29-49 in Anant R.
        Negandhi (ed.), Research in International Business
        and International Relations. Volume 3. Greenwich,
        Conn: JAI Press, Inc.

The author surveys samples of personnel in American, German,
British, Japanese, and Swedish multinationals and their
subsidiaries in terms of communication styles, levels of
formalization, decision making, staffing policies, etc.

0463   Negandhi, Anant R. and Daniel Robey (1977)
        "Understanding Organizational behavior in
        Multinational Settings," Human Resource
        Management 16 (Spring): 16-23.

The authors present a conceptual framework for understanding
cross-cultural organizational behavior using an open-ended
contingency theory model.

0464   Negandhi, Anant R., Edith C. Uen, and Golpira
        Eshghi (1987) "Localization of Japanese
        Subsidiaries in South East Asia," Asia Pacific
        Journal of Management 5 (September): 67-79.

This article summarizes the senior author's and others' 17
year research in the U.S., Europe, Japan, Taiwan, South East
Asia, and Australia. The focus is the analysis of the
managerial sources of Japanese successes in foreign
countries as compared to the subsidiaries of other
countries' multinationals. Japanese subsidiaries follow a
"modified local system" in which decision making is highly
centralized at the home office. This system is very
different from that common in Japan.

0465   Nelson, Carl A. (1990) Global Success:
        International Business Tactics for the 1990s.
        Blue Ridge Summit, PA: TAB BOOKS.

The author provides general presentations on why U.S.
business personnel need to "think globally" and on the
global changes that have taken place recently. Chapters deal
with business protocols, unique national business
structures, country-specific business customs, the mechanics
of establishing foreign presences, getting visas, etc. There
are also very useful and comprehensive lists of addresses of
agencies that help potential exporters, U.S. Chambers of
Commerce abroad, business contacts throughout the world, and
U.S. export trading companies. There are also lists of
foreign business titles, international glossaries, and
national holidays.

0466   Noburn, David, Sue Birley, Mark Dunn, and
        Adrian Payne (1990) "A Four Nations Study
        of the Relationship Between Marketing
        Effectiveness, Corporate Culture, Corporate
        Values and Market Orientation," Journal of
        International Business Studies 21 (3): 451-68.

650 senior executives from four English-speaking nations
were interviewed during 1985-86 to test whether or not there
were national differences in top managerial attitudes. There
were cultural differences, although the best predictors for
marketing effectiveness in all four samples were (1) giving
primacy importance to people and (2) concern with quality.

0467   Parnell, Myrtle and Jo Vanderkloot (1989)
        "How to Build Cross-Cultural Bridges,"
        Communication World 6 (July/August): 40-42.

The U.S. workforce is becoming increasing culturally
diversified. Supervising a multicultural workforce requires
cultural sensitivity. Symptoms of cultural-in-origin
problems include lateness, silence, absenteeism, and high
employee turnover.

0468   Peak, Martha H. (1991) "Developing an
        International Style of Management,"
        Management Review 80 (February): 32-35.

In today's global markets, "it is not where you do business,
it's how you do business." Developing local and global
knowledge, defined as the process of globalization, is now
necessary. Globalization includes cross-cultural knowledge
and sensitivity.

0469   Peng, T. K., M. F. Peterson, and Y.P. Shyi
        (1991) "Quantitative Methods in Cross-National
        Management Research: Trends and Equivalence
        Issues," Journal of Organizational Behavior
        12 (March): 87-107.

Cross-national management articles published in 24
management-related journals from 1981-1987 are reviewed in
terms of the methods and data used. Methodological
sophistication increased, through the problem of cross-
national equivalence still exists. More qualitative analysis
would help avoid some inherent methodological problems when
conducting cross-cultural research. One-fifth of all
articles used students in their samples. In comparative
papers, Japan was most often compared with the U.S.

0470   Pereta, Mahendra and Sybil B.G. Eysenck (1984) "A
        Cross-Cultural Study of Personality: Sri Lanka and
        England," Journal of Cross-Cultural Psychology 15
        (September): 353-71.

Over one hundred Sri Lankan men and women completed the
Eysenck Personality Questionnaire. Sri Lankan subjects

measured much higher on social desirability and lower on neuroticism than did British respondents. There were no differences on extroversion scores. The authors' methodology is questioned by Bijinen and Poortinga (0383).

0471   Plenert, Gerhard Johannes (1990) <u>International Management and Production: Survival Techniques for Corporate America</u>. Blue Ridge Summit, PA: TAB BOOKS, Inc.

An overview is presented of management and personnel systems in over 20 countries. The focus is on what each country does or produces best (and worst) in order to be competitive or noncompetitive in global markets. There are culturally-related "lessons" managers can learn to make the U.S. competitive world-wide.

0472   Poon, June M., Raja Ainunddin, and Hamdan Affrin (1990) "Management Policies and Practices of American, British, European and Japanese Subsidiaries in Malaysia," <u>International Journal of management</u> 7 (December): 467-74.

Japanese and European subsidiaries in Malaysia did not institute long-range planning to the extent done by U.S. and UK units. Selected personnel policies also varied by national ownership. The Japanese were more informal and less systematic in terms of personnel policies.

0473   Price Waterhouse (on-going) <u>Doing Business in   </u>.

These "Information Guides" are published on most of the world's nations. These guides contain primarily information dealing with currency issues, regulating agencies and policies, labor laws, taxations issues, forms of business enterprises allowed, etc. Each guide contains social, political, labor and economic data. There is usually a short section on national social behavior.

0474   Rhinesmith, Stephen H. (1991) "An Agenda for Globalization," <u>Training and Development Journal</u> 45 (February): 22-9.

Managing on the global level demands six skills, including being able to manage multi-cultural teams and managing change. The globalization process includes reviewing a company's culture to see if it is adequate enough to operate on the international level.

0475   Ricks, David A. (1986) "How to Avoid Business
        Blunders Abroad," pp 107-121 in Subhash C. Jain and
        Lewis R. Tucker, Jr., (eds), International Marketing:
        Managerial Perspectives (Second Edition). Boston,
        Massachusetts: Kent Publishing Company.

The author presents examples of international marketing
errors and how to avoid them. Most are the result of
ignorance of national values and customs.

0476   Roberts, Karlene H. (1970) "On Looking at an
        Elephant: An Evaluation of Cross-Cultural Research
        Related to Organization," Psychological Bulletin 74
        (5): 327-50.

The author selects a number of publications from a total of
526 articles in order to evaluate the cross-cultural study
of organizations. Three questions are answered from a close
analysis of this literature: (1) do we know anything new,
(2) are relevant questions being asked; and (3) are the
methodologies, including sampling, appropriate and useful?
The author concludes the research is weak, not well guided
by theory, and adds little to our knowledge of
organizations. Research should focus on one culture at a
time to develop middle-range theories for further testing.
This article is a "classic" statement of the field.

0477   Robinson, Richard D. (1973) International Business
        Management: A Guide to Decision Making. Hinsdale,
        Illinois: Dryden Press.

Although dated, this work is sensitive to non-U.S.
management styles and the importance of culture in
international business. One case study describes the
feelings of three foreign nationals considering working for
a U.S. multinational firm.

0478   Rodgers, Irene (1986) "Making Cultural
        Differences Work for You," Industrial and
        Commercial Training 18 (May/June): 15-7.

Cultural differences exist in terms of negotiating styles,
personnel policies, time management, etc. Anglo-Saxons tend
to be open and informal. Latin Americans may interpret this
behavior as a privileged, very personal relationship. Firms
should train their international managers to be able to
adapt to and accept different cultural systems and mind
sets.

0479   Ronen, Simcha and Allen I. Krant (1983)
        "Similarities among Countries Based on
        Employee Work Values and Attitudes,"
        pp 498-511 in Herman O.J. Overgaard et al.,
        (eds.) International Business: The Canadian
        Way. Dubuque, Iowa: Kendal/Hunt Publishing Company.

Cross-national comparisons of employee's values, attitudes
and views toward work are analyzed by combining national
samples into cultural areas. The data are based on a number
of data sets using samples from many countries.

0480   Roniger, Luis (1987) "Coronelismo, Caciquismo, and
        Oyabun-Kobun Bonds: Divergent Implications of
        Hierarchical Trust in Brazil, Mexico and Japan,"
        The British Journal of Sociology 38 (September):
        310-30.

Hierarchical relations of dependence are found in Brazil,
Mexico, and Japan. Only in Japan have these social patterns
been used for the purposes of modernization. Yet these
patterns of patron-client dependencies are very similar.
This hierarchical trust pattern contributes to societal
trust in Japan but does not in Latin American countries.
These differences are caused by differences in national
character, especially the images of self-fulfillment and
the nature of a culture's institutional structures.

0481   Rosenstein, Eliezer (1985) "Cooperativeness and
        Advancement of Managers: An International
        Perspective," Human Relations 38 (1): 1-22.

This article investigates the relationships between
cooperative tendencies and rates of advancement among 700-
2,000 managers from 12 national groups. On a global level,
organizations generally reward non-cooperative behavior over
cooperativeness, although there were significant national
differences. By contrast, Scandinavian nations and Japan
both reward cooperativeness. Non-cooperative attitudes were
rewarded in Spain and France. U.S. and Japanese managers had
similar scores on a number of dimensions. The work generally
supports Hofstede's findings.

0482   Sanders, Patricia (1988) "Global Managers for Global
        Corporations," Journal of Management Development 7
        (1): 33-44.

Global managers should develop a world-wide orientation
while at the same time maintain their own inner space. Their
management philosophies should be more collaborative.

0483   Sengoku, Tamotsu (1985) **Willing Workers: The Work Ethics in Japan, England, and the United States**. Westport, Conn: Quorum Books.

The author compares the work attitudes of workers in three countries, using a large number of quotes and examples. The sources of these attitudes are explored.

0484   Shani, A.B. and M. Tom Basuray (1988) "Organization Development and Comparative Management: Action Research as an Interpretive Framework," **Leadership and Organization Development Journal** 9 (2): 3-10.

The Action Research (AR) approach provides the framework for the comparative analysis of management. The model is applied to the Japanese and American styles of management, and these styles are compared systematically.

0485   Shaw, James H. (1990) "A Cognitive Categorization Model for the Study of Intercultural Management," **Academy of Management Review** 16 (October): 626-45.

The author develops a model that focuses on the interaction patterns between an expatriate superior and a host national subordinate. The cultural variables structuring these interactions are placed into their cultural contexts.

0486   Smith, Peter B., Jyuji Misumi, Monir Tayeb, Mark Peterson, and Michael Bond, (1989) "On the Generality of Leadership Style Measures Across Cultures," **Journal of Occupational Psychology** 62 (June): 97-109.

The authors conduct research and test the P (Performance) M (Maintenance) leadership theory by using respondents from Britain, the U.S., Japan, and Hong Kong. Leadership styles are similar across cultures. However, the carrying out of this style varies according to cultural context.

0487   Snowdon, Sandra (1986) **The Global Edge: How Your Company Can Win in the International Marketplace**. New York: Simon and Schuster.

The author profiles 25 countries in terms of culture, business protocol, important business addresses, negotiation practices, and communication styles. There are also ten general principles for conducting business outside the United States. Some of these principles deal with questions of security and how to avoid and react to terrorist acts.

0488   Sodetani, Lori L. and William B. Gudykunst (1989)
        "The Effects of Surprising Events on Intercultural
        Relationships," Communication Research Reports 4
        (December): 1-6.

People's reactions to surprising events differ by cultural
origins. Some of this difference is based on where a culture
falls in an individualism-collectivism continuum. Americans,
who come from a more individualistic culture, reacted in a
more extreme manner to surprising events because their
friendships are more specifically oriented to activities.
Surprising events have fewer impacts when the friendship
ties, as for the Japanese, are more comprehensive.

0489   Stieglitz, Harold (1972) Organization Structures of
        International Companies. New York: Basic Books.

The author presents and analyzes the organizational charts
of 42 companies from 14 countries. There is an excellent
introductory chapter which compares U.S. and other national
corporate structures. Cross-national and inter-company
comparisons are illustrated.

0490   Swierczek, Fredric William (1991) "Leadership
        and Culture: Comparing Asian Managers,"
        Leadership & Organization Development Journal
        12 (7): 3-10.

Using Hofstede's and Hofstede and Bond's data, the author
compares existing leadership theories and Asian values. The
findings suggest a universal theory of leadership may be
possible, though U.S. leadership values differ from Asian
values.

0491   Takeshito, Takashi (1989) "Reappraising the
        Japanese Work Ethic: Myth vs. Global Perspectives,"
        Management Japan 22 (Autumn): 29-32.

A survey of 1950 workers in 16 countries found that workers
working longest hours placed the highest importance on work.
The Germans gave work/job the highest importance; the
Japanese came next. The Spanish were lowest on this item.
The desire to enjoy leisure activities correlated positively
with GNP.

0492   Tansuhaj, Patriya, James W. Gentry, Toby John,
        L. Lee Manzer, and Bong Jin Cho (1991)
        "Cross-National Examination of Innovation
        Resistance," International Marketing Review
        8 (3): 7-20.

Adoption of new products is dependent on cultural values
such as a person's degree of fatalism, traditionalism,
religious commitment, and other values. The authors measure
the dimensions of innovation resistance using samples from
Korea, U.S., Thailand, India, and the Senegal. The U.S.
respondents had the lowest levels of traditionalism,

religious commitment, and fatalism. The Senegalese perceived less risk to be associated with technical products but more risk with non-technical products.

0493   Templer, Andrew and Karl Hofmeyer (1988) "In Search of Personnel Management Excellence: An International Comparison," International Journal of Management 5 (September): 296-303.

There has been a globalization of manufacturing, business, and managerial problems. This internationalization process has been accompanied by an international convergence in Human Resource Management. Using samples of workers from Canada, the UK, Germany, France, and Switzerland, measures indicate a general agreement in terms of the practice of HRM, except for the dimension of job security.

0494   Tepperman, Lorne and Hilja Laasen (1990) "The Future of Happiness," Futures 22 (December): 1059-70.

Cross-cultural surveys of happiness indicate that happiness levels vary by nations. The concept of happiness is defined in different ways across cultures. Americans exhibit a higher level of happiness than Japanese.

0495   Thiederman, Sondra (1988) "Managing the Foreign-Born Work Force: Keys to Effective Cross-Cultural Motivation," Manage 10 (October): 26-9.

Multicultural differences among workers and managers create confusion and frustration. Many non-American workers hesitate to ask questions or to offer negative comments. They may also be motivated by different motivational policies. U.S. managers should be prepared for these cultural differences.

0496   Tse, David K., Kam-Hon Lee, Ilan Vertinsky, and Donald A. Wehrung (1988) "Does Culture Matter? A Cross-Cultural Study of Executives' Choice, Decisiveness, and Risk Adjustment in International Marketing," Journal of Marketing 52 (October): 81-95.

145 Executives from China, Hong Kong, and Canada took part in four simulated international marketing situations. The behaviors of the participants were influenced by home country cultures. Executives from Hong Kong exhibited both Eastern and Western decision-making patterns. This suggests that managerial practices and decision-making are influenced by multiple cultural patterns.

0497   Tylecote, Andrew (1987) "Time Horizons of Management
        Decisions: Causes and Effects," Journal of Economic
        Studies 14 (1): 51-64.

Although profit is an important consideration as a
management objective, different cultures define "profit" in
various ways. The Japanese take a long-term view of profit.
Americans and Germans take an intermediate view. British
firms have a short-term view.

0498   Usunier, Jean-Claude (1991) "Business Time
        Perceptions and National Cultures: A Comparative
        Survey," Management International Review 31
        (3): 197-217.

Conceptions of time were measured using samples from five
nations. Intra-nation North-South differences were slight,
except for those in West Germany and Mauritania. Time is
more economically defined ("time is money") in developing
countries (Brazil, Mauritania, and South Korea) than in
France and West Germany. There was agreement in Brazil, West
Germany, and South Korea that wearing a watch is a
necessity. Business meals were seen as necessary to French
and Koreans, but not to Germans.

0499   Weihrich, Heinz (1990) "Management Practices in the
        United States, Japan, and the People's Republic of
        China," Industrial Management 32 (March/April): 3-7.

Managerial functions differ in China, Japan, and the United
States. The Japanese have a long-term orientation. Decisions
in China are centralized but are not in Japan. In Japan and
in China, employees are hired after school graduation and
are expected to stay with the same employers during their
work careers. Americans are high in job mobility.

0500   The Western Business School (on going)
        International Business Case Bibliography.
        Case and Publication Services, the Western
        Business School, the University of Western
        Ontario. London, Ontario Canada N6A 3K7.

The Western Business School maintains and updates an archive
of over 2,500 management case studies, cross-referenced to
245 key words, including country, organizational behavior,
author, and intercultural relations. The archive also
distributes case material and reprinted articles from five
other sources, including the Harvard Business School.

0501   Williamson, Harold F.(1975) Evolution of
        International Management Structures. Newark,
        Delaware: University of Delaware Press.

Although dated, this work contains still-useful chapters on
managerial structures and behavior in France, Soviet Russia,
and Japan.

0502   Wills, James R. and John K. Ryans (1982)
        "Attitudes Toward Advertising: A Multinational
        Study," Journal of International Business Studies
        8 (Winter): 121-29.

This study surveys an international sample of consumers,
students, academics, and managers to determine national
differences in attitudes toward advertising in 14 countries.
Managers and consumers have the greatest attitudinal
differences.

0503   Yamamoto, Shichihei (1985-86) "Tradition and
        Management," International Studies of Management
        and Organization 15 (Fall/Winter): 69-88.

Societies can be divided into "courtesy and music" or "law
and contract" types. Japanese enterprises which achieve the
"courtesy and music" classification are democratic,
decentralized, and efficient. They also have few rules,
cooperative personnel, and a definite hierarchy allowing for
mobility. Those firms that do not follow these principles
will collapse.

0504   Yeh, Rhy-Song (1988) "Values of Americans,
        Japanese and Taiwanese managers in Taiwan:
        A Test of Hofstede's Framework," Academy of
        Management Best Papers, Proceedings: 106-110.

The author used Hofstede's methodology and conceptual
framework to study the values of managers in three
countries. American managers scaled low on power distance,
as predicted, though scores are lower than Hofstede's
findings. Contrary to Hofstede, American managers had lower
individualistic scale values than the Japanese managers. The
author concludes that Hofstede's findings, especially those
based on his Asian samples, are neither reliable nor valid.

0505   Zeffane, Rachid M. (1989) "Organization
        Structures and Contingencies in Different Nations:
        Algeria, Britain and France," Social Science Research
        18 (December): 331-69.

The patterns of organization of over 100 organizations from
Algeria, Britain, and France were compared in terms of their
organizational structures. Algerian organizations were the
most centralized; British Enterprises the least.

6

The Americas

0506   Ahmed, S.A. (1990) "Comparison of Haitian and
        Canadian Managers' Job Needs and Psychological
        Profiles," <u>Canadian Journal of Development</u> 11
        (1): 81-98.

A comparison of Haitian and Canadian managers and business
students indicated that the Haitian sample was less
competitive, less independent, less individualistic, and
less materialistic.

0507   Ajami, Riad A. (1983) "Attitudes of U.S. Workers
        toward Foreign Owned Enterprises," <u>Management</u>
        <u>International Review</u> 23 (4): 53-62.

A survey of 643 Americans working in foreign-owned
manufacturing firms in Ohio found that U.S. workers feared
that foreign ownership would result in loss of control. The
workers disliked foreign investments in the United States.
Workers, however, were much more positive in terms of
working for a foreign-owned firm.

0508   Allen, Douglas B., Edwin L. Miller, and Raghu Nath
        (1988) "North America," pp 23-54 in Raghu Nath (ed.),
        <u>Comparative Management: A Regional View</u>. Cambridge,
        Mass: Ballinger Publishing Company.

National character and organizational behavior in Canada and
in the United States are analyzed within the theoretical
framework of Hofstede's work. This chapter also contains an
overview discussion of the American economy and the
society's infrastructures.

0509   Alten, Gary (1988) <u>American Ways: A Guide for</u>
        <u>Foreigners in the United States</u>. Yarmouth, Maine:
        Intercultural Press, Inc.

This is an excellent introduction of U.S. values, attitudes,
and behavior for both U.S. citizens and foreign visitors.
The author covers such topics as male-female relations,
individualism, degree of informality, sense of time, and
assertiveness. There is also practical advice (driving,
shopping, etc.). The readings and bibliography are very
useful.

0510   Amado, Gilles and Haroldo Vingagre Brasil
        (1991) "Organizational Behaviors and Cultural
        Context: The Brazilian "Jeitinho,""
        <u>International Studies of Management &</u>
        <u>Organization</u> 21 (Fall): 38-61.

While Brazilian organizational behaviors exhibit Latin
American features, they also contain unique elements.
Brazilian managerial performance is oriented toward the
short-term, centralized decision-making, hierarchical, and a
punitive system of control. Managers prefer a "receptive"
style in order to avoid direct confrontation. The authors
summarize and interpret a number of studies dealing with
Brazilian national character. The concept of <u>jeitinho</u> offers
a clue to Brazilian culture and national character.

0511   Argyris, Chris and Donald A. Schon (1978)
        <u>Organizational</u> <u>Learning: A Theory of Action</u>
        <u>Perspective</u>. Reading, Mass: Addison-Wesley.

The authors illustrate limited learning and the resistance
to change in organizations by using a Latin American company
as an example.

0512   Becker, Thomas H. (1991) "Taboos and How To's
        About Earning an Honest Peso," <u>Management</u>
        <u>Review</u> 80 (June): 17-21.

The author offers advice on how to increase the chances of
successfully doing business in Mexico. There is information
on bribes (don't), the need to speak Spanish (if possible),
the use of local contacts (sometimes), and the investment
and legal climates.

0513   Berry, Bryan (1986) "An American Work Force Produces
        Japanese Quality," <u>Iron Age</u> 229 (July): 44-50.

Nissan Motor Manufacturing Corp. has an all-American work
force in its Smyrna, Tennessee plant. The quality of the
Smyrna-built trucks is equal to those built in Japan. The
reason for this quality performance is the adoption of
Japanese-style work behavior and policies, such as job
rotation, consensus decision-making, and job security.

0514   Black, Hawley (1980) "What Your MP thinks About
        Your Problems," Canadian Business 53 (November):
        68-83.

284 Canadian Members of Parliament were surveyed as to their
views on business and economic issues. Most MPs were
optimistic about the prospects for the Canadian economy.
Most MPs supported a government proposal to establish a
"national trading corporation," although there are few
details about its final form.

0515   Blair, John D. and Carlton J. Whitehead (1984)
        "Can Quality Circles Survive in the United States?"
        Business Horizons 27 (Sept/Oct): 17-23.

Quality control programs could be adopted by American
manufacturers only if they are integrated into the belief
and organizational systems of U.S. firms. Traditional U.S.
corporate cultures and values do not reflect the values
needed for efficient introduction of Quality Control
Circles, such as the acceptance of bottom-up management.

0516   Bourgeois, L.T. III and Manuel Boltvinik (1981)
        "OD in Cross-Cultural Settings: Latin America,"
        California Management Review 23 (Spring): 75-81.

The transfer of organizational development technology from
the U.S. to Latin America is made difficult by the cultural
differences among nations.

0517   Bowman, James S. (1986) "The Rising Sun in America
        (Part Two)--Japanese Management in the United
        States," Personnel Administrator 31 (October): 81-91.

Managers in Japanese-owned U.S. subsidiaries are
successfully using selected aspects of Japanese-style
management. But there is also reliance on some American-
style managerial practices. Most Japanese-owned firms do not
stress seniority as the basis for pay raises, and
performance evaluation is done at shorter intervals than in
Japan.

0518   Brooks, Brian J. (1988) "Long-Term Incentives:
        International Executives Need Them, Too," Personnel
        65 (August): 40-2.

U.S. multinationals do not have effective reward systems for
expatriate employees. Rewards should be linked to long-term
programs and should be global in scope.

0519   Bunke, Harvey C. (1989) "Lessons from Singapore,"
        Business Horizons 32 (May/June): 2-10.

The decline of the United States is evident in its social
and economic institutions. The "American disease" is in part
caused by an amoral approach to education, a lack of a sense
of personal responsibility, and a litigiousness attitude

toward the legal system and persons. Singapore, a Confucian-based society, is compared to the U.S.'s moral and economic decay.

0520   Bunke, Harvey C. (1990) **"More About the United States and Some About Singapore,"** Business Horizons 33 (March/April): 6-10.

Responding to critics of an earlier article, the author's position is that cultural values, embodied in such value complexes as the Confucian Ethic and the Protestant Ethic, are responsible for a country's economic decline or emergence as a leader. The minimum cultural values needed for economic and social health are (1) a value of hard work, (2) a value of frugality, and (3) a sense of personal responsibility for individual behavior.

0521   Burden, Charles A. and Milton S. Hochmuth (1983) **"Why Foreign Firms Like American Workers,"** Business Horizons 26 (Sept/Oct): 10-18.

Top-level German managers with extensive international experiences, including in the U.S., were asked to evaluate U.S. workers. These chief executives found U.S. workers to be willing, under-employed in relation to their skills, and motivation, and ready to work intelligently if given proper encouragement. Good community relations were stressed, as well as holistic employee relations programs and the recognition of workers' contributions to the achievement of company goals.

0522   Cavanagh, Gerald F. (1990) American Business Values Third edition. Englewood Cliffs, New Jersey: Prentice-Hall.

The origins of American business values can be traced to the American frontier and European roots, such as the Protestant Ethic. The author discusses the work values of Americans in the context of stages of moral growth and development, as well as ethical business norms. A final chapter offers a business ethic for today's business environment.

0523   Chandler, Charles R. (1979) **"Traditionalism in a Modern Setting: A Comparison of Anglo and Mexican American Value Orientations,"** Human Organization 38 (Summer): 153-9.

The Anglo- and Mexican-American sub-cultures exhibit large differences in values. Anglos were more likely to trust non-kin while the Mexican-American sample exhibited greater loyalty and closeness to relatives. Mexican Americans were more present-oriented and more fatalistic. Anglo-Americans accepted planning for the future more. Anglo-Americans scored (92% vs. 44%) as "modern" rather than "traditional."

0524   Clement, Wallace (1986) The Canadian Corporate
        Elite: An Analysis of Economic Power. Ottawa:
        The Carleton University Press.

Corporate leadership and behavior is heavily influenced by
the values, social origins, education, and patterns of
interaction of its elite. The author finds that Canadian
business elites form a unitary sub-culture, in part because
of its control of the Canadian mass media.

0525   Condon, John C. (1985) Good Neighbors: Communicating
        with the Mexicans. Yarmouth, Maine: Intercultural
        Press, Inc.

The focus of this work deals with how Mexicans and Americans
view each other and why they often misunderstand each other.
There is a section devoted to the description of daily work
behavior in Mexico.

0526   Cowan, Robert (1988) "Meshing Management Style:
        Should I Work for a Japanese Company?"
        Business Credit 50 (December): 53-4.

Roughly 400,000 U.S. citizens work in Japanese-owned
companies. Americans have to adjust to the slower Japanese
model of decision-making and the greater emphasis placed on
cooperation and team work. Japanese managers are also
adjusting to U.S. work patterns and values, since not all
Japanese-style managerial practices can be effective in the
U.S.

0527   Crozier, Michel (1984) The Trouble with America: Why
        the System is Breaking Down. Berkeley: University
        of California.

The noted French sociologist observes what he defines as the
causes of the decline of the U.S. society. Americans are too
individualistic, causing a crisis in "due process" as
everyone claims certain "rights" to the detriment of the
total society. Americans exhibit a fear of decision, stress
the short-term, and place too much confidence in "the
market," which tends to offer uniform products from one
manufacturer to another. Americans also hold simplistic
views of good vs. evil and human nature.

0528   De George, Richard T. (1982) "What is the American
        Business Value System?" Journal of Business Ethics
        1 (November): 267-75.

The American business system is based on certain values and
ethical standards. These include support for: (1) freedom,
(2) competition, (3) fairness in transactions, and (4)
optimism for the future. The Myth of Amoral Business helps
to undermine these values.

0529   Devine, Elizabeth and Nancy L. Braganti (1988) <u>The</u>
        <u>Travellers' Guide to Latin American Customs and</u>
        <u>Manners</u>. New York: St. Martin's Press.

This a very useful and practical guide to social and
business etiquette in sixteen countries in South and Central
America. The business style of each country is described, as
well as business hours and holidays, facilities available,
etc. A vocabulary of basic terms is presented in Spanish and
Portuguese.

0530   Dewey, Donald (1990) "The Half-Wit American," <u>Across</u>
        <u>The Board</u> 27 (October): 13-4.

In recent years, a number of publications have offered
Americans advice when travelling abroad. Much of the advice
is stereotypical and patronizing. The advisors assume that
foreign hosts are less flexible than Americans and that
Americans are cross-culturally ignorant.

0531   Diaz-Guerero, Rogelio (1977) "A Mexican
        Psychology," <u>American Psychologist</u> 32 (11): 934-44.

The Mexican national character and personality differ from
those in North America. A survey of test scores on various
measures indicates that the Mexican character contains
different values by age of respondents.

0532   Dicle, Ulku, I. Atilla Dicle, and Raymond E. Alie
        (1988) "Human Resources Management: Practices in
        Japanese Organizations in the United States,"
        <u>Public Personnel Management</u> 17 (Fall): 331-9.

The human resource management practices of twelve Japanese
subsidiaries located in the state of Michigan follow a blend
of Japanese and American practices. The Japanese elements of
egalitarianism, information sharing, and job rotation were
present. U.S.-style practices included authoritarian
decision-making, being individual-oriented, and equal
treatment of women employees.

0533   Dryden, Steve (1990) ""Europeanizing" U.S.
        Businesses," <u>Europe</u> 229 (September): 13-14.

Surveys for more than a decade of over 300 U.S. companies in
Europe indicate a gradual trend of "Europeanization" of U.S.
divisions. Sending expatriates to Europe is expensive and
likely to fail because of the expatriates' inability to
adjust to foreign cultures. The result is the promotion and
staffing of host country nationals.

0534   Durlabahji, Subhash (1983) "Japanese-Style American
        Management: Primary Relations and Social
        Organization," Human Relations 36 (9): 837-40.

The author disagrees with the assumption that Japanese-style
management techniques can be adopted by Americans. The data
suggest specific management methods are irrelevant to
employee well-being. The keys to workers' satisfaction are
the employee-organization relationships.

0535   England, George W. (1983) "Japanese and American
        Management: Theory Z and Beyond," Journal of
        International Business Studies 14 (Fall): 131-42.

Theory Z type of management is not likely to be adopted by
American managers. Good management techniques are those that
are internally consistent, fit societal norms, and obtain
support from major institutional structures.

0536   Fallows, James M. (1989) More Like Us: Making
        American Great Again. Boston: Houghton Mifflin
        Company.

The author describes the unique American national character
using a journalistic-autobiographical approach. American
values are contrasted to those in Japan and elsewhere.

0537   Fayerweather, John (1959) The Executive Overseas:
        Administrative Attitudes and Relationships in a
        Foreign Culture. Syracuse, New York: Syracuse
        University Press.

The author presents a description and analysis of Mexican
national character as reflected in business and
administrative behavior which offers insights in spite of
the age of the work. There are comparisons of national
character and national values with U.S., Indian and German
business behavior.

0538   Feather, Roger (1990) "Internal Communication in
        Canada: Held Back by Timid Management," Communication
        World 7 (December): 36-7.

Corporate communication in Canada is made complex by the use
of two languages and a multicultural workforce. Canadian
managers are defined as timid and inhibited. They are more
concerned with the external business environment than the
internal corporate environment.

0539   Florida, Richard and Martin Kenney (1990) The
        Breakthrough Illusion: Corporate America's
        failure to Move from Innovation to Mass Production.
        New York: Basic Books.

The decline of America's technological standing, relative to
Japan's and other countries', is the result of American
values and organizational structure. U.S. values encourage

innovation but not the commercialization of new knowledge. New managerial practices and organizational structures are needed if the U.S. is to compete successfully with Japan.

0540   Freeman, Howard E., A. Kimball Romney, Joao
        Ferreira-Pinto, Robert E. Klein,
        and Tom Smith (1981) "Guatemalan and U.S.
        Concepts of Success and Failure," <u>Human
        Organization</u> 40 (Summer): 140-5.

Respondents in Guatemala and the U.S. were asked to explain why five friends were successful or unsuccessful. Guatemalan respondents were more likely to blame "bad luck" for failure. The concepts of luck and fate are used to explain both success and failure in Guatemala. The ability to manipulate social relationships was also deemed important for success or failure in life.

0541   Garreau, Joel (1981) <u>The Nine Nations of North
        America</u>. New York: Avon Books.

Writing in a popular style, the author states that Mexico, Canada, and the United States are becoming nine "nations," each with its own economic and political interests and sub-cultures.

0542   Gemmel, Art (1986) "Management in a Cross-Cultural
        Environment: The Best of Both Worlds," <u>Management
        Solutions</u> 31 (June): 28-33.

Fujitsu America, Inc. has successfully blended managerial styles from Japan and the U.S. Consensus is developed by a bottom-up process. Personal responsibility is encouraged, and supervisors behave more in the American style.

0543   Gilbert, Nathaniel (1988) "Foreign Companies Use
        Democracy to Prosper in the U.S.," <u>Management Review</u>
        77 (July): 25-9.

Americans working for foreign-owned firms feel they work better than before because the companies are managed better. One aspect of foreign-style management is greater democracy for workers.

0544   Gillingham, David W. and Kenneth E. Louckes (1981)
        "The Future Scenario for North Americans in the Year
        2000," <u>Management International Review</u> 21 (1): 8-18.

87 Canadian executives of trade associations, Chambers of Commerce, and voluntary associations were asked to evaluate possible scenarios in terms of eight dimensions (society, morals, economics, etc.) for the year 2,000, using a modification of the Delphi methodology. A majority of the sample was optimistic in terms of medical and technical advances. A majority also predicted diminishing Federal power (73%), more corporate accountability (74%), and loss of low-skilled jobs to third world countries (60%).

0545   Green, Robert T. and Isabella C.M. Cunningham (1980)
        "Family Purchasing Roles in Two Countries," Journal
        of International Business 80 (Spring): 92-97.

Two samples of respondents were drawn from Houston, Texas
and Valencia, Venezuela. Family purchasing decisions made by
the two samples varied greatly. Decisions in Venezuela were
made primarily by the husband, indicating differences in
family authority patterns.

0546   Grey, Ronald J. and Peter Gelfond (1990) "Corporate
        Culture and Canada's International Competitiveness
        (Part 2)," Canadian Business Review 17 (Winter):
        21-5.

Canadians and American workers like their jobs to an equal
extent. However, surveys indicate that U.S. workers are more
concerned with quality performances. Canadians feel there
are fewer opportunities to advance and for individual
growth.

0547   Harper, Stephen C. (1988) "Now That the Dust Has
        Settled: Learning from Japanese Management,"
        Business Horizons 31 (July/August): 43-51.

A limited number of aspects of Japanese-style management can
be adopted by U.S. managers to form a new American-style
management. Elements (strengths) of Japanese management that
can be incorporated into U.S. managerial behavior include
concern for the total person, deliberate decision-making
processes, a desire to learn at all levels of the
organization, and a longer time horizon.

0548   Harris, T. Frank (1983) "Penetrating the U.S.
        Market," pp 413-25 in Herman O.J. Overgaard et al.
        (eds.), International Business: The Canadian Way.
        Dubuque, Iowa: Kendal/Hunt Publishing Company.

A Canadian view of U.S. business values and practices is
presented.

0549   Hasegawa, Yukio (1990) "Modifying the American
        Management System in the U.S.," Tokyo Business
        Today 58 (October): 52-5.

Japanese and American management styles can complement each
other. The experiences of the Japanese company NEC in
Dallas, Texas, indicate that superior U.S. management
practices include recruitment and job evaluation. Japanese
practices of training and communication are superior.

0550   Hoerr, John and Seah Nathan Spiro (1990) "Culture
        Shock at Home: Working for a Foreign Boss,"
        Business Week 3192 (December 17): 80-4.

Japan is the fourth largest foreign employer in the United
States, after Great Britain, Canada, and Germany. In the
Japanese-owned companies, America-born managers are more
dissatisfied than blue collar workers. Compensation of
managers is lower than in U.S.-owned firms. Upward mobility
is greater in German than in Japanese firms. European firms
operate on the U.S. system of management.

0551   Hill, Roy (1978) "The Frustration of Managing in
        Brazil," International Management 33 (December):
        50-54.

Brazil offers foreign investors special problems, including
high executive mobility, political indecision, and rigid
social class differences.

0552   Horton, Thomas (1986) "American Management Style:
        Far From Being Eclipsed," International Management
        41 (August): 38-9.

U.S.-style management remains the standard for most of the
world. A number of U.S. firms, including IBM, have no equal.
U.S.-style business schools are being created throughout the
world. A manager can still benefit from non-U.S. managerial
patterns and values, such as long-term planning (Japan), the
work ethic (Germany), and emphasis on quality (Belgium).

0553   Hutchison, William and Cynthia Poznanski,
        with Laura Todd-Stockman (1987)
        Living in Columbia: A Guide for Foreigners.
        Yarmouth, Maine: Intercultural Press.

The national character, daily life, interaction patterns and
communication styles (friends, strangers, superiors, etc.)
of the Hispanic Columbian people are described in lay
language. There is also advice for foreigners on day-to-day
living in Columbia.

0554   Jackofsky, Ellen F., John W. Slocum Jr., and Sara
        J. McQuaid (1988) "Cultural Values and the CEO:
        Alluring Companions?" Academy of Management
        Executive 2 (February): 39-49.

CEOs behave in ways congruent with their own cultures. U.S.
CEOs are high in individualism and low in uncertainty
avoidance. Multinationals need information on local values
in order to operate successfully.

0555   Jaeger, Alfred M. (1985) "Organization Development
        and National Culture: Where's the Fit?" The Academy
        of Management Review 11 (January): 178-90.

American firms overseas utilize the managerial techniques of
organization development (OD). The basic values of OD are
developed and compared to the managerial strategies in 40
countries, based on Hofstede's four dimensions of culture.
The U.S. managerial model includes medium level Power
Distance, low Uncertainty Avoidance, high Masculinity, and
high Individualism. This OD profile does not fit many other
countries' values, resulting in a large lack of
exportability of many aspects of U.S.-style management.

0556   Jain, Hem C. (1990) "Human Resource Management
        in Selected Japanese Firms, Their Foreign
        Subsidiaries and Locally Owned Counterparts,"
        International Labour Review 129 (1): 73-89.

Japanese-style management has been adapted in Canadian
subsidiaries. The decision-making processes and labor-
management relations are different in Japanese-owned firms
in Japan and in Canada. Nevertheless, Japanese subsidiaries
exhibit some similarities in managerial behavior as compared
to locally-owned firms.

0557   Johnson, Robert E. (1986) "Doing Business in
        America," Journal of General Management 12
        (Winter): 13-24.

There are eight reasons why British firms are not as
successful in the United States as they might be. One major
reason is the British tendency to ignore U.K.-U.S. cultural
differences.

0558   Kanungo, Rabindra N. (1980) Biculturalism and
        Management. Toronto: Butterworth & Company.

The Francophone and Anglophone divisions of Canadian society
reflect major group differences in values systems.
Managerial styles and organizational policies must take into
account these important value differences.

0559   Kanungo, Rabindra N. (1981) "Work Motivation and
        Canadian Bicultural Context," pp 785-814 in Gunter
        Dlugos and Klaus Wiermair (eds.), Managing under
        Differing Value Systems: Political, Social, and
        Economical. Berlin and New York: Walter de Gruyter.

Based on a study of French-speaking and English-speaking
employees in the same enterprise, the author found that the
two samples were similar in some values (having interesting
work and adequate earnings). Major differences were also
measured. Francophone workers placed greater importance on
benefits, working conditions, opportunity for upgrading
skills, and more equitable pay). The Anglophones stressed
independence, recognition, and responsibility more.

Francophones had higher levels of work satisfaction and lower turnover rates. Anglophones scored higher on three levels of commitment.

0560   Kee, Y.T. (1983) "Canada's Cultural Barrier: A
        Dangerous Deterrent to Canadian Industrial Growth,"
        pp 512-29 in Herman O.J. Overgaard et al. (eds.),
        International Business: The Canadian Way. Dubuque,
        Iowa: Kendal/Hunt Publishing Company.

This chapter discusses the variety of work-related values, attitudes, and motivations found among Canadian sub-groups.

0561   Korth, Christopher M. (1991) "Managerial
        Barriers to U.S. Exports," Business Horizons
        34 (March/April): 18-26.

The U.S. balance of trade for 1989 contained a deficit of $123 billion. A major reason for this trade imbalance is that U.S. managers do not aggressively seek foreign markets. This lack of seeking after international opportunities is due to five "barriers," among which are (1) limited ambition of managers, (2) managerial inertia, and (3) unrealistic fears of going international.

0562   Kras, Eva S. (1989) Management in Two Cultures:
        Bridging the Gap Between U.S. and Mexican Managers.
        Yarmouth, Maine: Intercultural Press, Inc.

Mexican and U.S. cultures contain many differences, thereby causing cross-cultural misunderstandings. Mexican culture gives family relations more importance and work is less of a central value. Mexican managers are more authoritarian and concerned with their and other's dignity. These and other differences in values and behavior are discussed.

0563   LaFleche, Heidi J. (1990) "When in Rome---A
        Protocol Primer," Retail Control 58 (10): 27-9.

Americans should pay closer attention to foreign customs when abroad. An "America as number one" attitude is obsolete due to the rise of the economic power of the European Community and the Pacific Rim.

0564   Lam, Natalie (1986) "Work Orientations:
        A Cross-Cultural Comparison and Relevance for
        Participative Management," International Journal
        of Management 3 (September): 17-28.

Chinese and Caucasian Americans are compared according to their work orientations. Chinese Americans were more expressive (valued jobs for personal growth and job-related activities). They also had higher expressive scores (work for money: 30% vs. 15% of Caucasians). Both samples viewed their jobs as means to other ends, such as earning money to do other things.

0565   Lane, Henry W. and Paul W. Beamish (1990) "Cross-
        Cultural Cooperative Behavior in Joint Ventures in
        LDCs," Management International Review 30 (special
        issue): 87-102.

Selected U.S. business practices are not effective in many
foreign countries. They decrease the chance of success of
joint ventures in less developed countries. The selection of
local managers is especially important. Such personnel
should be given as much autonomy as possible, since they are
familiar with the local cultures.

0566   Langford, Tom (1986) "Workers' Subordinate
        Values: A Canadian Case Study," The Canadian
        Journal of Sociology 11 (Fall): 269-91.

A test of a model of the development of workers' attitudes
indicates Canadian workers and managers have similar
abstract valuations. The article compares a series of
attitudes and values of workers and managers.

0567   Lanier, Alison R. (1988) Living in the U.S.A. (fourth
        edition). Yarmouth, Maine: Intercultural Press.

This is a practical guide for English-speaking foreigners
and their families expecting to live in the United States.
The author discusses U.S. values, business-related behavior,
and aspects of American culture that are most likely to
confuse foreigners. There are also sections devoted to daily
aspects of living, such as shopping and schools.

0568   Lauterbach, Albert L. (1966) Enterprise in Latin
        America: Business Attitudes in a Developing
        Economy. Ithaca, New York: Cornell University Press.

This study of managerial attitudes in Latin America includes
analyses of life goals and satisfaction. It is based on
historical sources and surveys of managers from twelve Latin
American nations during 1961-1963. While dated, the work
offers still-valid insights on managers' work-related values
and attitudes. The aims of the managers were found to be
only partly financial in nature. Company profit was less
valued than stability and growth. Latin American managers
tended to avoid long-term planning and projects. They were
paternalistic in terms of leadership style and risk-
avoiders.

0569   Lieske, Joel (1988) "The United States as a Third
        World Country: Race, Education, Culture, and the
        Quality of American Life," pp. 253-64 in Jim Norwine
        and Alfonso Gonzales (eds.), The Third World: States
        of Mind and Being. Boston: Unwin Hyman, Inc.

While the U.S. society is advanced in many ways, selected
sectors fall near or even below the standards of the third
world, especially in selected cities. U.S. regional and
racial differences create differences in quality of life.

0570   Lincoln, James R., Mitsuyo Hanada, and Jon Olson
        (1981) "Cultural Orientations and Individual
        Reactions to Organizations: A study of Employees
        of Japanese-Owned Firms," Administrative Science
        Quarterly 26 (March): 93-115.

A survey of 522 employees in 28 Japanese-owned firms located
in the U.S. found that U.S.-born non-Japanese employees were
less influenced by close relations to superiors (in vertical
structures). Japanese-born and Japanese-American employees
did favor vertical structures and more personal ties with
superiors. Organizational systems reflected the members'
cultural and social orientations.

0571   Lee, James A. (1988) "Changes in Managerial Values,
        1965-1986," Business Horizons 31 (July/August):
        29-37.

Surveys of U.S. managers in two corporations and a training
program during 1965-1986 indicate strong similarities within
sub-samples and little changes from one year to another. The
six highest rankings for the ideal manager's characteristics
for the 1965 and 1986 surveys were: future planning,
decision making, develop new methods, sensitive to feelings,
belief in subordinates, and capacity for loyalty.

0572   Longenecker, Justin G., Joseph A. McKinney, and
        Carlos W. Moore (1988) "The Ethical Issue of
        International Bribery: A Study of Attitudes Among
        U.S. Business Professionals," Journal of Business
        Ethics 7 (may): 341-6.

A survey of 2,219 readers of major business periodicals
indicates a diversity of level of acceptance for the 1977
Foreign Corrupt Practices Act. Four sources of disagreement
are found in the respondents' assumptions, defined as
moralism, pragmatism, cultural relativism, and legalism. In
terms of restrictions of international bribery, half (49%)
said restrictions were never acceptable.

0573   Margerison, C. and A. Kakabadse (1985) How American
        Chief Executives Succeed. New York: American
        Management Association.

The authors surveyed a sample of U.S. executives on their
self evaluations of the key sources for their occupational
successes. The highest ranked items were (1) a need to
achieve results, (2) the ability to work easily with a wide
range of people, (3) a positive reaction to challenges, and
(4) a willingness to take risks.

0574   Marshland, Stephen (1990) "The Evolution of Japanese
        of Japanese Management: Lessons for U.S. managers,"
        Organizational Analysis 11 (Winter): 49-67.

Japanese-style management has undergone changes recently.
U.S. managers can also borrow selected Japanese-style
managerial techniques within the context of U.S. values.

0575   Mendosa, Eugene L. (1988) "How to do Business in
        Latin America," Purchasing World 32 (July): 58-9.

Latin American and North American approaches to business
differ. Latins work at a slower pace, they are reluctant to
compromise, and friends and family take priority over
business. North Americans should take pains to develop
personal relationships and make direct, face-to-face
contacts.

0576   Mente, Boye De (1989) The Japanese Influence on
        America: The Impact, Challenge & Opportunity.
        Lincolnwood, Illinois: Passport Books.

Selected Japanese cultural and behavioral patterns offer a
number of advantages over their North American counterparts.
The author describes the main elements of Japanese culture,
those traits that have been successfully adopted by U.S.
managers, and other practices that would enhance the quality
of life in the U.S. In addition to work-related items, the
author presents Japanese daily behaviors whose adoption
would improve American living.

0577   Milner, Boris Z., Vladimir Rapoport, and Leonid
        Yevenko (1986) Design of Management Systems in
        U.S.S.R. Industry. Dordrecht, Holland: D. Reidel
        Publishing Company.

The work presents an analysis of policies, managerial
structure, external forces, and characteristics of Soviet
industrial organizations in relationship to national
planning. Included is a detailed case study of KAMAZ, a
complex of plants manufacturing heavy trucks.

0578   Nelson, Reed E. (1990) "Is there Strategy in Brazil?"
        Business Horizons 33 (July/August): 15-23.

Long-term planning in developing countries is often
impossible due to unforeseen changes in government policy
and high rates of inflation. Prices are often set by a
ministry of finance, and industry concentration results in
similarity among competitors. Other socio-economic
conditions make managerial behavior in Brazil and other
developing countries different than those found in more
developed and stable economies.

0579   **Newman, Richard G. and K. Anthony Rhee (1989) "Self-Styled Barriers Inhibit Transferring Management Methods," Business Horizons 32 (May/June): 17-21.**

Underlying principles of Japanese-style managerial ideology are "simplicity" and long-range planning. These principles give the Japanese an advantage in global markets. American managers must transfer these and other Japanese-style principles. However, American cultural values form barriers to successful adaptation. These barriers are U.S. values relating to time, complexity, specialization, and diversity.

0580   **Nimgade, Ashok (1989) "American Management as Viewed by International Professionals," Business Horizons 32 (November/December): 98-105.**

Foreign managers occupy a good vantage point from which to evaluate the practices of U.S. managers. U.S. business practices contain both strengths and weaknesses. Major weakness are (1) a short-term orientation, (2) wide wages disparities, (3) emphasis on faddism and superficiality, (4) reliance on a charismatic leadership style, (5) over-specialization in the education of managers, and (6) an overemphasis of aggressiveness over intelligence.

0581   **Norris, William P. (1984) "Patron-Client Relationships in the Urban Social Structure: A Brazilian Case Study," Human Organization 43 (Spring): 16-26.**

Patron-client relationships are prevalent in Latin America, both in the modern and traditional sectors. The poor in Brazil use clientism to establish a wide range of patron-client ties which are generally not connected with other ties. Such ties, classified into two types, are important sources of social cohesion in urban society.

0582   **Odiorne, George S. (1984) "The Trouble with Japanese Management Systems," Business Horizons 27 (July/August): 17-23.**

Japanese-style management practices need not be imitated by U.S. managers. U.S. managers are "lazy" and know what needs to be done to revitalize the economy.

0583   **Okechuku, Chike and Viola Yee Wai Man (1991) "Comparison of Managerial Traits in Canada and Hong Kong," Asia Pacific Journal of Management 8 (October): 223-35.**

The managerial traits of 208 managers in Hong Kong and Canada were compared using Ghiselli's Self-Description Inventory (SDI). Canadian managers scored higher in supervisory ability, achievement motivation, self-actualization, self-assurance, and decisiveness.

0584   Ouchi, William (1981) "Going from A to Z ...
        Thirteen Steps to a Theory Z Organization,"
        Management Review 70 (May): 8-16.

The author proposes the steps necessary for a firm's
transformation from an American-style management to a merged
Japanese-U.S. managerial style.

0585   Parsons, Talcott (1989) "A Tentative outline of
        American Values," Theory Culture and Society 6
        (November): 577-612.

The author, a noted sociologist, presents a typology of
cultural-level values based on worldly-non-worldly and
religious-non-religious emphasis dimensions. He then
discusses the American value system, which he feels falls in
the "religious" cultural category.

0586   Pascale, Richard Tanner (1978) "Personnel Practices
        and Employee Attitudes: A Study of Japanese- and
        American-Managed Firms in the United States,"
        Human Relations 31 (7): 597-615.

Managers in Japanese-owned U.S. firms expend more resources
per employee on nonpayroll benefits than do managers in
U.S.-owned enterprises. Employees in Japanese-managed
enterprises had higher satisfaction levels than those
working in American-owned firms. Worker absenteeism and
tardiness levels were the same in both sub-samples.

0587   Pick, James B., Edgar W. Butler, and Elizabeth L.
        Lanzer (1989) Atlas of Mexico. Boulder, Colorado:
        Westview Press.

Using a Geographic Information System approach, the authors
present social, demographic, and economic data on Mexico,
generally based on state and regional data distributions.
Much of the tabular data is also presented in graphic form.
There are historical, voting, economic, and quality of life
data. Most of the data derive from the 1980 and 1985 Mexican
censuses.

0588   Poff, Deborah and Wilfred Waluchow, editors (1987)
        Business Ethics in Canada. Scarborough, New Jersey:
        Prentice-Hall.

This work contains a collection of writings on business
ethics in Canada using cases studies and articles. The work
is divided into eleven ethical topics.

0589   Prasad, S.B. (1981) "Managers' Attitudes
        in Brazil: Nationals vs. Expatriates,"
        Management International Review 21 (2): 78-85.

Brazil has been found to be a special case when clustering
countries in terms of values. In comparison with
expatriates, Brazilian managers differed in terms of

leadership style and internal control. No differences were found in terms of information-sharing and participation. Expatriates from Europe resembled Brazilian managers more than previous surveys have indicated. These differences from previous studies may be influenced by specific elements in the changing Brazilian cultural environment.

0590   Putti, Joseph M. and Thomas F.H. Chong (1985) "American and Japanese Management Practices in Their Singapore Subsidiaries," Asia Pacific Journal of Management 2 (January): 106-14.

American and Japanese subsidiaries in Singapore react to their foreign cultural environments differently. The Japanese exhibit changes in their managerial behavior. The Americans remain constant and change little in their managerial practices. This may indicate that American managerial patterns are more transferable than Japanese practices.

0591   Quezada, Fernando and James E. Boyce (1988) "Latin America," pp 247-70 in Raghu Nath (ed.), Comparative Management: A Regional View. Cambridge, Mass.: Ballinger Publishing Company.

The authors present a comprehensive discussion of the major characteristics and recent changes in Latin American managerial patterns. Latin American management behavior in different nations is placed in its socio-economic-historical contexts. There are also discussions of those nations' ethnic composition, legal systems, and general social values.

0592   Rhinesmith, Stephen H., John N. Williamson, David M. Ehlen, and Denise S. Maxwell (1989) "Developing Leaders for the Global Enterprise," Training and Development Journal 45 (April): 24-34.

U.S. global firms must change their views of human resource policies and become more international and "culture free." A global firm passes through three stages, and managers must learn to develop global perspectives.

0593   Ricks, David A. and Vijay Mahajan (1984) "Blunders in International Marketing: Fact or Fiction," Long Range Planning 17 (February): 78-83.

The stereotype of U.S. business abroad is that U.S. personnel are insensitive, lack understanding of unique social, political, cultural and trade foreign environments, and are blundering all of the time. A survey of 38 international blunders indicates that U.S. firms are not as liable as the media indicates.

0594   Robertson, James Oliver (1980) <u>American Myth:</u>
        <u>American Reality</u>. New York: Hill & Wang.

The American national character and social values are
studied from the myths and ideals Americans hold concerning
their society. The myths are compared to reality.

0595   Rokeach, Milton and Sandra J. Ball-Rokeach (1989)
        "Stability and Change in American Value Priorities,
        1968-1981," <u>American Psychologist</u> 44 (May): 775-84.

Survey data using U.S. national samples during 1968-85
indicate large value changes for selected attitudes.
Attitudes toward egalitarianism have recently decreased,
although most values show stability. Major changes in
American values indicate a shift away from a collective
morality to a more personal-competence value orientation.

0596   Ronen, Simcha (1986) <u>Comparative and Multinational</u>
        <u>Management</u>. New York: Wiley.

Although this work is a general textbook, it is sensitive to
cultural differences. There is an excellent section on the
U.S. business national character.

0597   Roniger, Luis (1985) "Institutionalized Inequalities,
        the Structure of Trust, and Clientism in Modern Latin
        America," pp 148-63 in Erik Cohen, Moshe Lissak, and
        Uri Almagor (eds.), <u>Comparative Social Dynamics</u>.
        Boulder: Westview Press.

A central feature of Latin American societies is the patron-
client relationship. "Clientism" is a pervasive social
arrangement involved in many if not most allocations of
scarce goods (jobs, education, etc.). Clientilistic ties are
hierarchical, particularistic, and diffuse. Bureaucrats,
government officials, and business persons all behave in
personalistic ways in violation of formal rules because of
the existence of client-patron ties. Such relationships are
found in both the modern and traditional sectors of Latin
American societies.

0598   Ruch, William V. (1984) <u>Corporate Communications:</u>
        <u>A Comparison of Japanese and American Practices</u>.
        Westport, Connecticut: Quorum Books.

The first chapters recount the basic and unique features of
Japanese corporate business behavior and management theories
from a communication perspective. The last section details
American corporate communications practices and systems. A
large number of examples are presented, as well as
organization-communication theories. There are lists
comparing Japan and American patterns of communication and
Management ideologies. Final chapters deal with how
corporate America can/should enter the "information age."
The work is stronger on American than on Japanese practices.

There are well-done descriptions of both countries' corporate systems.

0599   Schmidt, Klaus (1980) <u>Doing Business in Mexico</u>.
        Menlo Park, California: SRI International.

This twenty-page booklet offers practical advice on how to conduct business in Mexico, how to entertain, how to dress, and how to negotiate with Mexican negotiators. There are discussions on selected aspects of Mexican national character.

0600   Schwartz, Jim (1986) "Detroit's New Mentors in
        Managing Americans-The Japanese," <u>International</u>
        <u>Management</u> 41 (September): 81-87.

U.S. Manufacturers can learn a number of lessons in labor relations from the Japanese, including flexible work rules, job rotation, and team assignments. The suggestions are based on the work changes being introduced by General Motors in its NUMMI plant as well as on-going reforms at Ford Motors Co. and Chrysler Corp.

0601   Shafer, Robert Jones (1973) <u>Mexican Business</u>
        <u>Organizations: History and Analysis</u>.
        Syracuse, New York: Syracuse University Press.

Members of business organizations in Mexico tend to react to their internal clients and dominant political-governmental groups rather than to the public or consumers. The author traces the history of Mexico's business organizations. He also describes the various social values and power groups that influence the economic sector.

0602   Sherman, Stratford P. (1991) "Japan's Influence on
        American Life," <u>Fortune</u> 123 (June 17): 115ff.

Japanese expatriates in the U.S. are influencing U.S. social customs and values. While there are segregated Japanese communities, some public school systems contain sizable minorities of Japanese students. More high schools are offering Japanese language courses and counseling to combat prejudice. Americans are learning Japanese values and interests.

0603   Slocum, John W. Jr. and Paul M. Topichak (1972)
        "Do Cultural Differences Affect Job Satisfaction?"
        <u>Journal of Applied Psychology</u> 56 (April): 177-8.

Mexican employees were found to be more satisfied than their U.S. counterparts. The national samples were as equally likely to feel that their security needs were unfulfilled.

0604   Stinson, Jeff (1989) "Maquiladoras Challenge Human
        Resources," Personnel Journal 68 (November): 90-3.

Mexico's labor laws dealing with Maquiladora workers favor
employees in terms of mandated benefits. Foreign employers
need to be aware of Mexican labor laws. Mandated benefits
include a lack of a termination-at-will policy, full-time
medical personnel on duty, 15-day cash holidays bonuses,
etc.

0605   Sutton, Francis X, Seymour E. Harris, Carl
        Kaysen, and James Tobin (1962) The American
        Business Creed. New York: Schocken Books.

Based on content analyses of business associations' policy
statements and corporate advertisements, personal statements
and general literature, this study describes how U.S.
business persons define themselves. The authors then examine
the contents of the "American Business Creed." They find the
business person's role to be complex and internally
contradictory. These create personal strains and conflicts
which are only partly eased by a business creed and ethical
standard.

0606   Teagarden, Mary B. and Mary Ann von Glinow (1990)
        "Contextual Determinants of HRM Effectiveness in
        Cooperative Alliances: Mexican Evidence," Management
        International Review 30 (Special Issue): 23-36.

The authors present a framework for a better use of Human
Resource Management in international joint ventures, using
Mexico as an example. Mexican culture is characterized by
collectivism, high masculinity, Catholicism, etc. These
items and their differences from North American culture have
to be addressed for successful joint ventures. Mexican
partners should learn to address personnel and staffing
needs, since the culture of their North American partners is
different from theirs.

0607   Tinsley, Dillard B. and Jose A. Rodriguez (1981-82)
        "Mexican American Employees-Stereotypes or
        Individuals," Business and Society 20
        (Winter/Spring): 40-45.

Mexican Americans exhibit a wide range of heterogeneous
values and attitudes that are ignored by Anglo Americans.
Non-Hispanic managers are less effective than they might be
because they hold simplistic and inaccurate stereotypes of
Mexican American workers.

0608   Thorne, Paul and Bill Meyer (1987) "The Care and
        Feeding of Your American Management," International
        Management 42 (October): 112-4.

American national character and business behavior are
analyzed from a European perspective. European managers
define Americans as overly optimistic and trained to be

positive. This causes Americans to ignore negative business conditions and the need for careful planning. Americans are also seen as naive, monolingual, arrogant, impersonal, superficial, and oriented to the short-term.

0609   Tocqueville, Alexis de (1969) <u>Democracy in America</u>.
        Edited by J.P. Mayer. Garden City, New York:
        Doubleday & Company, Inc.

This work is a classic statement on American character which still offers great insight. One section deals with the characteristics of American individualism, its influence on U.S. institutions, and how individualism's dangerous tendencies are controlled.

0610   Turner, Frederick Jackson (1976) <u>The Frontier in
        American History</u>. Huntington, New York: Kreiger.

Originally published in 1920, Turner's work contains classic statements on national character of the U.S. This work forms the basis for most contemporary statements on American national character. Turner's work stands with Tocqueville's as a significant statement of American national character.

0611   Verma, Jyoti (1987) "Some Observations by An Indian
        Visitor to the United States," <u>International Journal
        of Intercultural Relations</u> 11 (4): 327-36.

This essay contains comments on the U.S. by an Indian visitor during a six-month stay. He evaluates U.S. behavior and values from an Indian perspective. Americans give all credit to the actors of behavior, making them independent, methodological, hard working, responsible, and anxious for the outcomes of their behavior. Americans have a love for the novel and for adventure, and are very individualistic and self-centered.

0612   Wallin, Theodore O. (1976) "The International
        Executive Baggage: Cultural Values of the American
        Frontier," <u>MSU Business Topic</u> 24 (Spring): 49-58.

An analysis of the major features of the American character (equality, youthfulness, informality, materialism, etc.) as influenced by the American frontier. The frontier environment is seen as a unique cultural experience which still influences the U.S. national character. There are comparisons of U.S. frontier-derived values and related behavior patterns with their counterparts in other cultures.

0613   White, B. Joseph (1988) "The Internationalization of
        Business: One Company's Response," <u>The Academy of
        Management Executive</u> 2 (February): 29-32.

The author describes his experiences in globalization while at Cummings Engine Company, and then suggests the changes necessary if American businesses are to successfully compete in foreign markets.

0614   Whitehill, Arthur M. (1988) "America's Trade Deficit:
        The Human Problems," Business Horizons 31 (Jan/Feb):
        18-23.

America's trade deficit is caused in part by the values of
U.S. managers. Three cultural factors for this lack of
international success are (1) the lack of commitment to
international endeavors, (2) reliance on very short-term
strategies, and (3) a widespread ignorance of other
cultures.

0615   Whitehill, Arthur M. (1989) "American Executives
        Through Foreign Eyes," Business Horizons 32
        (May/June): 42-48.

The author presents a list of U.S. business/social customs
that foreigners find interesting, both positive and
negative. Foreigners both respect and dislike the American
optimism that their way of life is the best. Foreigners also
dislike the American propensity to stress the present and
ignore the future.

0616   Whyte, William F. and Allan R. Holmberg (1956) "Human
        Problems of U.S. Enterprise in Latin American,"
        Human Organization 15 (Fall): 1-40.

This article presents a discussion of Latin American
national character and behavior patterns. Included in the
presentation is a stress on the social pattern of
"personalism." This pattern differs greatly from North
American business behavior. The lack of knowledge of this
concept can create great cross-cultural misunderstandings.
Latin American values are contrasted with U.S. values.

0617   Wilkie, J. (1985) Statistical Abstract of Latin
        America volume 24. Los Angeles: University of
        California Press.

This work contains a wealth of data, most of it up-to-date,
on Latin American countries, resources, population, etc.

0618   Williams, Robin M. Jr. (1985) American Society: A
        Sociological Interpretation. Third Edition. New York:
        Alfred A. Knopf.

The author discusses the basic elements, structures, and
characteristics of the major institutions of U.S. society,
including education, the economy and the family. He then
presents an analysis of the dominant values in American
society and how these values and institutions are integrated
and interrelated with one another.

0619   Zussman, Yale E. (1983) "Learning from the Japanese:
        Management in a Resource-Scarce World,"
        <u>Organizational Analysis</u> 11 (Winter): 68-80.

The author offers advice on how to change U.S. corporate
behavior and selected aspects of the U.S. society in order
to become more globally competitive and less wasteful.

7

Europe

0620   Allen, Keith R. (1986) "Motivating European Managers:
        Maybe We've Got it all Wrong," Benefits and
        Compensation International 15 (May): 7-11.

European executives blame competition among European
countries for lack of market integration. In addition,
European managers graduate from inflexible educational
systems and their pay systems are too rigid. Pay should be
based more on performance.

0621   Amado, Gelles, Claude Faucheux, and Andre
        Laurent (1991) "Organizational Change and
        Cultural Realities: Franco-American Contrasts,"
        International Studies of Management &
        Organization 21 (Fall): 62-95.

The authors present an idealized "deafmen's dialog" between
an American consultant in OD and a French organizational
psychologist to illustrate a number of cultural sources of
misunderstandings and organizational behavior. The American
"functional" paradigm of organizational perception is
contrasted to a French "personalist" view.

0622   Andrle, Vladimir (1976) Managerial Power in the
        Soviet Union. Lexington, Mass: Lexington Books.

The roles and perceptions of Soviet managers reflect state
and political policies. In spite of state planning and
control, factory directors enjoy a certain amount autonomy
(within the framework of a plan). This autonomy is extra-
legal and operates by personal bargaining with individual
parties and interlocking clique memberships. Long tenure
encourages the development of personal status and influence.

0623   Arndt, Johan, Sigmund Gronmo, and Douglass K. Hawes
        (1980) "Allocation of Time to Leisure Activities:
        Norwegian and American Patterns," <u>Journal of Cross-
        Cultural Psychology</u> 11 (December): 498-511.

Americans spend more time than Norwegians on career-oriented
activities and a smaller amount of time on housework.
Americans report spending twice as much time with their
children, though this difference is influenced by each
culture's view of how this is defined. Norwegians are
"doers" and participants in their use of leisure. Americans
are more likely to be spectators.

0624   Barsoux, Jean-Louis and Peter Lawrence
        (1990) <u>Management in France</u>. London: Cassell
        Educational.

French managers generally reflect a "technocrat"
orientation, basing decisions on data and logic rather than
emotions. Those in top positions in government and business
are graduates of the Grandes Ecoles, which stress science
and engineering as well as the Liberal Arts. Their education
makes them "modern" and well trained.

0625   Becker, Helmut and David J. Fritz (1987) "Business
        Ethics: A Cross-Cultural Comparison of Managers'
        Attitudes," <u>Journal of Business Ethics</u> 6 (May):
        289-95.

Codes of ethics are compared among 296 managers from France,
Germany, and the U.S. These findings are compared with
earlier data. French managers were the most optimistic in
feeling that ethical codes could have a positive impact on
business activities. U.S. managers were highest in believing
that good ethics was good business.

0626   Benton, Lauren (1990) <u>Invisible Factories: The
        Informal Economy and Industrial Development in
        Spain</u>. Albany, New York: State University of
        New York Press.

Foreigners wishing to export products from Spain, Italy, and
other countries with active underground economies should
investigate the "off-the-books" or "informal sector"
manufacturing firms. These form the bulk of those nations'
invisible economies and are often based on sweatshop labor
and worker-entrepreneur self-employment. This process of
decentralization or subcontracting is a major economic force
in selected industrializing countries. This field study
focuses on the unregulated aspects of Spain's shoe and
electronic cottage industries and deals with the values and
attitudes central to their operation, such as familism,
cooperationism, and systems of trust.

0627   Bock, Kevin P. (1990) "The Disciplining and Dismissal
        of Employees by Joint Ventures in the USSR," George
        Washington Journal of International Law and Economics
        23 (3): 615-67.

Foreigners wishing to develop joint ventures in the Soviet
Union need to be aware of general USSR managerial policies,
such as the difficulty in dismissing workers.

0628   Bourantas, Dimitris (1988) "Leadership Styles, Need
        Satisfaction and the Organizational Commitment of
        Greek Managers," Scandinavian Journal of Management
        4 (3-4): 121-34.

Organizational commitment was higher among Greek managers
when the superior adopted a consultative leadership style.
Greek managers felt that their needs for promotion, personal
growth, achievement, and pay were less well satisfied than
their needs for power, self-esteem, friendship, and
security.

0629   Bourantas, Dimitris, John Anagnostelis, Yiorgos
        Mantes, and Asterios K. Kefalas (1990) "Culture
        Gap in Greek Management," Organization Studies
        11 (2): 261-8.

585 Greek managers reported on the cultures of their firms.
The respondents defined their firms as Zeus/Apollo
(power/role) centered while they defined themselves as
Athena/Dionysus (task/people) oriented.

0630   Braganti, Nancy L. and Elizabeth Devine (1984)
        The Travellers' Guide to European Customs &
        Manner. Deephaven, MN: Meadowbrook Books.

There are detailed presentations of business and social
protocols in all Western and Central European nations. There
are also lists of business holidays and working hours, legal
information, and detailed etiquette guides. The focus is on
the social protocols for each country.

0631   Brooke, Michael Z. and H. Lee Remmers editors
        (1972) The Multinational Company in Europe: Some
        Key Problems. Ann Arbor: The University of
        Michigan Press.

Aside from general descriptions of the structures of
European multinationals, there is a chapter on differing
managerial styles and ideologies and practices among
managers from the United states and a number of European
countries and Israel. There is a description of differences
in communication styles in European firms.

0632   Brown, Robert J. (1987) "Swatch vs. the Sundial,"
        Internatioanl Management 42 (December): 80.

A case study of intercultural conflict between Italian and
Swiss team members indicates that each nationality held non-
compatible views of time and attitudes toward schedules. The
Swiss complained that the Italians never met deadlines,
changed their minds often, and ignored schedules. The
Italians complained that the Swiss were inflexible, always
insisting that deadlines be met, and unwilling to wait a few
days to "allow better ideas to emerge." The Swiss seemed
always urgent. Team members took part in an exercise in
which each group lived for short periods according to the
other nationality's sense of time. Each nationality learned
the other's viewpoint toward time and each learned to adjust
accordingly.

0633   Bruce, Leigh (1987) "The Italians: The Best
        Europeans?" International Management 42
        (May): 24-31.

The Italian national character and historical experiences
will make Italians successful European-wide business
persons. The positive characteristics of Italians include
flexibility, a high tolerance of foreign customs, the
ability to adapt, a weak sense of nationalism, and
creativity. These characteristics have helped make Italy
into a major economic power and will serve Italians well in
doing business throughout Europe.

0634   Budde, Andreas, John Child, Arthur
        Francis, and Alfred Rieser (1983)
        "Corporate Goals, Managerial Objectives,
        and Organizational Structures in British
        and West German Companies Organization
        Studies," Organization Studies 3 (1): 1-32.

The values of high profitability and growth are strongly
held in British and German firms. Such values, and others,
may originate less from cultural values than from accepting
capitalist goals. Nevertheless, managerial values did differ
in the two national samples, though the reasons for such
differences are unclear.

0635   Burawoy, Michael and Janos Lukacs (1989) "What is
        Socialist about Socialist Production? Autonomy and
        Control in a Hungarian Steel Mill," pp 295-316 in
        Stephen Wood (ed.), The Transformation of Work?
        Skill, Flexibility and the Labour Process. Boston:
        Unwin Hyman Ltd.

Production practices in socialist countries differ from
those in capitalist countries. Analysis of one of Hungary's
three integrated steel mills indicated a preference for

small-batch production because of the demands of the state. Middle management forms a buffer between upper managers and the shop floor. Shop-floor culture creates strong ties among workers in the same shift, creating problems of inter-shift cooperation.

0636   Calori, Roland and Philippe Sarnin (1991)
        "Corporate Culture and Economic Performance:
        A French Study," Organization Studies 12 (1): 49-74.

A study of 280 managers in five French firms evaluated workers' attitudes. Human relations values were important in terms of corporate culture and achieved profitability. Corporate culture has a greater effect on company growth than profitability. Growth was seen as a major strategy to respond to international competition.

0637   Carr, Christopher (1987) "The Implications of
        Internationalization for the Management of the
        Vehicles Components Industry in Britain, Germany,
        Japan and the U.S.A.," Engineering Management
        International 1 (September): 197-207

Senior executives from sixty matched component manufacturers in four countries were interviewed. The decline in this industry, especially in Britain, has been caused in part by managerial inflexibility. Japanese managerial systems focus on flexibility, quality, and improved standards.

0638   Cherns, Albert (1978) "Perspectives on the Quality of
        Working Life," International Studies of Management
        and Organization 8 (Spring/Summer): 38-58.

A review of survey data indicates that levels of work satisfaction in terms of work-related quality of life in non-Communist European countries vary by country.

0639   COFREMCA (1978) "A Psychological Study of the
        Attitudes of French Managers," International
        Journal of Management and Organization 8
        (Fall): 22-38.

This article contains a summary of findings from 30 in-depth interviews and a survey of 600 managers conducted during the early 1970s. The answers suggest a sense of crisis and disillusionment among French managers. Younger managers were less satisfied and more willing to change employers.

0640   Collins, Stephen (1990) "Motivating the British-
        the Role of Incentive Pay in UK Remuneration,"
        Benefits and Compensation International 19 (March):
        17-22.

Compensation systems must reflect national character in
order to be effective. British national character includes
such characteristics as (1) a stubborn independence, (2) a
desire to beat the system, (3) the protection of the weak,
and (4) a dislike of change. Incentive pay should take into
account these and other elements of British culture.

0641   Constable, John and Roger McCormick (1987) The
        Making of British Managers. Northants, England:
        British Institute of Management.

This report on management education and training in the
United Kingdom finds British managers less trained than
their Continental peers. Most UK managers have no formal
management training prior to entering management. The
Department of Education proposes an educational program
leading to a new diploma in management studies with national
standards. The report concludes: "If there is a UK culture
of management, organisations and their mutual development,
it would seem to embrace qualities of parochialism,
insularity and 'muddling through.'"

0642   Cooper, Cary L. and Marilyn J. Davidson (1982)
        "Attitudes of European Working Women," Leadership &
        Organization Development Journal 3 (5): 30-2.

The EEC Council of Ministers commissioned a survey of 3,392
working women in nine European countries. Questions asked
include the feeling that being a woman is an advantage or
not for selected work dimensions and situations.

0643   Cox, Charles J. and Cary L. Cooper (1985) "The
        Irrelevance of American Organizational Sciences to
        the U.K. and Europe," Journal of General Management
        11 (Winter): 27-34.

Many concepts in American organizational science are seen as
irrelevant to the European business environment. The reasons
for this reluctance to borrow from the U.S. are in large
part due to the values and attitudes of European managers
themselves.

0644   Cox, Charles J. and Cary L. Cooper (1989) "The Making
        of the British CEO: Childhood, Work Experience,
        Personality, and Management Style," The Executive
        3 (August): 241-5.

The social background, personalities, and attitudes of 45
British executives are studied. One source of their success

was their self-reliance due to early death of the father, boarding school experience, etc. Family values were ranked highest with work a close second. The sample was innovative, paternalistic/authoritarian, worked long hours, and had high levels of need for achievement.

0645   Cromie, Stanley and Sandra Johns (1983) "Irish
        Entrepreneurs: Some Personal Characteristics,"
        Journal of Occupational Behaviour 4 (October):
        317-24.

42 Irish entrepreneurs were studied to determine the personality traits associated with starting and managing one's own business. These are compared with 41 managers. Entrepreneurs were slightly higher on achievement motivation. Entrepreneurs were significantly higher in terms of a frank avowal of success in business. Entrepreneurs were more internal in terms of locus of control.

0646   Crozier, Michel (1964) The Bureaucratic Phenomenon.
        Chicago: The University of Chicago Press.

This work is a classic analysis of French bureaucratic structures and social behavior. The work includes data and quotes reflecting workers' attitudes, their evaluation of interpersonal and intergroup relationships, and descriptions of the elements of French bureaucratic systems.

0647   Crozier, Michel (1971) The World of the Office
        Worker. Chicago: The University of Chicago Press.

Originally published in 1965, Crozier offers a comprehensive view of French office workers. Included are survey data of attitudes of workers toward formalism and company loyalty. The average French white-collar employee "resists ambiguity and takes refuge in formality and obedience." There are other illustrations of the French national character.

0648   Crozier, Michel (1978) "Attitudes of French Managers
        Regarding the Administration of their Firms,"
        International Journal of Management and Organization
        8 (Fall): 39-63,

Survey data (see COFREMCA) indicate a high level of "malaise," a sense of crisis, alienation, and cynicism among French managers.

0649   Csath, Magdolna (1989) "Corporate Planning in
        Hungarian Companies," Long Range Planning 22
        (August): 89-97,

The corporate culture of Hungarian managers includes resistance to change, high levels of self-confidence, acceptance of government control, and a lack of strategic planning.

0650   Cummings, L. and S. Schmidt (1972) "Managerial
        Attitudes of Greeks: The Role of Culture and
        Industrialization," Administrative Science
        Quarterly 17 (June) 265-272.

The managerial beliefs of Greek managers (N=42) tended to cluster with a Latin-European cluster along some dimensions. In terms of sharing information with subordinates and participative management, the sample resembled a developing countries cluster.

0651   Czarniawska, Barbara (1984) "Managing General
        Managers: Control and Motivation at the Top,"
        Scandinavian Journal of Management Studies 1
        (November): 101-22

A comparison of Polish and U.S. managers indicated that the processes of appraisal and incentives were similar in both countries. However, the central processes in Poland were linked to outside forces, such as politics. The Polish political, economic and cultural contexts inhibit "borrowing" organizational knowledge from the U.S.

0652   Darling, John R. (1985) "The International Market
        Place: Changes in the Competitive Positioning of
        the U.S. vs. Japan," Journal of East and West
        Studies 17 (Spring/Summer): 39-54.

This study is based on a 1975-1985 longitudinal analysis of the general attitudes of consumers in Finland toward the products of the U.S. and their attitudes toward various dimensions of marketing mix strategies. Finnish consumers exhibit a large change in their perceptions of U.S. and Japanese goods and their marketing practices.

0653   De Kieffer, Donald E. (1985) Doing Business with
        Romania. New Canaan, CT: Business Books
        International.

This is a practical guide and introduction to the Romanian society and economy. The focus is on the technical aspects of doing business in that country. There are sections which deal with specific issues (patents, shipping, taxes, duties, etc). There are useful lists of addresses of foreign trade organizations, industrial concerns, and embassies, as well as maps and tourist information. There are limited discussions of business protocols.

0654   Derossi, Flavia (1978) "The Crisis in Managerial
        Roles in Italy," International Journal of
        Management and Organization 8 (Fall): 64-99.

The roles of managers in Italy have been changing rapidly in
recent years, causing a sense of crisis and internal
conflict. The emerging role for managers is one of
participative decision-making outside traditional technical
limits. A new behavioral role model has not yet developed.

0655   Derossi, Flavia (1982) The Technocratic Illusion:
        A Study of Managerial Power in Italy. Armonk, NY:
        M.E. Sharp, Inc.

An analysis of the decision-making and policy-making powers
of mid- and upper-level managers exposes the relative
powerlessness of Italian managers. The interpretations are
based on 653 interviews taken during the early 1970s. This
excellent study is sensitive to modern organizational
theory.

0656   DeYoung, H. Garrett (1990) "In Search of the New
        European Manager," Electronic Business 16 (Dec. 10):
        103-4.

Global managers should be able to fit easily into new
cultures. Such persons are few in number. Beside costly in-
house training, one solution is to hire managers with global
expertise. Other options are available.

0657   Dickson, John W. (1982) "Top Managers' Beliefs and
        Rationales for Participation," Human Relations 35
        (3): 203-17.

The belief systems and general worldview of managers in
Scotland were investigated. The focus was the sample's
beliefs and rationales for the participative style of
management or its rejection.

0658   Douglas, Susan P. (1978) "Cross-National Comparisons
        and Consumer Stereotypes-A Case Study of Working and
        Non-Working Wives in the U.S and France," pp 263-81
        in Michel Ghertman and James Leontiades (eds.),
        European Research in International Business. New
        York: North-Holland Publishing Company.

French and U.S. wives exhibit a number of differences in
terms of selected values and consumer practices. There are
both national as well as employed/non-employed differences.

0659   Doyle, Peter, John Saunders, and Veronica Wong
        (1986) "A Comparative Study of Japanese Marketing
        Strategies in the British Market," Journal of
        International Business Studies 17 (Spring): 27-46.

Matched samples of British and Japanese companies indicate
that Japanese firms are more market-oriented and focused on
market   share   than   their   British   competitors.   The
organization of Japanese companies in Britain resembles
successful British companies more than the Japanese
stereotype. The Japanese enjoy economic advantages in
Britain because of their marketing skills rather than their
cultural patterns.

0660   Dreyfus, Patricia A. (1988) "Negotiating the Kremlin
        Maze," Business Month 132 (November): 55-63.

There are many problems, which are illustrated, when dealing
with the Russian bureaucracy. The author offers guidelines
for cutting red tape.

0661   Dubin, Robert and Amira Galin (1989) "Attachments
        to Work: Russians in Israel," Work and
        Occupations 18 (May): 172-93.

Russian immigrants to Israel assimilate into the Israeli
work environment in a partial manner, and they maintain many
of their original work-related attitudes. They maintain
their Russian views toward authority, organizational
loyalty, and labor unions. There was a high level of belief
in the centrality of their employers. Compared to Israeli
workers, Russian immigrants were higher in terms of the
beliefs "getting along with the people at work" and "number
of people doing the same job as me."

0662   Edwards, V. (1979) "The Organization of Management
        Education in East Germany," Journal of European
        Industrial Training 3 (1): 29-32.

Managers in East Germany, as "cadres," have political as
well as occupational responsibilities. Training includes the
development of political as well as managerial skills. As
socialist co-owners of enterprises, workers must be
motivated by managers to work as efficiently as possible.
Yet most activities are subordinated to political
socialization and the building of a socialist society.

0663   Ehrman, Henry W. (1957) Organized Business in
        France. Princeton: Princeton University Press.

An analysis is presented of the French national character in
relation to corporate practices, including a tendency toward
resistance to change and innovation. Later research supports
these and other findings.

0664   Fairchild, Erika S. (1989) "National Culture
        and Police Organization in Germany and the
        United States," Public Administration Review
        49 (Sept/Oct): 454-62

German and U.S. organizational behaviors fit two models:
empiricism (U.S.) and rationalism (Germany). These two
models offer different alternatives in terms of six
dimensions of organization and organizational culture. These
dimensions include career perceptions, organizational
climate and basic corporate structures.

0665   Farndon, John (1988) "West Germany: Self Doubt
        Amid Success: Doing Business with the Germans,"
        Director 41 (July): 96-101.

Germans doing business abroad are aggressive and flexible.
Local firms, however, are bureaucratic, conservative, and
conventional. Germans have the greatest number of holidays
in Europe. Business and leisure time are strictly kept
separate.

0666   Fedorowicz, Jan (1990) Poland: A Guide to Business
        Opportunities. Ottawa Canada: Prospective Strategic
        Business Research Group.

This work offers general, current information on the Polish
society and economy, including consumption patterns,
economic policies, tax incentives for foreigners, and trade
information. There is advice on how to establish a joint
venture and how trade is organized in Poland. There is a
list of useful addresses. There are short sections on Polish
business customs, business travel, business hours, and
holidays.

0667   Fidler, John (1981) The British Business Elite:
        Its Attitudes to Class, Status and Power. London:
        Routledge & Kegan Paul.

A survey of 130 chief executives, entrepreneurs, and higher-
level bureaucrats describes the samples' attitudes toward
social class, equality, and their images of society. The
study begins with a description of the samples' social,
education, career paths, leisure preferences, and voluntary
organizational political and non-political involvements.
Thirty-eight percent were educated at Oxford or Cambridge,
indicating a high degree of social homogeneity.

0668   Friday, Robert A. (1989) "Contrasts in Discussion
        Behaviors of German and American Managers,"
        International Journal of Intercultural Relations
        13 (4): 429-46.

U.S. managers expect business to be an impersonal activity,
want to be liked, are assertive in conversation style, and
prefer direct confrontations. German managers prefer to be
more personal, need to be respected and credible rather than
liked, prefer order and hierarchy, and accept assertiveness
and confrontation. German managers were more sophisticated
about history and better able to conduct logical analyses of
current issues. They expected striking, intelligent and
informed debates. Americans tended to discuss sports, the
weather, etc. during informal conversations.

0669   Furnham, Adrian (1984) "Work Values and Beliefs in
        Britain," Journal of Occupational Behavior 5
        (October): 281-91.

The work-related values and their socio-demographic
correlates were investigated using 256 British adults. Work
values were strongly and positively related to conservative
beliefs, and were negatively related with Leisure Ethic and
Marxist-related beliefs. Age and education were important
determinants of beliefs and values.

0670   Gable, Myron and Peter Arlow (1986) "A Comparative
        Examination of the Value Orientations of British and
        American Managers," International Journal of
        Management 3 (September): 97-106.

150 British and U.S. executives were administered the
Allport-Vernon-Lindzey Study of Values scale. The British
executives' dominant values were economic, political, and
aesthetic. The U.S. executive's values were economic,
theoretical, and political.

0671   Gallino, Luciano (1975-76) "Three Types of Italian
        Top Managers," International Studies of Management
        and Organization 5 (Winter): 43-70.

The author subjectively develops a typology of Italian
managers (liberal, lay humanist, and Christian socialist).
Each category adheres to different values and reacts
differently to crises, such as labor relations. The
"liberal" manager has similar values and identities to U.S.
managers with Calvinistic values. He is "objective," non-
patriarchal, and market-oriented.

0672   Garner, Arthur (1972) "Personal Practices and
         Policies of Italian Management," pp 191-216 in
         Lawrence Stessin (ed.), Managerial Styles of
         Foreign Businessmen series 9, volume 1. Hemstead,
         New York: Hofstra.

Italian workers give work a low priority in relation to non-
work interests. The Italian management style includes the
elements of paternalism, short-term planning, and nepotism.

0673   Gilbert, Nathaniel (1990) "Enticements of an
         Inaccessible Market," Management Review 79
         (March): 14-20.

Soviet bureaucracy, inefficient distribution systems, and
material shortages make foreign business entry into Russia
difficult. Pepsi Co., for example, negotiated for 14 years
for an entry.

0674   Granick, David (1975) Enterprise Guidance in
         Eastern Europe: A Comparison of Four Socialist
         Economies. Princeton: Princeton University Press.

The national managerial systems and their weakness are
described for Romania, East Germany, Hungary, and
Yugoslavia. There is information on managerial behavior,
restrictions on behavior, career and educational paths,
characteristics of social background, and earnings. Each
country's managerial characteristics are placed within their
political, economic, and historical contexts.

0675   Graves, Desmond (1973) "The Impact of Culture upon
         Managerial Beliefs and Behavior in England and
         France," pp 283-304 in Desmond Graves (ed.),
         Management Research: A Cross-Cultural Perspective.
         San Francisco: Jossey-Bass.

There is a description of survey research using
international samples of managers. The French sample viewed
authority as vested in the person rather than in the
position. This encourages detachment and centralization
among French managers.

0676   Greenhouse, Steven (1991) "Studying Business? Why
         Stick to Just One Continent?" The New York Times
         June 30: F-5.

This article describes the origins of the student body of
the Institut Europeen d'Aministration des Affaires, of which
88% are non-French. The author describes the school's
program and compares INSEAD to other M.B.A. programs.

0677   Grey, Ronald J. and Ted J.F. Thone (1990)
        "Differences Between North American and
        European Corporate Cultures," Canadian
        Business Review 17 (Autumn): 26-30.

Significant cultural differences will remain after the
unification of the European markets in 1992. Each nation
will remain a distinct cultural area in terms of markets.
Crucial strategies for entry include (1) a long-range view
and (2) adjusting to divergent cultures.

0678   Grosset, Serge (1970) Management: American and
        European Styles. Belmont, CA: Wadsworth Publishing
        Company, Inc.

Although dated, this comprehensive work remains a useful
model for comparative analyses of management. Chapters
include the social backgrounds, formation, power levels, and
career paths of managers. The bibliography is complete and
cites sources in a number of languages.

0679   Grunwald, Wolfgang and Hans-Georg Lilge (1981)
        "Change of Leadership Style in German Enterprises:
        From Authoritative to Participative Leadership?"
        pp 722-55 in Gunter Dlugos and Klaus Weiermair
        (eds.), Managing Under Differing Value Systems:
        Political, Social, and Economical Perspectives.
        Berlin and New York: Walter de Gruyter.

The preferred leadership style in German enterprises has
experienced a change from authoritarian to cooperative-
participative styles. However, such attitudes have changed
faster than actual behavior. Surveys indicate a tendency
toward more consultative, participative decision-making in
some areas of the society.

0680   Grzelak, Eva (1987) "The U.S. Businessman in
        Europe," European Trends (3): 71-9.

American expatriates in Europe have learned the value of
adopting European business customs. U.S. expatriates view
the work pace in Europe to be slower and see the British as
excellent negotiators. Northern Europeans are evaluated as
too authoritarian. Southern Europeans are defined as
unpredictable and indecisive.

0681   Habert, Kjell and Arild Lillebo (1988) Made in
        Norway: Norwegians as Others See Us. Norway:
        Norwegian School of Management Press.

U.S. management-style practices do not work well in Norway.
The book discusses Norwegian national character while
focusing on business-related behavior. Norwegian corporate
culture is people-centered, stresses teamwork, and decisions

are made through consensus. There are fewer rules in Norwegian enterprises.

0682   Hobson, Charles J., James B. Dworkin, and
        Ekkehard Frieland (1984) "A Preliminary
        Empirical Analysis of the Work Ethic in West
        Germany," International Journal of Management
        1 (March): 20-25.

Almost half of a sample of 135 West German workers were committed to the traditional work ethic, and defined as being willing to work if not financially needing to work. Seventy-two percent of U.S. workers agreed with this statement. German women were less (27%) willing to continue working than men.

0683   Hoffman, Douglas (1972) "The Effect of the Cartel
        System in France," pp 148-71 in Lawrence Stessin
        (ed.), Managerial Styles of Foreign Businessmen
        series 9, volume 1. Hempstead, New York: Hofstra.

French executives value stability over risk-taking. Such an attitude influences not only the structure of the French economy (cartels; government direction of business) but also managerial behavior. There is a lack of concern for profitability and a tendency toward centralization of authority. Predictability and order are major values and goals of businessmen.

0684   Hoffmann, Paul (1990) That Fine Italian Hand. New
        York: Henry Holt and Company.

The Italian national character is explained in a journalistic manner. The author discusses why one-third or more of the economy is underground. While emphasizing the cultural sophistication of Italians, the author also discusses the negative aspects living in Italy, of the Italian society, and Italian culture. Politics and religion are relatively ignored.

0685   Hofstede, Geert H. (1975-76) "The Importance of Being
        Dutch: National and Occupational Differences in Work-
        Related Goal Importance," International Studies
        of Management and Organization 5 (Winter): 5-28.

The analysis of a 120-item questionnaire using Dutch and European samples indicates that the Dutch maintain a separate national identity. The Dutch national character fits a profile in which family is more valued than work, cooperation is preferred over advancement/excelling over others, job freedom is more desired than success, and comfortable physical conditions are valued more than the idea of an efficient organization.

0686   Horovitz, Jacques H. (1978) "Management Control
in France, Great Britain and Germany," Columbia
Journal of World Business 13 (Summer): 16-22.

The author presents an analysis of how systems of managerial
control vary in Great Britain, Germany, and France. British
managers have a different time perspective than the two
other national samples. Attention to detail was highest in
Germany and lowest in Great Britain. The French were lowest
in standardization of work procedures.

0687   Horovitz, Jacques Henri (1980) Top Management
Control in Europe. New York: St. Martin's Press.

This study of British, German, and French management emerges
as one of the better analysis of comparative management. The
three countries' management and organizational behaviors are
contrasted. The focus is on the comparative systems of
control used in Western Europe. The study is based on a
sample of 52 companies. Centralization is lowest in the
British sample; top management receives the most information
in Germany; and systemization is lowest in France.

0688   Inzerilli, Giorgio (1990) "The Italian Alternative:
Flexible Organization and Social Management,"
International Studies of Management and Organization
20 (Winter): 6-21.

Italian firms offer an alternative to traditional models of
large-scale organizations. The Italian model is highly
decentralized and made up of legally separate small firms
which voluntarily cooperate on generally short-term
projects. Each enterprise becomes a point of connection for
others. This model offers flexibility of size and
production. Such enterprise structures demand trust among
participants, and result in a unique employer-employee
relationship.

0689   Inzerilli, Giorgio and Andre Laurent (1983)
"Managerial Views of Organization Structure in
France and the USA," International Studies of
Management and Organization 13 (Spring/Summer):
97-118.

Findings from a 56-statement questionnaire scored on a five-
point scale taken by French and U.S. managers indicate that
French managers were more authoritarian, preferred well-
defined lines of authority, and accepted authority systems
in organizations as necessary. U.S. respondents preferred
more distance between superior and subordinate and more
questioning of superior's decisions.

0690   Jenner, Stephen R. (1984) "The British Roots of
        Business Ideology," Journal of General Management
        10 (Autumn): 44-56.

The various elements of business management are discussed
based on surveys of middle to senior managers in the UK, the
U.S., and Australia. There is much similarity among the
attitudes of the respondents, though the U.S. sample
differed in terms of such values as privacy and career
advancement.

0691   Jones, Stephanie (1990) "Working for the Japanese:
        The Myths and Realities," Management Accounting 68
        (May):40-4.

A survey of roughly 100 British employees of Japanese
companies revealed that many so-called Japanese-style
managerial practices are more ideal than followed. This
includes the myth of consensus decision-making. British
employees received extensive training and expressed loyalty
to their employers. The Japanese rewarded loyalty and good
performance with promotion rather than cash bonuses.

0692   Kennedy, Carol "As Others See Us," Director 41
        (April): 44-70.

Visitors and expatriates find British management much more
effective than normal stereotypical images. Managers from
six countries state that British management behavior to be
creative. They also find it to be inflexible and resistant
toward change.

0693   Kiesche, Elizabeth S. (1991) "A Global Executive for
        a Global Business," Chemical Week 148 (Jan 18):
        22-23.

Executives at Hoechst Celanese recognize that managerial
styles in Germany and the U.S. differ. The two managerial
cultures are being blended together, creating a synergy that
improves the company.

0694   Kiezun, Witold (1979) "Decision Making by
        Socialist Managers in Complex Organizations,"
        International Journal of Management and
        Organization 9 (Winter): 63-77.

Research in Poland's engineering industry defined elements
of decision-making by managers in terms of a model of
intensifying degrees of difficulty/ambiguity. A sample of
165 managers in the city and province of Warsaw was drawn.
Techniques of reaction to difficult or stressful situations
used were: overcompensation (87%), suppression or shame
(71%), fixation-continual worrying (71%), rationalization-
search for logical reasons, and justification for one's acts

in a difficult situation (35%-49% based on sub-sample), compensation (49%), repression (25%), identification (25%-37%), and aggression (32%).

0695   Klein, Harold E. and Robert E. Linneman (1984)
        "Environmental Assessment: An International Study
        of Corporate Practice," The Journal of Business
        Strategy 5 (Summer): 66-75.

Environmental assessment and strategic planning are standard activities in roughly half of U.S. and European firms (N=445), though 92-97% have distinct planning units. Non-U.S. firms have a much longer time horizon. One-third of foreign industrial firms planned more than ten years in the future compared to one-fifth of U.S. industrial firms.

0696   Klimaski, Richard J. and Anat Rafaeli (1983)
        "Inferring Personal Qualities through Handwriting
        Analysis," Journal of Occupational Psychology
        56 (September): 191-202.

Handwriting analysis, or graphology, is sometimes used in continental firms as one basis for job applicant evaluation. The authors describe the major features of graphology in terms of the basic twelve features analyzed and the results that can obtained. The reliability of such analysis seems to be low but positive, though the technique's validity is unclear.

0697   Kono, Toyohiro (1984) "Long Range Planning of U.K.
        and Japanese Corporations - A Comparative Study,"
        Long Range Planning 17 (April): 58-76.

UK, U.S., and Japanese firms have very different policies concerning long term planning. Japanese firms are long term and growth oriented. They consider employee welfare more and are more centralized than British or U.S. firms.

0698   Kreder, Martina and Maria Zeller (1988) "Control
        in German and U.S. Companies," Management
        International Review 28 (3): 58-66.

Managerial control in Germany is behavior-oriented. In the U.S, control is system-oriented. This difference is due in part to the different cultural contexts found in the sample's large companies.

0699   Kuc, Bolec, David J. Hickson, and Charles McMillan
        (1980) "Centrally Planned Development: A Comparison
        of Polish Factories with Equivalents in Britain,
        Japan, and Sweden," Organization Studies
        1 (3): 253-70.

As part of the Aston Programme, eleven Polish factories are
matched for size, product, and unit status with those in
Britain, Japan, and Sweden. The "bold hypothesis" dealing
with the structural effects of organizational size is
supported in the Polish sample. The Polish factories differ
from the others in that they were more centralized, highly
formalized and functionally specialized. Another article in
the same issue lists the data sets available from the Aston
Programme.

0700   Lafuente, Alberto and Vincent Salas (1989)
        "Types of Entrepreneurs and Firms: The Case of New
        Spanish Firms," Strategic Management Journal 10
        (Jan/Feb): 17-30.

There are a number of entrepreneurial personality types
based on work aspirations of owners of new Spanish firms.
These personality profiles and the origins of these
entrepreneurs shape the performance and structures of these
firms.

0701   Lane, Christel (1989) Management and Labour in
        Europe: The Industrial Enterprise in Germany,
        Britain and France. Brookfield, Vermont: Gower
        Publishing Company.

A survey of corporate structure and managerial differences
among companies in Germany, Britain, and France with
comparisons with U.S. practices indicates the existence of
national differences. There are comparisons of
organizational structures and organizational elements
(vocational, acceptance of Taylorism, and administrative
structures). A number of difficult-to-obtain studies are
carefully analyzed.

0702   Lassere, Philippe (1988) "Why Europeans are Weak in
        Asia-An Organizational Perspective," Long Range
        Planning 21 (August): 25-35.

The European presence in Pacific Asia is relatively weak.
One reason for this neglect is that European managerial
values and practices are too inflexible for the region. The
author suggests the adoption of selected Japanese strategic
and managerial practices.

0703   Laurent, Andre (1983) "The Cultural Diversity of
        Western Conceptions of Management," International
        Studies of Management and Organization 13
        (Spring/Summer): 75-96.

The author provides an analysis of the concepts related to
the practices of management among 817 managers from nine
European countries and the United States.

0704   Lawrence, Paul R. and Charalambos A. Vlachoutsicos
        editors (1990) Behind the Factory Walls: Decision
        Making in Soviet and U.S. Enterprises. Boston:
        Harvard Business School Press.

The work consists of essays on Soviet and U.S. managerial
systems and decision-making. National scholars write on
their own country's practices with foreign readers in mind.

0705   Lawrence, Peter (1980) Managers and Management in
        West Germany. New York: St. Martin's Press.

The background and characteristics of German-style
management and managerial values are described. There are
chapters dealing with the role of the foreman and the views
of German managers.

0706   Lawrence, Peter (1983) "National Culture and Business
        Policy," Journal of General Management 8 (Spring):
        79-85.

Variations in national cultures are associated with
variations in managerial behavior and in business policy.
The author describes the national characters of German and
UK managers. These differences influence business policy.
German managers, compared to British managers, tend to be
poor improvisors, less adept, do better in planning to avoid
problems than handling crises, and are more centralized in
terms of decision-making.

0707   Lederer, Gerga (1982) "Trends in Authoritarianism:
        A Study of Adolescents in West Germany and the United
        States since 1945," Journal of Cross-Cultural
        Psychology 134 (September): 299-314.

The authoritarianism values in relation to a number of
institutions were measured among adolescents in West Germany
and America during a 33-year period. During this time frame,
German youths became less authoritarian, so that in 1978,
American youths were more authoritarian.

0708   Maccoby, Michael (1991) "Introduction: Why American
        Management Should be Interested in Sweden," pp 1-15
        in Michael Maccoby (ed.), Sweden at the Edge: Lessons
        for American and Swedish Managers. Philadelphia:
        University of Pennsylvania Press.

The author contrasts Swedish and American values. Swedish
manufacturing and social ethics are based on the concept of
lagom, which means "just right" in the contexts of fairness
and moderation. Swedes work well in groups and cooperative
teams. The concluding chapter of this book ("Lessons for
American Managers," pp 297-301) summarizes selected points
from other chapters and makes suggestions to improve
American managerial behavior based on Swedish work
practices.

0709   Mahoney, Jack (1990) Teaching Business Ethics
        in the UK, Europe and the USA. London:
        The Athlone Press.

The issue of business ethics is more discussed in the U.S.
than in Europe and the U.K. When discussed in business
educational programs, each country exhibits very different
concerns and approaches. The literature on business ethics
is more developed in Germany and Switzerland.

0710   Maitland, Ian (1983) The Causes of Industrial
        Disorder: A Comparison of a British and a German
        Factory. London: Routledge and Kegan Paul.

Workers and managers in a British factory had adversarial
stances toward each other, resulting in inefficiencies in
the marketplace. This antagonism resulted in continuous
"class warfare:" work stoppages, disruptions of production
in general, and erosion of authority. The German factory was
organized along different structures, making work relations
much more harmonious and productive.

0711   Mant, Alistair (1977) The Rise and Fall of the
        British Manager. New York: Holmes, & Meier
        Publishers, Inc.

Guided by philosophy and history as well as organizational
theory, the author traces the development of managerial
ideology and behavior in Britain. There are also incisive
comparisons with German, Swedish, and American national
character and national values. One conclusion is that
management in Britain has not become an integrated segment
of British culture. This results in a "national neurosis."

0712   Marceau, Jane (1989) <u>A Family Business? The</u>
        <u>Making of an International Business Elite</u>.
        Cambridge: Cambridge University Press.

A major influence among economic elites in Europe and
elsewhere is the Institut d'Aministration des Affaires
(INSEAD). The author studies the backgrounds and attitudes
of students and alumni of INSEAD, the career paths, and
attitudes of French and other national graduates and their
wives. Interviews were conducted in over ten major capitals
to study this international elite. This elite follows the
traditional "family-centered" European values and are linked
through extensive network systems. INSEAD graduates are
family-oriented, business-oriented, international in scope,
and basically ambitious risk-taking entrepreneurs. A review
of this school's programs is found in Greenhouse (0676).

0713   Margerison, Charles (1980) "Leadership Paths and
        Profiles," <u>Leadership and Organization Development</u>
        1 (1): 12-17.

244 chief executives of major companies in Britain were
asked to rank the major influences helping them to develop
as managers. The top-ranked items were (1) ability to work
with a wide variety of people, (2) early overall
responsibility, and (3) a need to achieve results.

0714   Martin, Janette (1988) "Italy's High-Tech
        Management Style," <u>Datamation</u> 34 (May 1):
        45-20.

Italian management is characterized by a lack of stability
of corporate structure; worker-management relations are
confrontational, and business messages are indirect.

0715   Maruyama, Magoroh (1990) "Some Management
        Considerations in the Economic Reorganization of
        Eastern Europe," <u>Academy of Management Executive</u>
        4 (May): 90-91.

Eastern European countries have different managerial styles
since each country has its own culture. However, there are
four problems common to Eastern Europe, including the
practice of bribing administrators and poor work habits.
Suitable management methods must be developed that are
appropriate to each country's managerial and social values.

0716   Maurice, Marc, Arndt Sorge, and Malcolm
        Warner (1980) "Differences in Organizing
        Manufacturing Units: A Comparison of France,
        West Germany and Great Britain," Organization
        Studies 1 (1): 59-86.

The authors find large cultural and structural differences
in the organizational processes of firms located in three
European nations.

0717   McCroskey, James C., Nancy F. Burroughs, Ake
        Daun, and Virginia P. Richmond (1990)
        "Correlates of Quietness: Swedish and American
        Perspectives," Communication Quarterly 38
        (Spring): 127-37.

Swedish   and   U.S.   students   reported   differences   in
communication perceptions. Swedish respondents were less
willing to communicate and more introverted.

0718   Meller, Paul (1990) "Rouble, Rouble, Toil and
        Trouble," Management Today (August): 64-7.

Problems in doing business in Russia include a lack of hard
currency, a different negotiating style, and a legal system
that ill-defines foreign activities and joint ventures.
Another difficulty is Russia's large size, resulting in
unavoidably large amounts of time spent in trains. A train
ride from Moscow to the commercial center of Lutsk in the
Ukraine takes 28 hours.

0719   Mendras, Henri and Alistair Cole (1991) Social Change
        in Modern France: Toward a Cultural Anthropology of
        the Fifth Republic. Cambridge, England: Cambridge
        University Press.

Written from the social science and historical perspectives,
the French national character, both static and changing, is
explored in a series of excellently-written essays. There
are chapters on the cadres' position in society, the
changing educational system, changing business values, etc.

0720   Millar, Jean (1979) British Management Versus
        German Management: A Comparison of Organizational
        Effectiveness in West German and U.K. Factories.
        Earnborough, England: Saxon House.

The author contrasts British and German management styles
and explains why German factories are more efficient.

0721   Montebello, Michel and Pierre Buigues (1982)
        "How French Industry Plans," Long Range Planning
        15 (June): 116-21.

French managers do not plan long range due to cultural and
linguistic characteristics. Due to two general forecasting
styles being used, planning in French firms is badly
coordinated and in conflict within firms.

0722   Monthoux, Pierre Guillet de (1991) "Modernism
        and the Dominating Firm - On the Managerial
        Mentality of the Swedish Model," Scandinavian
        Journal of Management 7 (1): 27-40.

Swedish managerial thought as well as national character
reflect a German background rather than an Anglo-Saxon
perspective. Managers try to "realize capitalism without
capitalists." This is achieved by defining the concept of
the "firm" in a unique manner.

0723   Norburn, David (1987) "Corporate Leaders
        in Britain and America: A Cross-National
        Analysis," Journal of International Business
        Studies 18 (Fall): 15-32.

A study of 2,123 British and U.S. managers indicates large
differences in values and behavior by national origin. U.S.
managers were more likely to be better educated, though UK
graduates were more likely to have a science than a liberal
arts background. The highest-ranked U.S. success trait was
listed as concern for people. British managers ranked
intelligence highest. British managers accept "job-hopping"
through the use of personal networks as a means for
achieving high rank.

0724   Oberg, Winston (1978) "The Executive in a
        Communitarian society," MSU Business Topics 26
        (Autumn): 5-14.

Forty Norwegian and Swedish top executives explain their
respective government's hostility toward business, their
different reactions to this ideology, and their attitudes
toward "communitarian" societies.

0725   Olsson, Anders S. (1991) The Swedish Wage
        Negotiation System. Brookfield, Vermont:
        Dartmouth Publishing Company.

A unique aspect of the Swedish economic institution is its
national wage negotiation system, which decides on the
distribution of wages and profits. Much of the strengths of
the Swedish economy and its labor peace up to the mid-1980s
can be attributed to this system. Included in the study are
reports of surveys of workers illustrating their values.

0726   Olve, Nils-Göran, Alf Westeluis, and Ann-Safie
        Westelius (1988) "Managers' Attitudes-A
        Comparison between Sweden and China,"
        <u>Scandinavian Journal of Management</u>
        4 (1-2): 63-75.

A test of Hofstede's four dimensions of culture using
managers in Sweden and China indicated that value scores did
discriminate between national samples. When asked about the
"ideal job," the Swedish sample's answers were having
interesting work to do, participating in decisions, and
having a job which helped solve society's problem. The same
values were also defined as most important by the Chinese
sample.

0727   Papageorge, Andrew Jackson (1967) <u>Transferability</u>
        <u>of Management: A Case study of the United States</u>
        <u>and Greece</u>. Ph.D. dissertation, University of
        California, Los Angeles.

The author studied firms that were located in the U.S., U.S.
subsidiaries in Greece, and Greek-owned firms to compare
their managerial behavior in terms of four management
functions. The American-owned Greek firms used an American-
style of management. Greek managers did not delegate
authority. They were less willing to write company policies
and statements of organizational structure. Greek managers
were the least customer-oriented, reflecting a Greek value
which denigrates "hustler" behavior. They were less
competitive than U.S. managers. A guiding principle for
managers and workers was "filotomo:" personal honor.

0728   Parry, John (1990) "Wild East Pioneers,"
        <u>International Management</u> 45 (November): 50-4.

Although East European governments are eager to learn
Western management practices, living in Eastern Europe
presents a number of problems. There is a shortage of
accommodation, local co-workers will resent the expatriate's
high pay, and most Eastern Europeans lack initiative.

0729   Peak, Martha H. (1991) "A Survivor's Guide to
        Soviet Business Travel," <u>Management Review</u>
        80 (January): 51-4.

The author provides a "Survival Guide" for foreigners
visiting and living in Russia. There is advice on what
supplies to take into Russia, such as decaffinated coffee,
herbal teas, chocolate, dried fruit, peanut butter, and even
vodka. These products are often unavailable.

0730   Perkins, H. Wesley and James L. Spates (1986)
        "Mirror Images? Three Analyses of Values in England
        and the United States," International Journal of
        Comparative Sociology 27 (January/April): 31-52.

The value systems in England and the U.S. are both different
and similar, depending on the level of analysis. English and
American urban adults have the same rankings of values (good
health, happy marriage, meaningful life, sense of peace,
close friends, and control of life). There are consistent
Anglo-American differences in the strength of specific
values, such as achievement success (U.S. stronger) and
humanitarianism (UK higher).

0731   Pettibone, Peter J. (1991) "Negotiating a
        Business Venture in the Soviet Union," The Journal
        of Business Strategy 12 (January/February): 18-23.

Stationing a single U.S. representative in Moscow costs
upwards of U.S. $400,000 a year. The chances of such a
person's failure can be decreased by careful preparation,
the negotiation of the broadest possible business charter
for a joint venture, and a realistic policy of what to do
with profits.

0732   Phillips-Martinsson, Jean (1982) Swedes as Others See
        Them: Facts, Myths or a Communication Complex? Lund,
        Sweden: Studentlitteratur.

Swedish businessmen exhibit unique cultural behavior
patterns, including avoidance of eye contact, their sense of
time, space, and negotiation style. Based on a survey of 100
non-Swedes living in Sweden, Swedes were defined as "too
quiet" during meetings, people who did not mix social and
business conversations, and as cold and unfriendly.

0733   Porter, James L., Helen Muller, and Robert
        K. Render (1989) "The Making of Managers:
        An American Perspective," Journal of General
        Management 14 (Summer): 62-76.

British managers should become more professional. Past
educational programs for managers did not develop creative
or critical thinking. There is a need to better combine
classroom and practical knowledge.

0734   Posner, Barry and Warren H. Schmidt (1983)
        "U.S. and European Executives Begin to Think
        Alike," International Management 38 (March):
        58-60.

Results of surveys conducted during 1980 and 1983 of
executives from 10 European countries and the United States
indicate a convergence of attitudes dealing with career

goals and work vs. family conflicts. American executives are more optimistic about "fulfilling your life's ambition" and getting more satisfaction from career over family life. Americans were also most willing to relocate to a higher paying job. European managers felt better able to separate work from home concerns, and gained more satisfaction from their home life than from their careers. Value differences continue to exist, and the Americans held some "non-European" values.

0735   Prais, S.J. and Karin Wagner (1988) "Productivity and Management: The Training of Foremen in Britain and Germany," National Institute Economic Review 123 (February): 34-47.

Plants in Germany have higher productivity levels than UK plants. One reason for this is that German first-line supervisors receive more training and are more skilled. Vocational training is more thorough in Germany.

0736   Pusic, Eugen (1981) "Ambiguity of Managerial Values in Self-Management," pp 833-50 in Gunter Dlugos and Weiermair (eds.), Managing Under Differing Value Systems: Political, Social and Economical. Berlin and New York: Walter de Gruyter.

An analysis of managerial and work-related values among managers, workers, and youths in Yugoslavia indicates variations in attitudes toward work. The official ideology is one of shared decision-making. This ideology differs from actual behavior because of the privileged position held by managers due to their monopoly of technical expertise. Attitudes toward participative management, wage equalization and work differ by occupational level and social origin (village youths, students, white collars, etc.).

0737   Reynolds, Beatrice K. (1984) "A Cross-Cultural Study of Values of Germans and Americans," International Journal of Intercultural Relations 8 (3): 269-78.

The Rokeach Value Survey was administered to German and U.S. students. The Germans were more competence-oriented in terms of the means they would use to achieve desired goals. Americans were more moralistic-oriented in terms of acceptable means. Desired goals of the German sample were personal and self-centered rather than society-oriented.

0738   Richman, Barry M. (1965) Soviet Management: With Significant American Comparisons. Englewood Cliffs, New Jersey: Prentice-Hall.

An examination of the socio-economic and cultural aspects of Soviet management and national character indicates a great difference in attitudes and managerial practices between the two countries.

0739   Richman, Louis S. (1987) "Lessons from German
        Managers," Fortune 115 (April 27): 267-78.

German managers emphasize long-term objectives over short-term financial gains. All firms cooperate with local vocational schools to educate apprentices.

0740   Robertson, Ivan T. and Peter J. Makin (1986)
        "Management Selection in Britain: A Survey and
        Critique," Journal of Occupational Psychology
        59 (March): 45-8.

Most managers in Britain are selected on the basis of interviews and references. Some Continental-owned firms also used handwriting analysis. The authors propose that a number of scientifically reliable psychological tests be used in the future selection of managers.

0741   Rojot, Jacques (1978) "Evolutionary Trends Among the
        French Managerial Groups ("Cadres")," International
        Studies of Management and Organization 8 (Fall):
        8-21.

A survey of attitudes of French managers ("cadres") in terms of their closeness to superiors and subordinates and patterns of career mobility indicates a somewhat egalitarian attitude, though differences due to class origin and membership remain.

0742   Ross, Randolph E. (1976) "International Comparison
        of Personal Values and Job Performance within an
        International Firm," International Studies of
        Management and Organization 6 (Spring/Summer): 54-71.

The Personal Value Questionnaire (PVQ) is used to measure business-related values of employees of a U.S. organization with a Canadian and five European subsidiaries. In terms of "People," Canadians and Dutch ranked "Customers" highly. In terms of organizational goals, Italians ranked High Productivity highest. The Dutch ranked Performance and Organizational Stability highest. Germans ranked highest High Productivity, Growth, and Stability. Belgians ranked Profit Maximization and Growth highest. The British sample ranked all dimensions highest except Efficiency.

0743   Sadler, P.J. and G. H. Hofstede (1976)
        "Leadership Styles: Preferences and Perceptions
        of Employees of an International Company in
        Different Countries," International Studies
        of Management and Organization 6 (Fall): 87-113.

A study of leadership style preferences of a sample of
Research and Development employees from seven European
countries working for the same corporation indicates both
national similarities and differences, according to which
dimension is involved. National samples differed in terms of
their preferred vs. perceived leadership styles ("tells,"
"sells," "consults," and "joins"). All national sub-samples
preferred the "consult" leadership style, though there
existed differences within occupational sub-groups.

0744   Saussois, Jean-Michel (1984) "French Research on
        Cadres: Results and Perspectives," International
        Studies of Management and Organization 14 (Spring):
        80-99.

This is an excellent essay summarizing the research
conducted on French industrial cadres: the highly educated
elite of French industry. The author notes why a "malaise
des cadres" exists in terms of these leaders' thought
patterns and values, education, career paths, occupational
duties, and relations to union and political leaders.

0745   Savage, Dean (1979) Founders, Heirs and Managers:
        French Industrial Leadership in Transition.
        London: Sage.

Managers in French family businesses tend to value stability
over growth, except when a firm is managed by the first-
generation founder. The author traces the career paths of
the different types of business leaders.

0746   Selmer, Jan (1987) "Swedish Managers' Perception of
        Singaporean Work-Related Values," Asia Pacific
        Journal of Management 5 (September): 80-88.

Swedish top managers identified the work-related values of
ethnic Chinese Singaporeans. Singaporeans identified their
own values. The results indicated that Swedish managers
greatly misjudged the values of Singaporean subordinates. An
extension of the length of foreign assignments of Swedish
managers from the current three years would not greatly
enhance cross-cultural understanding.

0747   Shackleton, Vic and Sue Newell (1991) "Management
        Selection: A Comparative Survey of Methods used in
        Top British and French Companies," Journal of
        Occupational Psychology 64 (March): 23-36.

British companies are more likely than French firms to
select new members on the basis of reliable selection
methods. Larger firms in both countries are more likely to
use reliable methods. French firms (92%) resort to more than
one interview per applicant compared to 60% in Britain.
Differences in the selection process are based on French-
British cultural differences, some of which are explained
using Hofstede's concept of culture. The French propensity
for multiple interviews is related to the French value of
uncertainty avoidance and greater power distance.

0748   Sheedy, John F. and Richard N. Dean (1991)
        "Gaining a Foothold in the Soviet Market:
        How to Establish a Representative Office,"
        The International Lawyer 25 (Spring): 103-25.

Establishing an official and a legally-recognized business
presence in Soviet Russia has been streamlined recently.
Nevertheless, the Soviet bureaucracy is likely to cause
delays by demands for additional information, etc. The
Soviet government seems to want to encourage the internal
participation of foreign firms, though recent attempts to
decentralize power make registration a very time-consuming
process.

0749   Simon, Hermann (1986) "Market Entry in Japan:
        Barriers, Problems and Strategies," International
        Journal of Research in Marketing 3 (2): 105-115.

German expatriates in Japan find entry into the Japanese
market difficult. German companies are characterized by a
number of weaknesses in terms of a dynamic and competitive
Japanese market.

0750   Symons, Gladys L. (1984) "Career Lives of Women in
        France and Canada: The Case of Managerial Women,"
        Work and Occupations 11 (August): 331-52.

A sample of 63 French and Canadian managerial women
indicated that they had a strong commitment to work. Family
life was less central: 50% of the Canadians and 40% of the
French were single, divorced or separated and childless. The
author develops types of career paths from the sample.

0751   Taylor, Bernard and Luigi Ferro (1991) "Key Social
        Issues for European Business," pp 9-36 in Sheila
        Rothwell (ed.), Strategic Planning for Human
        Resources. New York: Pergamon Press.

Originally published in 1983, this article points out that
understanding of political and social trends is essential
for planning. The authors discuss a number of uncertainties
and trends in Europe's future, such as changing divorce
rates, health issues, working women, trade union and other
organized power pressure groups, and changing social values.

0752   Thurley, Keith and Hans Wirdenius (1989),
        Toward European Management. London: Pitman
        Publishing.

The authors describe the main features of Japanese and
American managerial approaches, then explore the possibility
of a general European management model. The authors describe
European managerial practices, discuss the recent relative
decline of the European economy, and make suggestions to
improve European managerial ideologies and practices. The
bibliography is wide-ranging.

0753   Trevor, Malcolm (1983) "Does Japanese Management
        Work in Britain?" Journal of General Management 8
        (Summer): 28-43.

Managerial practices vary among Japanese firms, so it is
difficult to discuss whether "Japanese-style" management can
be transferred to the British work environment. At best,
Japanese behavior in British subsidiaries can stimulate UK
managers to rediscover basic principles of effective
"British-style" management.

0754   Turner, Graham (1987) "How Top Management is
        Changing Dutch Business," Long Range Planning
        20 (December): 10-17.

Dutch business culture has traditionally encouraged low
personal profiles, quality products, rigid hierarchies, a
low work ethic, and a negligent attitude toward the
marketplace. Changing international competition has caused
changes in Dutch work attitudes, as illustrated by case
studies of Dutch companies.

0755   Useem, Michael (1982) "Classwide Rationality in
        the Politics of Managers and Directors of Large
        Corporations in the United States and Great Britain,"
        Administrative Science Quarterly 27 (June): 199-226.

Challenges to the large businesses (organized labor in Great
Britain and government in the U.S.) force the corporate
elite to develop classwise values and policies, rather than

maintain more parochial outlooks. The highest corporate elite are political in orientation. The U.S. elites view organized labor as an ally against government. The opposite is true in Great Britain.

0756   Veiga, John F. and John N. Yanouzas (1991)
        "Differences Between American and Greek Managers
        in Giving Up Control," Organization Studies
        12 (1): 95-108.

On the average, Greek managers are less likely to cede control in decision-making than U.S. managers. American managers are willing to give up control in group situations under five conditions, including (1) low personal commitment, (2) task mastery is low, and (3) when another member has greater expertise. The findings support Hofstede's U.S.-Greek differences on Power Distance scores. Greek managers were unwilling to give up control under any condition.

0757   Vlachoutsicos, Charalambos and Paul Lawrence (1990)
        "What We Don't Know About Soviet Management,"
        Harvard Business Review 68 (Nov/Dec): 50-64.

U.S. managers have a distorted view of Soviet management behavior and policies. Soviet management is based on a number of principles which will not change soon, as opposed to the Soviet economic system. Soviet organizational structures begin with the collective, which is organized around groups rather than individuals. These groups, called Structured Task Units (STU) carry out complete missions (administrative, service, production) and receive the workers' total loyalty. Managers have direct authority over everyone below them. There is little horizontal integration or coordination.

0758   Vliet, Anita Van (1986) "What Japan is Doing
        Better," Management Today 20 (April): 68-75, 132-4.

British workers in Japanese-owned firms are more productive than many European workers and as productive as Japanese workers. Reasons for this high productivity lie in the use of selected aspects of Japanese-style management, including consensus decision-making, a team policy, and job rotation.

0759   Walby, Sylvia (1989) "Flexibility and the Changing
        Sexual Division of Labor," pp 127-40 in Stephen
        Wood (ed.), The Transformation of Work? Skill,
        Flexibility and the Labour Process Boston: Unwin
        Hyman Ltd.

More and more women in Europe are becoming employed, and they are an important source of labor. However, the rates of female unemployment vary in nine European nations. In addition, the proportions of women working part-time also varies by country. Britain has the highest rate of part-time female employment. Germany has the lowest.

0760   Weihrich, Heinz and Diethard Buhler (1990) "Training Managers for the Global Market," Business 10 (July/August): 10-13.

Germany has an apprentice system based on close cooperation between industry and the educational system. A similar system, Vocational Academy, has been established to train managers who will operate globally. Graduates will be proficient in English and French, have experience working abroad, and be generalists. Such a program prepares managers for the coming intense competition on a global level.

0761   White, Michael and Malcolm Trevor (1983) Under Japanese Management: The Experience of British Workers. London: Heinemann Educational Books.

British employed in a Japanese-owned firm exhibited high levels of satisfaction. The data indicate that Japanese-style management and personnel policies can in part be transferred to Britain. This transfer was not successful in all dimensions, such as work satisfaction and employee-management relations. The Japanese were successful in instilling more worker-management cooperation and a sense of equality.

0762   Wielecki, Tomasz (1981) "Societal Values Affecting the Level of Leadership Creativity in Polish Economic Organizations," pp 851-61 in Gunter Duglos and Klaus Weiermair (eds.), Managing under Differing Value Systems: Political, Social, and Economical. Berlin and New York: Walter de Gruyter.

The value systems of Polish managers are divided into the "progressives" and the "protectives." The latter prefer state centralization of resources and management power, and value stability, job security and risk avoidance. Creative thinking is replaced by bureaucratic rigidity. The rise of the dominance of the centralized management ideology in Poland causes both inefficiency on the economic dimension and value conflicts among managers.

0763   Zemke, Ron (1988) "Scandinavian Management – a
        Look at our Future?" Management Review 77 (July):
        44-7.

Scandinavian countries offer an alternative to U.S.-style or
Japanese-style management. Nordic management style has
proven to be effective. Basic elements of Scandinavian-style
management include: (1) non-confrontational attitudes of
managers toward workers, (2) respect for individual dignity,
(3) reward for individual contribution to the success of the
work group, (4) an awareness of the limits of resources,
land, energy, etc., (5) a democratic workplace, and (6)
being customer-oriented.

8

Middle East and Africa

0764   Abboushi, Syhail (1990) "Impact of Individual
        Variables on the Work Values of Palestinian
        Arabs," International Studies of Management
        and Organization 20 (Fall): 53-68.

Arab employees in the West Bank region were surveyed in
terms of their attitudes toward work, the work ethic, and
their hierarchy of work values. The Palestinian Arabs
preferred intrinsic over extrinsic aspects of work,
preferred activity and involvement in work, and upward
mobility. Pride in good workmanship was ranked the highest
valued aspect of work, which is an important part of the
Protestant ethic value system.

0765   Abu Naba'a, Abdel Aziz M. (1984) Marketing
        in Saudi Arabia. New York: Praeger.

A 1979 sample of 57 U.S. marketing executives in Saudi
Arabia were mailed questionnaires to discover the specific
marketing problems they faced in Saudi Arabia. The responses
list the social, political, economic, and especially the
religious features which influence marketing policy from a
function approach. The bibliography is excellent and there
are socioeconomic data for the region covering the 1970s and
early 1980s.

0766   Abutu, F. (1986) "Work Attitudes of
        Africans, with Special Reference to Nigeria,"
        International Studies of Management and
        Organization 16 (Summer): 17-36.

The colonial view of African workers was a negative one
which defined workers as "lazy." Reasons for this attitude
are explained, making workers' behavior logical in relation
to their work goals and work-related behavior. Modern
attitudes toward work in non-traditional contexts in Nigeria
tend also to be negative. The article explains the sources

for this work ethic and discusses how to better motivate workers.

0767   Agarwala, P.N. (1985) A Case Study on Decision-
        Making in Selected Multinational Enterprises in
        India. Working Paper No. 38. Geneva: International
        Labour Office.

A wide variety of degrees of decentralization in decision-making is found among eleven multinational enterprises in India. Local divisions generally enjoy wide latitude in terms of employment, personnel policies, and expansion projects. Strategic decisions in basic policy are made at higher levels, resulting in a combination of top-down and bottom-up decision making.

0768   Ahiauzu, Augustine I. (1986) "The African Thought-
        System and the Work Behavior of the African
        Industrial Man," International Studies of
        Management and Organization 16 (Summer): 37-58.

The poor attitudes African workers have toward work will remain until there are major changes in administrative and managerial systems. The author traces the origins and nature of African thought systems and cosmologies. These are related to the work values/attitudes/behavior in a modern context.

0769   Ahiauzu, Augustine I. (1989) "The 'Theory A'
        System of Work Organization for the Modern
        African Workplace," International Studies of
        Management and Organization 19 (Spring): 6-27.

Traditional African methods of work organization were based on the efako system. The elements of this ideology include organization of work according to status rather than contract, no categorization of members into hierarchies, age is a determining factor for leadership, teamwork is emphasized, and reward is based on a diffuse relationship between worker and leader. The author then compares the efako system to modern industrial management in Africa and how they can be blended together.

0770   Al-Jafary, Abdulrahman and A.T. Hollingsworth
        (1983) "An Exploratory Study of Managerial
        Practices in the Arabian Region," Journal of
        International Business Studies 14 (Fall): 143-52.

Managers in the Gulf region used a consultative managerial mode, but at a lower level than American managers.

0771   Alhashemi, Ibrahim S.J. (1988) "Management
        Development in Transition: The Gulf Experience,"
        International Journal of Manpower 9 (1): 3-7.

The culture and history of the Gulf States have limited the development of local management skills. Management education should focus on ending management imbalances and upon systematically developing managerial skills.

0772   Ali, Abbas J. (1989) "Decision Style and Work Satisfaction of Arab Gulf Executives: A cross-National Study," International Studies of Management and Organization 19 (Summer): 22-37.

103 managers from Saudi Arabia, Kuwait, and Qatar were interviewed as to their levels of work satisfaction and leadership styles.   Kuwaiti managers are more oriented toward the pseudo-consultative style. Those in higher levels of their respective hierarchies were more satisfied. Leadership style varied by origin, degree of contact with Westerners, and age. Younger respondents preferred the participative form of leadership. Most respondents preferred the consultative form. Few were categorized as "delegators."

0773   Ali, Abbas J. (1990) "Management Theory in a Transitional Society: The Arab's Experience," International Studies of Management and Organization 20 (Fall): 7-35.

Arab management and business principles are derived from Islamic values, which in turn have undergone changing definitions. These changes have resulted in six management schools. Modernization, changing socioeconomic conditions, and nationalism have recently contributed to changes in management thought. New managers in the Arab world have become change agents as business-related behaviors are currently changing.

0774   Ali, Abbas and Mohammed Al-Shakhis (1989) "The Meaning of Work in Saudi Arabia," International Journal of Manpower 10 (1): 26-32.

132 Saudi managers were interviewed in terms of three models of the meanings of work.   Almost all (94%) Saudis would continue to work if they had enough money to live comfortably.   Family and work were the most important interests in life.

0775   Ali, Abbas, and Dennis R. Vanden Bloomen (1988) "Managerial Value Systems in Saudi Arabia and Mexico: An Empirical Cross-Cultural Investigation," International Journal of Management 5 (1): 29-33.

Saudi managers were highly conformist-sacrificial (low tolerance for ambiguity; need rules to follow), more egocentric (high need for affiliation; little concern for money), and less manipulative (materialistic; self-calculative to achieve an end) than Mexican managers.   The Mexican sample was highly existential (high tolerance for ambiguity; express self).

0776   Ali, Abbas J. and Somanathan Nataraj (1991)
        "Indian and Saudi Managers' Beliefs About
        Work: An Empirical Study," International
        Journal of Management 8 (June): 536-46.

280 managers from India and Saudi Arabia were contrasted in
terms of their belief systems. Indian managers are more
humanistic, more loyal to their organizations, and accept
the work ethic more. Saudis were more leisure-oriented.

0777   Almaney, A.J. (1982) "How Arabs See the West,"
        Business Horizons 25 (September/October): 11-7.

Arabs hold both positive and negative attitudes towards the
West. The author lists the ways a non-Arab business person
can avoid injuring Arab sensibilities by avoiding certain
comments and attitudes.

0778   Al-Meer, Abdul Rahim A. (1989) "Organizational
        Commitment: A Comparison of Westerners, Asians and
        Saudis," International Studies of Management and
        Organization 19 (Summer): 74-84.

The objectives of this study were to measure the
organizational commitment levels among 239 expatriates and
Saudis working in Saudi Arabia. Organizational commitment
scores were highest for Asian expatriates and equally lowest
for Westerners and Saudis. The reasons why Saudis had low
commitment scores include a lack of contracts, which
encourages high job mobility and long work hours.

0779   Al-Nimir, Saud and Monte Palmer (1982) "Bureaucracy
        and Development in Saudi Arabia: A Behavioral
        Analysis," Public Administration and Development
        2 (April/June): 93-104.

300 Saudis were interviewed in terms of items related to
administrative behavior. Saudi bureaucrats strongly resisted
innovation, had high risk-avoidance levels, and were highly
concerned with job security. High salaries and prestige were
ranked low.

0780   Alverson, Hayt S. (1977) "Peace Corps Volunteers in
        Rural Botswana," Human Organization 36 (Fall): 274-
        81.

The author developed a training program to help Peace Corps
volunteers adjust better to living in Botswana. The author
lists the values and expectations of U.S. volunteers which
help determine their reactions to being in a foreign
culture. A number of cultural traits (time, greetings,
saving face, oral contracts and "sincere" lies) make
Botswanan behavior different from that of Americans.

0781   Analoui, F. (1990) "Senior Managers and Increased
        Effectiveness," Project Appraisal 4 (4): 215-18.

A survey of managers in Zimbabwe indicates that the most
important skill requirements were (1) people managing skills
and (2) self-development.

0782   At-Twaijri, Mohammed (1981) "How to Sell
        Successfully in the Middle East," International
        Management 36 (October): 61-3.

The article presents examples of successful marketing
strategies conducted in the Middle East. A major reason for
their success was that the sponsors took into account Middle
Eastern values and customs. These customs are listed.

0783   At-Twaijri, Mohammed (1989) "A Cross-Cultural
        Comparison of American-Saudi Managerial Values in
        U.S.-Related Firms in Saudi Arabia: An Empirical
        Investigation," International Studies of
        Management 19 (Summer): 58-73.

191 U.S. and Saudi managers of U.S.-owned ventures in Saudi
Arabia were surveyed in terms of work satisfaction and
needs. The Saudis differed from the Americans in 11 of 15
measures of satisfaction.

0784   Ayman, Roya and Martin M. Chemers (1983)
        "Relationship of Supervisory Behavior Ratings
        to Work Group Effectiveness and Subordinate
        Satisfaction Among Iranian Managers,"
        Journal of Applied Psychology 68 (May): 338-41.

The leadership behavior ratings of Iranian managers are
compared to those of U.S. and European samples. For the
Iranian sample, a good leader should be domineering, "like a
kind father," and "make everyone obey him." There were
different ratings by levels, as foremen preferred leaders
who were more paternalistic. Benevolent paternalism emerges
as an Iranian leadership ideal.

0785   Baba, Vishivanath V. (1989) "Central Life interests
        and Job Involvement: An Exploratory Study in the
        Developing World," International Journal of
        Comparative Sociology 30 (Sept/Dec): 181-94.

Samples of high school teachers in Nigeria and Trinidad were
interviewed in terms of their degree of job involvement (JI)
and Central Life Interest (CLI). CLI and JI were correlated
for both samples, but there were cross-cultural differences.
The Trinidad sample exhibited higher scores on both
measures. Respondents with urban backgrounds had higher
correlations between CLI and JI, indicating a more "modern"
world view.

0786   Baba, Vishivanath and M. Jamal (1988) "Work
        Alienation and Mental Health: A Comparative
        Study of Nigeria, Pakistan and Trinidad,"
        <u>International Journal of Management</u> 5 (June):
        143-50.

The three nations under study are each developing countries
and former British colonies. In Pakistan and Trinidad, there
was a strong negative relationship between alienation from
work and positive mental health. No relationship between
variables was found for the Nigerian samples. The developing
world is made up of diverse cultures with significantly
different values which affect attitudes toward work and
related topics.

0787   Badr, Hamed A., Edmund R. Gray, and Ben L.
        Kedia (1983) "Personal Values and
        Managerial Decision-Making," <u>Management
        International Review</u> 22 (3): 65-73.

A sample of 106 Egyptian and U.S. male graduate students in
the U.S. were interviewed in terms of personal values and
potential managerial performance. The managerial values of
the Americans were influenced by their theoretical,
economic, political, and religious personal values. Their
social and aesthetic values were uncorrelated with action.
For the Egyptian students, their theoretical, social,
political, and religious values correlated with choices of
action. Each group made managerial choices consistent with
its own value profile.

0788   Banaji, Jairus and Rohini Hensman (1990) <u>Beyond
        Nationalism: Management Policyand Bargaining
        Relationships in International Companies</u>.
        New Delhi: Sage Publications.

Indian and Dutch managers view labor unions in different
ways, in part because of different negotiation contexts used
to settle wages and other labor issues. Dutch firms are able
to exhibit a certain amount of autonomy in India concerning
personnel issues, in spite of local laws. However, Indian
firms are less free to act as they wish in terms of labor
issues. The authors discuss the major Indian-Dutch
bargaining characteristics, their institutional contexts,
relative pay levels, managerial values, etc.

0789   Beaty, David T. and Oren Harari (1987)
        "South Africa: White managers, Black Voices,"
        <u>Harvard Business Review</u> 65 (July/August): 98ff.

Black workers in South Africa exhibit high degrees of
skepticism and resentment toward the white-controlled
economic system. They see business as an extension of white
domination and exploitation. White managers separate the
workplace from politics. Black workers had a set of work
motivations different from white managers' perceptions of
these ranks.

0790   Bluen, Stephen D. and Julian Barling (1983) "Work
        Values in White South African Males," Journal of
        Cross-Cultural Psychology 14 (September): 329-35.

A survey of 273 white South African young males indicates
that the status of a job was relatively unimportant. Work
values differed from those of Americans.

0791   Conaty, Joseph, Hoda Mahmoudi, and
        George A. Miller (1983) "Social Structure
        and Bureaucracy: A Comparison of Organizations
        in the United States and Prerevolutionary Iran,"
        Organization Studies 4 (2):105-28.

Organizational structures in Iran and the United States
resemble each other and are influenced by similar variables.
This indicates that organizational structure may be "culture
free." The determining variable may be technology.

0792   Daftuar, Chittranjan N. (1982) Job Attitudes in
        Indian Management: A Study in Need Deficiencies
        and Need Importance. New Delhi: Concept Publishing
        Company.

The author tests nine hypotheses based on Abraham Maslow's
theory of hierarchy of needs dealing with need perceptions
among 1,951 executives and managers in an Indian enterprise.
Older managers valued security more than self-actualization
and autonomy. For the total sample, self-actualization needs
were ranked highest and social and esteem needs were ranked
lowest. Differences in need perceptions differed by rank,
size of organization, and job function.

0793   Elmuti, Dean and Yunus Kathawada (1982)
        "The effects of Participatory Programmes
        on Productivity in Selected Multinational
        Organisations," Asia Pacific Journal
        of Management 6 (April): 351-61.

184 middle-level managers in Saudi Arabia took part in a
program to expose the participants to participatory forms of
management. A majority of the participants learned to prefer
elements of participative management over other forms.

0794   Erez, Miriam and Christopher P. Early (1987)
        "Comparative Analysis of Goal-Setting Strategies
        Across Cultures," Journal of Applied Psychology
        72 (November): 658-65.

Students from Israel and the U.S. are contrasted in terms of
their goal-setting strategies. Israeli kibbutz and non-
kibbutz members and U.S. respondents fall in different
cultural dimensions based on Hofstede's work. Culture did
not influence goal-setting strategies but did effect
performance for difficult goals.

0795   Esposito, John L. (1991) Islam: The
        Straight Path Expanded Edition. New York:
        Oxford University Press.

This work deals with the Islamic faith, its history and
development. There is also concern with the relationships in
Islam with politics and social values and behavior. There
are also sections on contemporary culture and social
patterns throughout the Moslem world.

0796   Falbe, Cecilia M., Orly Ben-Yoav Nobel, and Aharon
        Tziner (1988) "Achievement Motivation of Managers:
        A New Approach to Assessing Cross-Cultural
        Differences," International Journal of Management
        5 (September): 304-9.

342 Middle-level managers from Israel and the U.S. were
administered tests measuring motivation: American managers
preferred difficult work and gained more satisfaction from
solving problems. Israeli managers preferred uncertainty and
risk-taking more.

0797   Faruqi, Isma'il R. al and Lois Lamya' al Faruqi
        (1986) The Cultural Atlas of Islam. New York:
        MacMillan.

The work includes descriptions of the varieties of beliefs
and customs of various Islamic societies within their local
cultural contexts.

0798   Gifford, Paul and Peter McBurney (1988) "The Ethical
        Concerns of Contemporary Zimbabwean Managers: A
        Preliminary Sounding," Journal of Business Ethics
        7 (May): 363-72.

MBA students at the University of Zimbabwe were asked to
discuss an ethical problem they had encountered in the
course of business. The types of problems presented were
sexual harassment, nepotism, political pressure, and public
corruption. No mentions were made of racial problems or to
trading with South Africa.

0799   Harpaz, Itzhak (1990) The Meaning of Work in Israel:
        Its Nature and Consequences. New York: Praeger.

The author offers a historical survey of work in Israel and
reviews the relevant literature to develop a research model
on the meaning of working. A national sample of Israeli
voters using 973 respondents is interviewed. In terms of
central life interests, family life was ranked first.
Interpersonal contacts are important at one's work as well
as the work's intrinsic qualities. Having interesting work
was a major value.

0800   Hourani, Albert Habib (1991) <u>A History of the Arab</u>
        <u>Peoples</u>. Cambridge, Mass: Harvard University Press.

Although this work is devoted primarily to Arab history,
there are sections which describe contemporary events and
social structures and institutions.

0801   Izraeli, Dove (1988) "Ethical Beliefs and Behavior
        Among Managers: A Cross-Cultural Perspective,"
        <u>Journal of Business Ethics</u> 7 (April): 263-271.

A sample of 97 Israeli managers was compared with a U.S.
sample in terms of responses to 17 ethical scenarios. "What
others do" was the best predictor of ethical responses. Both
national samples rated themselves more ethical than their
peers.

0802   Jones, Merrick (1988) "Managerial Thinking:
        An African Perspective," <u>Journal of Management</u>
        <u>Studies</u> 25 (September): 481-505.

105 managers in Malawi responded to a questionnaire and
interviews measuring their attitudes toward leadership as
compared to similar samples in 14 countries. While cultural
forces were influential, so were the effects of the stages
of industrialization and organization.

0803   Jreisat, Jamil (1990) "Administrative Change
        and the Arab Manager," <u>Public Administration</u>
        <u>and Development</u> 10 (Oct/Nov): 413-21.

63 senior Arab public administrators exhibited a high sense
of public responsibility and use of knowledge and skills.
They preferred secure and responsible jobs. A group of 77
Americans answered the same questionnaire; their rankings of
the values were similar to those of Arab respondents.

0804   Jules-Rosette, Benneta (1979) "Alternative Urban
        Adaptations: Zambian Cottage Industries as Sources
        of Social and Economic Innovation," <u>Human</u>
        <u>Organization</u> 38 (Fall): 225-38.

Zambia has experienced a rapid growth in small-scale cottage
industries. Their development is caused partly by economic
factors, but also reflects traditional social arrangements.

0805   Kamal, Raja and Hal Fisher (1988) "Change and
        Development in the Arab World--Advance Amid
        Diversity: An Economic and Social Analysis,"
        pp 196-208 in Jim Norwine and Alfonso
        Gonzales (eds.), <u>The Third World: States of</u>
        <u>Mind and Being</u>. Boston: Unwin Hyman, Inc.

The authors discuss the social and economic diversity of
Arab countries and their prospects. The development of that
area will be guided by three types of socio-economic value

systems, whose members are defined as (1) traditionalists, (2) technocrats, or (3) entrepreneurs.

0806   Kassem, M. Sami (1989) "Strategy Formulation: Arabian Gulf Style," International Studies of Management and Organization 19 (Summer): 6-21.

Four types of managers emerged according to strategic planning style: prospectors, analyzers, defenders, and reactors. The modal type was the reactor, though this varied by type of enterprise. Planning in the Arabian Gulf tends to be reactive rather than proactive, in part because of uncontrollable external factors.

0807   Kennedy, Paul T. (1980) Ghanaian Businessmen: From Artisan to Capitalist Entrepreneur in a Dependent Economy. Munchen and London: Weltforum Verlang.

This study is based on a survey of 186 Ghana businessmen primarily in manufacturing. The report describes the background of the respondents, their attitudes concerning consumers, techniques of business efficiency (delegation, training, control systems, etc.), social experiences (travel abroad, friendships with Europeans, etc.), entrepreneurial behavior and values, and social networks (friends, relatives, etc.).

0808   Khadra, Bashir (1990) "The Prophetic-Caliphal Model of Leadership: An Empirical Study," International Studies of Management and Organization 20 (Fall): 37-52.

The prophetic-Caliphal model of leadership highly influences the styles of political and managerial leadership in the Arab world. A survey of 75 managers, plus summaries of four other supportive surveys, indicates that this model is as operative today as it has been in the past. The model includes preferences for (1) personalism--one's job is treated as one's own private property; (2) individualism-- prefering individual over group or team activities, (3) a lack of institutionalism in favor of individualism; and (4) the Great Man predisposition. The respondents supported each dimension, especially the "Great Man Disposition," in which the top manager is perceived to be of great importance to the success or failure of the organization.

0809   Kiggundu, Moses N. (1988) "Africa," pp 169-243 in Raghu Nath (ed.), Comparative Management: A Regional View. Cambridge, Mass: Ballinger Publishing Company.

This book chapter provides an overview of the legal, debt, economic and government structures in Africa. There are also summaries of several studies of management practices and ideology. There are tables of indicators of the social development levels of African countries for 1970-2,000.

810   Kigitcibasi, C. (1970) "Social Norms and
       Authoritarianism: A Turkish-American Comparison,"
       Journal of Personality and Social Psychology 16
       (November): 444-51.

Authoritarian values among Turkish high school students was
stronger than among Americans. The values in the Turkish
samples were related to respect for authority and
patriotism. Obligations to self is higher in the U.S.

0811   Kwame, Safro (1983) "Doin' Business in an
       African Country (Business Ethics and
       Capitalism in a Poor Country),"
       Journal of Business Ethics 2 (November):
       263-8.

A Ghanan economic practice of charging excessive prices for
scarce goods is called "kalabule." This term, within an
ethical context, means that it is not wrong to maximize
one's profits, even for basic commodities that exist in
scarce quantities. The author explains why this value exists
even though it is contrary to the major ethical standards of
Ghanan society (Christian and Akan).

0812   Leonard, David K. (1991) African Success:
       Four Public Managers of Kenyan Rural
       Management. Berkeley: University of
       California Press.

The author traces the careers of four administrators in
Kenya. Their lives and successes are discussed within the
institutional contexts of the society of Kenya (education,
colonial administration, civil service structures, etc.).
This book contains a detailed analysis of administrative
success where failure is the norm.

0813   Lindsey, Gene (1991) Saudi Arabia. New York:
       Hippocrene Books.

Written by an American businessman, this work is an
excellent introduction to the history, geography and culture
of Saudi Arabia. The mindset of Saudis is described. This
national character is heavily influenced by its family-
centered Bedouin origins, and Islam. The result is the
Saudi's attempt modernize without Westernizing their
culture. Saudi Arabia produces one of the greatest amount of
culture shock for Westerners. The reasons for this and the
Saudi business culture are described throughout the work.

0814   Luqmani, Mushtaq, Zahir A. Quraeshi, and Linda
       Delene (1980) "Marketing in Islamic Countries:
       A Viewpoint," MSU Business Topics 28 (Summer):
       17-25.

There is a comprehensive listing of Islamic values and
appropriate social behaviors and their implications for
marketing policy for foreigners.

0815   Luqmani, Mushtaq and Zahir A. Quraeshi (1986)
        "Marketing in Islamic countries: A Viewpoint,"
        pp 122-35 in Subhash C. Jain and Lewis R. Tucker,
        Jr. (eds.), International Marketing: Managerial
        Perspectives Second Edition. Boston: Kent Publishing
        Company.

This chapter presents a long list of Islamic principles and
cultural values unique to Moslem societies, including which
products are in demand during specific seasons. Included are
late-1970s socioeconomic data on Moslem nations.

0816   Machungwa, Peter and Neal Schmit (1983)
        "Work Motivation in a Developing Country,"
        Journal of Applied Psychology 68 (February):
        31-42.

Workers in developing countries may respond to motivational
policies that are different from those commonly accepted by
workers in more developed economies. A sample of Zambians
indicated that positive and negative work motivations
differed from Herzberg's two-factor model.

0817   Mackey, Sandra (1987) The Saudis: Inside the
        Desert Kingdom. New York: Meridian.

This work is an introduction to Saudi society and the
behavior patterns of that society. There are sections on
religion and peculiar patterns of thinking. This book is a
good introduction to those planning to visit or work in
Saudi Arabia.

0818   McWhinney, Will (1986) "Tales of Arabian
        Days," New Management 3 (Spring): 38-43.

Because of Saudi culture and history, Saudi managers act
more as directors and maintain policy. Upward mobility is
made more difficult than in the U.S. due to educational and
gender barriers.

0819   Meebo, Henry S. (1973) Main Currents of
        Zambian Humanist Thought. Lusaka, Zambia:
        Oxford University Press.

Economic behavior and government policies are heavily
influenced by general social values and thought patterns.
Modernization in Zambia is likely to follow economic
doctrines based on humanist and socialist thought rather
than on capitalist tenets. Economic development, wage
determinants, and foreign investments will be shaped in part
by notions of "fair prices," "fair wages" and public vs.
private interests, as defined by humanist thought.

0820   Montgomery, John D. (1989) "Comparative
        Administration: Theory and Experience,"
        International Journal of Public Administration
        12 (May): 501-12.

A study of managerial training needs in five African
countries indicated 15 needs. These included the ability to
motivate workers, the interpretation of rules, and the
development of interpersonal skills. Organizational reforms
must reflect the cultural context of the workers and
managers.

0821   Muna, Farid A. (1980) The Arab Executive.
        New York: St. Martin's Press, Inc.

Business values and behavior and their social origins of
Arab executives are studied through interviews with 52 Arab
executive from six countries. The work attacks Western myths
about Arab managerial behavior. The analysis includes
patterns of Arab decision-making approaches (mainly
consultative), interpersonal style, attitudes toward time
and change, and social pressures experienced by Arab
executives. National differences are noted whenever
relevant. Kuwaiti executives, for example, shared decision-
making much more than those from Egypt or Jordan.

0822   Murrell, Kenneth L. (1980) "A Cultural Analysis of
        the Egyptian Management Environment," pp 105-120 in
        Philip R. Harris and G. H. Malin (eds.),
        Innovation in Global Consultation: Macro Perspectives
        on the Consulting Relationship. Washington, D.C.:
        International Consultants Foundation.

The value orientations of Egyptian managers and workers are
explained in terms of five dimensions: (1) their world view,
(2) the nature of self and the individual, (3) motivational
orientation, (4) relational orientation, and (5) activity
orientation.

0823   Murrell, Kenneth L. (1981) "Understanding the
        Egyptian Manager," Leadership & Organization
        Development Journal 2 (3): 12-6.

Egyptian managers are highly adaptive and intuitive. They
are able to operate in a confusing, complex, and changing
interpersonal environment. However, they are generally not
innovative or risk-takers. Their thinking is seldom linear
or logical in the Western sense. They exhibit low levels of
trust and cooperation. The Egyptian environment produces
unique needs which should be better investigated.

0824   Murrell, Kenneth L. and E.H. Valsan (1985)
        "A Team-Building Workshop as an OD Intervention
        in Egypt," Leadership & Organization Development
        Journal 6 (2): 11-6.

The authors describe a training program in Organizational
Development in Egypt. The authors offer advice on how to
organize such a program.

0825   Mutahaba, Gelase (1986) "The Training and
        Development of Top Executives in Developing
        Countries: A Tanzanian Approach," Public
        Administration and Development 6 (March): 49-59.

The Ministry of Manpower of Tanzania provides training for
top-level as well as lower-level administrators in public
services. There is no evidence that such training effort has
improved performance.

0826   Nonneman, Gerd (1988) Development, Administration
        and Aid to the Middle East. London: Routledge.

The focus of this book lies in the giving, receiving, and
administration of aid in the Middle East. However, a section
deals with the social and educational backgrounds of the
administrators.

0827   Nzelibe, Chinelo O. (1986) "The Evolution
        of African Management Thought," International
        Studies of Management of Organization 16
        (Summer): 7-16.

The basic elements of African management behavior are
traditionalism, communalism and teamwork. Western managerial
practices in Africa which ignore these values result in
nepotism, bribery, corruption, and a lack of discipline.

0828   Odinye, Moses O. and Erasmus C. Aduaka (1989) "What
        Motivates Nigerian Craftsman in a Task Force
        Situation: A Case Study of ASCON," International
        Journal of Manpower 10 (1): 16-22.

Managers in the public services tend to define craftspersons
as lazy and fraudulent. Consequently, they become
authoritarian and adopt methods of coercion that are
unworkable. A survey of craftsmen indicated that they were
motivated by the desires to be competent and recognized for
their self-worth.

0829   Onyemelukwe, Clement C. (1973) Men and
        Management in Contemporary Africa.
        London: Longman Group.

A blend of survey and qualitative methodologies is used to
interview 854 workers, managers and top-management
expatriates in Nigeria from 18 enterprises. Well grounded in
organizational theory and the Human Relations approach, the

first section presents background and attitudinal data on workers. Quotations from the interviews illustrate the samples' attitudes toward managers or workers, and indicate the alienation from work and/or traditional society. After an impressionistic discussion of the "African" attitudes toward work and traditional national character (communal, personal leadership), the author makes a plea for the blending of African values and the western Human Relations framework to increase work satisfaction and productivity.

0830   Patai, Raphael (1983) The Arab Mind.
        New York: Charles Scribner's Sons.

This book is a general introduction to the nature and diversity of Arab cultures, including the various aspects of the Arab modal personality traits. The Arab love of rhetoric (words and ideas over facts) results in non-Western speech patterns which tend toward exaggeration and elaborateness that can mislead non-Arabic speakers. Arabian definitions of time and matter reflect peculiar speech patterns. Arabic verb tenses are semantically vague and indeterminate, resulting in a vague sense of time different from that found in Europe and North America. The organizations of thoughts, words and action are unique among Arabic speakers.

0831   Pezeshkpur, Changiz (1978) "Challenges to
        Management in the Arab World," Business Horizons
        21 (August): 47-55.

Arab and U.S. cultures contain a number of fundamental differences within the individual, group, and organizational contexts.

0832   Preble, John F. and Arie Reichel (1988)
        "Attitudes Toward Business Ethics of
        Future Managers in the U.S. and Israel,"
        Journal of Business Ethics 7 (December):
        941-49.

279 Israeli and U.S. management students gave their responses to thirty items related to business ethics. Both groups held relatively high moral standards, though there were differences between the two national samples.

0833   Pryce-Jones, David (1989) The Closed Circle: An
        Interpretation of the Arabs. New York: Harper &
        Row, Publishers.

This book is a general introduction to Arab societies and unique personality features. The work includes chapters on shame and honor, problems caused by modernization, and how Arabs define and view themselves.

0834   Reichel, Arie and John F. Preble (1991)
        "Cross-Cultural Research: Israeli and American
        Attitudes Toward Business Ethics," International
        Journal of Management 8 (September): 631-41.

Management students in Israel and the U.S. (N=279) differed
in terms of selected dimensions of business ethics. Israeli
students viewed business ethics as a concept for public
relations and were more profit-oriented. They equated law
with morality. The article contains a good bibliography.

0835   Sanders, Jeffrey L., Ulfat M. Hakky, and Mary M.
        Brizzolara (1985) "Personal Space Amongst Arabs and
        Americans," International Journal of Psychology
        20 (1): 13-17.

Personal space among Arab and Americans students was defined
in the same way for males but not for females. Arab females
kept male friends very far away relative to female friends.

0836   Schermerhorn, John R. Jr., Robert S. Bussom,
        Hussein Elsaid, and Harold K. Wilson (1985)
        "Managing the Inter-Organizational Context of
        Management Development in a Developing Country,"
        Leadership & Organization Development Journal
        6 (1): 27-32.

The authors describe a project established to familiarize
Egyptian managers with American management practices. A
series of problems was experienced by the sponsors due to
the Egyptians' value system and the organizational contexts.

0837   Schiffman, Leon G., William R. Dillon,
        and Festus E. Ngumah (1981) "The Influence
        of Subcultural and Personality Factors on
        Consumer Acculturation," Journal of
        International Business 36 (Fall): 137-43.

150 Nigerian students in the United States varied in terms
of subcultural (religion) values and personality (Rokeach
Dogmatism) characteristics. Nigeria is a very heterogeneous
nation with significant contrasts in social values. Consumer
acculturation in such nations demand a special marketing
perspective.

0838   Seibel, Hans Dieter (1986) "Achievement
        Orientation: A Case Study in Multinational
        Firms in Africa," pp. 215-31 in Ukandi G.
        Damachi and Hans Dieter Seibel (editors),
        Management Problems in Africa. New York:
        St. Martin's Press.

There is the assumption that African cultures do not
encourage achievement-oriented values, which in turn impede
social and economic development. A survey of German and
American expatriates and African workers in Liberia found

the Liberians to be achievement oriented while the Germans were less so.

0839   Sethi, Kiran (1979) **Executive Training in**
        India. New Delhi: Sterling Publishers PVT LTD.

300 business educators and managers/executives in India and the U.S. were surveyed. The questions included training methods, educational programs, training objectives, and selection criteria of various levels of Indian managers. Chief characteristics of Indian management and its environment are (1) reliance on family ownership, (2) an emergence of professional education, (3) a mixed economic environment of socialism and capitalism, (4) strict government controls, (5) a British orientation, (6) a technical orientation, and (7) strong and unique religious and cultural influences.

0840   Shilling, Nancy A. (1978) **A Practical Guide**
        to Living and Travel in the Arab World.
        Dallas, Texas: Inter-Crescent Publishing Co.

This is a useful guide to travelling and living in eleven Arab countries. Most of the information is still valid except for Kuwait and Lebanon. The first section introduces the general features of Arab culture and values-including social and business aspects. The business-related and value discussions remain valid.

0841   Shilling, Nancy A. (1983) **Marketing in the**
        Arab World third edition. Dallas, Texas:
        Inter-Crescent Publishing Co.

Marketing in Arab countries offers a number of unique challenges and opportunities. Knowledge of culture offers an advantage.

0842   Simiar, Farhad (1983) **"Major Causes of**
        Joint-Venture Failures in the Middle East,"
        Management International Review 23 (1): 58-68.

Joint ventures failures in the middle East, based primarily upon cases from Iran, result usually from a lack of trust due to human relations conflict as well as inter-cultural misunderstandings. Such communication errors include a lack of goal congruence between partners.

0843   Sloane, Peter (1988) **"Islamic Law in the Commercial**
        World," The International Lawyer 22 (Fall): 743-66.

The rise of Islamic fundamentalism has been reflected in changes in the legal systems in many Islamic nations. Such changes will effect business oriented behavior, including foreign business. Many Moslem countries base their business legal systems on Shari'a law, which operates on different principles from those of Western legal principles. "Riba", for example, is the Moslem concept of "unearned or unjustified profit," and forbids charging interest on loans. Foreigners wishing to conduct business in Moslem nations need to be familiar with emerging Islamic legal systems.

0844   Speight, R. Marston (1989) God is One: The Way of Islam. New York: Friendship Press.

The various cultures of Islamic societies are described for the interested lay person.

0845   Tsalikis, John and Osita Nwachukwu (1991) "A Comparison of Nigerian to American views of Bribery and Extortion in International Commerce," Journal of Business Ethics 10 (February): 85–98.

420 business students in Nigeria and the U.S. reacted to six scenarios involving bribes. There were different response patterns based on the nationalities of the respondents, the participants, and where the assumed events took place. Some scenarios were defined as unethical by Americans but not by the Nigerians.

0846   Wright, P. (1981) "Organizational Behavior in Islamic Firms," Management International Review 21 (2): 86–94.

A "Moslem" mentality exists from which is derived non-Western forms of organization and patterns of social interactions. For example, Western values support the belief in merit promotions based on universalistic criteria. Moslem values support the belief that performance and talent have little to do with promotion, which takes place within the context of personality and social relations, such as family. Other dimensions of behavior are described.

0847   Yasin, Mahmoud and Michael J. Stahl (1990) "An Investigation of Managerial Motivational Effectiveness in the Arab Culture," International Studies of Management and Organization 20 (Fall): 69–78.

Arab managers' motivational and value profiles (n-Aff, n-Ach, n-Pow) and levels of satisfaction were measured among 70 subjects in Kuwait and Jordan. No differences were found based on country of origin. Top managers had significantly higher levels of need for power than lower-level managers. Arab managers have a motivational profile that is affiliation- and achievement-oriented rather than power-oriented.

0848   Yasin, Mahmoud and Michael J. Stahl (1990) "Models for Effective Motivation in the Arab and American Business Cultures: Review and Directions for Future Research," _International Journal of Management_ 7 (March): 43-55.

This paper presents a literature review of motivational effectiveness in the U.S. and Arab cultures. Two different models are developed. The Arab model includes: (1) those business values derived from religious values, (2) attention to social rituals and affiliations, (3) emphasis on familial over individual achievement, (4) preference for team effort, (5) unsystematic reward policies, and (6) group decision making.

0849   Yavas, Ugur, Mushtaq Luqmani, and Zahir Quraeshi (1990) "Organizational Commitment, Job Satisfaction, Work Values: Saudi and Expatriate Managers," _Leadership and Organization Development_ 11 (7): 3-10.

145 interviews in Saudi Arabia indicated that Saudi and expatriate managers had similar work values, levels of work satisfaction, and organizational commitment.

0850   Zand, Dale (1978) "Management in Israel," _Business Horizons_ 21 (August): 36-46.

The author lists six major Israeli national values (respect of labor, participative style of decision-making, a value of achievement over contemplation, acceptance of centralized economic planning, importance of personal relationships, and reliance on creative improvisation) and then explains how each value influences managerial behavior.

9

Japan

0851   Abegglen, James C. (1958) <u>The Japanese Factory:
        Aspects of its Social Organization</u>. (Reprint of
        original). Glencoe, Illinois: The Free Press.

This is the first empirical study of the structure and
unique cultural elements of a Japanese factory. It
emphasizes the policy of lifetime employment as the key
feature which differentiates Japanese and American factory
organizations.

0852   Abegglen, James C. and George Stalk, Jr. (1985)
        <u>Kaisha: The Japanese Corporation</u>. New York: Basic
        Books, Publishers.

Japanese values are reflected in the business and work
behavior of corporate workers. This work describes the
unique aspects of corporate behavior in Japan. There are
also chapters on foreign companies in Japan and the
strategies used by the Japanese to enter foreign markets.
<u>Kaisha</u> are growth-oriented entities encouraging harmony
among their workers through such policies as lifetime
employment and uniformity. Detailed international
comparisons include income levels and gradients,
shareholders' returns, stock prices, financial policies,
market profiles, and productivity levels.

0853   Adams, Roy J., Richard B. Peterson, and Hermann F.
        Schwind (1988) "Personal Value Systems of Japanese
        Trainees and Managers in a Changing Competitive
        System," <u>Asia Pacific Journal of Management</u> 5
        (May): 169-80.

This study measures the personal value systems of Japanese
and foreign students, trainees, and their managers over a
ten-year period. Japanese trainee cohorts became more
traditional rather than less. This shift may have been due
to differences in the job markets during the period. Other
sub-samples indicated very small value changes over time in

Japanese management systems, especially in the seniority-based compensation and promotion policies.

0854   Alston, Jon P. (1982) "Awarding Bonuses the
        Japanese Way," Business Horizons 25 (Sept/Oct):
        46-50.

Japanese reward systems can be profitably adopted by Western managers if they are clearly understood. Japanese reward systems stress seniority, group membership, and cooperation.

0855   Alston, Jon P. (1983) "Three Principles of
        Japanese Management," Personnel Journal 62
        (September): 758-62.

The unique elements of Japanese management include (1) defining the worker as intelligent, (2) workers form a family, and (3) the group is more important than the individual members. Specific managerial practices illustrate these three foundations of Japanese managerial ideology.

0856   Alston, Jon P. (1986) The American Samurai:
        Blending American and Japanese Managerial
        Practices. Berlin and New York: Walter de Gruyter.

The author describes the major elements of Japanese-style management within their cultural contexts, and suggests which practices may be introduced into U.S. managerial behavior.

0857   Alston, Jon P. (1990) The Intelligent Businessman's
        Guide to Japan. Tokyo: Charles E. Tuttle, Inc.

This work is a practical "how-to" guide to Japanese business protocols, presented within the context of Japanese culture. Included are descriptions of Japanese business customs, social etiquette, ways of negotiating, and patterns of interaction.   There are lists of useful telephone numbers and business addresses in Tokyo and Osaka for foreign business persons.

0858   Alston, Margaret L. and Jon P. Alston (1991)
        "Dealing with Japanese Investors," Management
        Quarterly 32 (Spring): 31-40.

The Japanese are now one of America's most active foreign investors. They are increasingly investing in rural areas, including golf courses and other leisure facilities. The authors list nine strategies to be used to attract Japanese investors to rural areas and to smaller communities. These strategies are discussed within the context of Japanese national character and business protocol.

0859   Amano, Matt M. (1979) "Organizational Changes of a
         Japanese Firm in America," California Management
         Review 21 (Spring): 51-59.

This study illustrates Japanese-U.S. differences in
managerial style through a description of how a Japanese-
owned subsidiary in the United States changed its corporate
culture from the parent's.

0860   Anonymous (1988) "Japan Compared: Pity Those Poor
         Japanese," The Economist 309 (December): 46-50.

Although the Japanese economy has been very successful, the
standard of living of the Japanese consumer is low compared
to those of other industrialized countries. The average size
of housing in Japan is 81 square meters, as compared to 86
in France and Germany.

0861   Apasu, Yao, Shigeru Ichikawa, and John L.
         Graham (1987) "Corporate Culture and
         Sales Force Management in Japan and America,"
         Journal of Personnel Selling and Sales management
         7 (November): 51-62.

321 Salespersons in Japan and in the U.S. took the Rokeach
Values System Test. The Japanese respondents had a higher
level of value congruence in terms of individual to
organization similarity. Work satisfaction values were
higher among the U.S. sample.

0862   Arima, Tatsuo (1987) "Habits of the Japanese Heart:
         The Internal Dynamics of a Nation in Transition,"
         Speaking of Japan 8 (July): 23-8.

The author discusses the major elements of Japanese national
culture, including a strong work ethic, strong senses of
community and conformity, and corporate loyalty.

0863   Artzt, Edwin (1989) "Winning in Japan: Keys to Global
         Success," Business Quarterly 53 (3): 12-6.

Foreign companies that have done best in Japan are those
that adapt to Japanese cultural conditions. The Japanese are
very company conscious, so the company as well as its
products must be well-presented. The Japanese multilayered
distribution system must be understood and used.

0864   Atsumi, Reiko (1979) "Tsukiai-Obligatory Personal
         Relationships of Japanese White-Collar Employees,"
         Human Organization 38 (Spring): 63-70.

Many Japanese corporate workers feel obligated to spend most
of their leisure time with co-workers. In a sample (N=45) of
large companies, one-third of respondents had supper with
work-related people three or more times in the last five-day
period. These relationships reinforce consensus and high

levels of intra-company communication and are based in part
on Japanese traditional cultural values.

0865   Azumi, Koya and Charles J. McMillan (1975)
        "Culture and Organization Structure: A Comparison of
        Japanese and British Organizations," International
        Studies of Management and Organization 5 (Spring):
        35-47.

An early comparative study of Japanese and British firms in
terms of attitudes, structure and function. The theoretical
model is based on the Aston approach to organization,
stressing structural elements of formal organization.

0866   Ballon, Robert J. (1983) "Non-Western Work
        Organization," Asia Pacific Journal of Management
        1 (September): 1-14.

The author describes the unique features of Japanese work
practices in relation to their cultural contexts, including
person-person and person-machine interactions.

0867   Ballon, Robert J. (1985) The Business Contract
        in Japan. Sophia University, Tokyo: Institute
        of Comparative Culture, Business Series,
        Bulletin No. 105.

The nature and cultural background of Japanese concepts
dealing with all aspects of contracts, both formal and
informal, are described. Sections discuss how disputes are
handled, as well as how negotiations progress in Japan.
There is specific advice for businesspersons wishing to
offer for sale to the Japanese selected objects and
supplies.

0868   Bartels, Robert (1984) "National Culture-
        International Business Relations: Two
        Dominant Markets Contrasted," pp 261-70
        in Erdener Kaynak (ed.), International
        Marketing Management. New York: Praeger.

The Japanese and U.S. economies have developed from very
different cultural bases. The U.S. economy was built in part
on the values of self-interested individualism, the Puritan-
Protestant work ethic, top-down decision-making, and minimal
government interference with business. Japan's economy has
developed along different lines. Both countries are
experiencing changes in their value systems and therefore
their economies. The author suggests that cultural changes
in both countries be closely watched to determine future
business changes.

0869   Bartlett, Christopher A. and Hideki Yoshihara (1988)
        "New Challenges for Japanese Multinationals: Is
        Organization Adaptation their Achilles Heel?" Human
        Resource Management 27 (Spring): 19-43.

Japanese corporate expansion throughout the world will force
changes in structure and practices if firms are to remain
efficient. The authors make a number of suggestions for
Japanese adaptations to new global conditions.

0870   Beatty, James R., Joseph T. McCune, and Richard W.
        Beatty (1988) "A Policy-Capturing Approach to the
        Study of United States and Japanese Compensation
        Decisions," Journal of Management 14 (September):
        465-74.

Japanese and Americans evaluated dossiers of 40 persons for
pay raise considerations. The two national samples exhibited
very different values in terms of their decisions. Japanese
managers considered performance less strongly than did U.S.
managers. Japanese considered job worth, organizational
commitment, and seniority more than Americans. Average pay
raises were the same, but Americans were willing to give a
wider range, including smaller pay raises to poor
performers.

0871   Benedict, Ruth (1946) The Chrysanthemum and the
        Sword. Boston: Houghton Mifflin.

This work forms the major classic in the study of Japanese
national character. It became the basis of most studies on
Japanese culture and personality since its publication.
Later empirical work has tended to support the book's
conclusions.

0872   Berezin, Charles E. (1989) "Leapfrogging Japan:
        Japanese Techniques for Americans," National
        Productivity Review 8 (Autumn): 349-56.

Japanese-style managerial practices will never improve U.S.
corporate performance unless workers accept these new
policies. This can be achieved when American workers are
given increased control over their work and can satisfy
their own needs. A nine-element blueprint for the re-
organization of U.S. firms into more efficient structures is
presented.

0873   Berger, Michael (1986) "How the Japanese Bring
        Democracy to Salary Review," International
        Management 41 (October): 58-60.

Employees of Japan's ODS Corp. bargain each year for pay
raises. This practice forces employees to think about their
contributions to the company and their relations with co-
workers.

0874   Berger, Michael (1987) "Entrepreneurs Who Win in
        Japan," International Management 42 (August): 51-3.

While entry by foreigners into the Japanese market is
difficult, there have been successful attempts. This article
describes the experiences and attitudes of five foreign
entrepreneurs from three different countries who have been
successful in establishing businesses in Japan.

0875   Berger, Michael (1990) "The Gentle Art of Head-
        Hunting," International Management 45 (December):
        56-9.

Japan's labor force remains highly immobile, especially at
the executive level. Executive recruitment in Japan involves
great secrecy and unique procedures.

0876   Bettignies, Henri-Claude de (1973) "Japanese
        Organizational Behavior: a Psychocultural
        Approach," pp 75-93 in Desmond Graves (ed.),
        Management Research: A Cross-Cultural Perspective.
        San Francisco: Jossey-Bass, Inc.

Japanese corporate behavior can be understood in terms of
the general values of Japanese workers. The article outlines
the basic components of Japanese institutional and work
behavior within the context of child socialization, training
methods, and family relations. In spite of its age, the
volume remains valuable.

0877   Bird, Allan (1990) "Power and the Japanese
        CEO," Asia Pacific Journal of Management 7
        (October): 1-20.

The sources of Japanese CEO power are personal and
positional. The author analyzes the organizational
structures (lifetime employment, job rotation) and cultural
values which give Japanese CEOs unique power
characteristics.

0878   Birnberg, Jacob G. and Coral Snodgrass (1988)
        "Culture and Control: A Field Study," Accounting,
        Organizations and Society 13 (5): 447-64.

The management control systems of 22 Japanese and U.S.
construction and manufacturing firms are different from each
other. Japanese control systems are more implicit because
their society is more homogeneous.

0879   Blake, Robert R. and Jane S. Mouton (1983) "Will
        the Real Theory Z Please Step Forward?" Training
        20 (March): 26-7.

The authors criticize William Ouchi's (1017) blending of
Japanese and U.S. styles of management into Theory Z.

0880   Bolan, Donald S. and Charles R. Crain (1989)
        "Brothers Beneath the Skin? Evidence for Cross-
        Cultural Similarities in Decision Styles," <u>Leadership
        and Organization Development Journal</u> 10 (1): 17-33.

Data from 79 Japanese and U.S. managers/executives indicate
that Japanese managers are as unwilling to dismiss a
hypothetical subordinate as the American respondents. But
the former wanted to learn more about the subordinate being
evaluated.

0881   Brizz, Michael (1987) "How to Learn What Japanese
        Buyers Really Want," <u>Business Marketing</u> 72 (January):
        68, 72, 74.

Marketing research in Japan is a necessity, since Japanese
buyers are very demanding. A "panel of experts" of potential
buyers is the recommended way of learning consumers' values
and desires. The article offers advice on how to staff the
advance team, prepare translators, how to ask questions,
etc.

0882   Brown, Lee T., Alan M. Rugman, and Alain
        Verbeke (1989) "Japanese Joint Ventures
        with Western Multinationals: Synthesising the
        Economic and Explanations of Failure," <u>Asia
        Pacific Journal of Management</u> 6 (April): 225-42.

Tensions and high failure rates exist among Japanese-
Western joint ventures. Two views exist why this is so: the
economic and the culture-conflict models. The authors review
the relevant literature and find that a combination of
socio-economic factors are responsible for joint venture
failures.

0883   Brzezinski, Zbigniew (1972) <u>The Fragile Blossom:
        Crisis and Change in Japan</u>. New York: Harper and Row.

Japan's post-war successes are compared with the fragility
of its socio-economic institutions, dependence on foreign
imports, etc. Some of these features remain points of danger
for Japan in the 1990s, including an aging population which
will result in higher labor costs and a labor shortage.

0884   Buckley, Peter J. and Hafiz Mirza (1985)
        "The Wit and Wisdom of Japanese Management: An
        Iconoclastic Analysis," <u>Management International
        Review</u> 25 (3): 16-32.

Alleged "unique" Japanese management techniques contain
common elements with those found in other countries. Many
are relatively recent post-war borrowings from the West.
Most of the "better" Japanese management techniques can be,
with modification, transferred back to other cultural
contexts.

0885   Burton, Gene E. "Japan vs. USA: A Comparison
        of Corporate Environments and Characteristics,"
        Human Systems Management 8 (2): 167-73.

Two factors emerge as significant when Japanese and American
businesses are compared: (1) corporate environment and (2)
corporate characteristics. Corporate characteristics said to
be responsible for Japan's economic successes include (1) an
emphasis on the total person, (2) humanistic managerial
policies, and (3) slow evaluation and promotion.

0886   Campbell, Donald J. (1985) "The Meaning of Work:
        American and Japanese Paradigms," Asia Pacific
        Journal of Management 3 (September): 1-9.

Fundamental differences in values exist between the Japanese
and American views of work. A survey of the literature
indicates that the Japanese are primarily people-oriented
and this value is based on the organism-response (O-R)
model. The American orientation is environmental-centered
based on the traditional stimulus-organism-response (S-O-R)
model. These fundamental differences suggest that many
elements of Japanese-style management should not be easily
transferable into the U.S. cultural environment.

0887   Campbell, Nigel (1987) "Japanese Business Strategy in
        China," Long Range Planning 20 (October): 69-73.

A survey of 115 foreign firms in China indicates that
Japanese business strategy differs from that of European and
U.S. companies. The Japanese are better able to use Chinese
cultural practices to their advantage. The Japanese are
longer-term oriented and accept lower initial profits. They
also prefer trading to investing in equity. The Japanese in
China spend more to support their. expatriate staff, build
local relationships, and get along better with their Chinese
co-workers.

0888   Chalmers, Norma J. (1989) Industrial Relations in
        Japan: The Peripheral Workforce. London: Routledge.

The Japanese non-regular, temporary workforce has been
ignored as a topic of investigation. Yet such workers
comprise a significant segment of Japan's labor force. They
include women workers, day laborers, and employees in small
firms. The author provides a detailed analysis of this
neglected topic.

0889   Cheng, Man Tsun (1991) "The Japanese Permanent
        Employment System: Empirical Findings," Work and
        Organizations 18 (May): 148-71.

The 1975 Japanese Social Stratification and Mobility Survey
includes data on Japanese job mobility. The proportions of
respondents who stay with the same employers increase with
size of firm and vary by occupation and industry. Only 33%
of male workers are still with their first employers. An

average Japanese male would make five employer changes during his work career, as compared to eleven job changes for an average American.

0890   Chikudate, Nobuyuki (1991) "Cross-Cultural Analysis of Cognitive Systems in Organizations: A Comparison Between Japanese and American Organizations," Management International Review 31 (3): 219-31.

This article deals with how Japanese and North Americans order and arrange in their minds the meaningful elements of their respective lives in organizations. The respondents worked for Japanese or U.S. banks, The four cognitive categories of the Japanese were "achievement," "occupational identity," "company friends," and "individual nature." The cognitive space of Americans was divided into the categories of "well-being," "authority figure," and "social environments." In general, Japanese and U.S. employees view their organizations in different ways.

0891   Choy, Chong Li and Hem C. Jain "Japanese Management in Singapore: Convergence of Human Resource Management Practices," Asia Pacific Journal of Management 4 (2): 73-89.

Human resource management practices among Japanese parent companies, their subsidiaries in Singapore and Singaporean companies are compared. The Japanese are adapting their managerial practices to the Singaporean cultural environment.

0892   Christopher, Robert C. (1983) The Japanese Mind: The Goliath Explained. New York: Linden Press.

This best-seller is an impressive journalistic description of Japanese society and national character. Beginning with outlines of the major Japanese institutions (family, education, government, economy), the work continues with analyses of the Japanese mania for information. The work then concludes with a section on work practices.

0893   Christopher, Robert C. (1986) Second to None: American Companies in Japan. New York: Fawcett Columbine.

The work presents case histories of American companies that have been successful in establishing markets in Japan. The author's advice includes becoming familiar with the peculiarities of the Japanese business and consumer cultures and advice for executives at the head office (patience, long-term planning), plus specific advice on establishing a business presence in Japan, including hiring policies, etc. There is the assumption that Americans are to blame when they do not enter the Japanese market, rather than alleged restrictive practices on the part of the Japanese.

0894   Cleaver, Charles Grinnell (1976) **Japanese and**
        Americans: Cultural Parallels and Paradoxes.
        Minneapolis: University of Minnesota Press.

This work provides an informed analysis of Japanese and
American national characters. The essays offer realistic
images of Japanese values and ways of living. The author
links historical Japan to the post-war society and its
internal social contradictions.

0895   Clifton, William J. (1988) "Japan in a Transnational
        World," **Baylor Business Review** 6 (Winter): 2-8.

Japan has become an economic power through its managerial
values. Others reasons include the practice of lifetime
employment and emphasis on quality.

0896   Coates, E. James (1989) "Eliminating the
        "Adversarial Work Ethic: A Cultural Problem,"
        Industrial Management 31 (Jan/Feb): 2-3.

The Japanese have been successful in the U.S. because of (1)
successful negotiations with labor unions, (2) their ability
to obtain very favorable conditions from local and state
governments, and (3) their employee selection process.
Japanese-style management practices avoid confrontation and
develop appropriate organization cultures.

0897   Coates, Norman (1988) "Determinants of Japan's
        Business Success: Some Japanese Executives' Views,"
        The Academy of Management Executive 2 (February):
        69-72.

In 1985, Japanese executives were asked to explain their
country's success. Of six factors (macro capital, micro
capital, etc.), half (56%) of the sample mentioned "culture"
as a major consideration.

0898   Cole, Robert E. (1971) **Japanese Blue Collar: The**
        Changing Tradition. Berkeley: University of
        California Press.

This work is a classic study of all aspects of blue collar
workers in Japan. The findings and conclusions form the
basis for most commentaries on the topic and on Japanese
workways in general.

0899   Cool, Karel O. and Cynthia A. Legnick-Hall (1985)
        "Second Thoughts on the Transferability of the
        Japanese Management Style," **Organization Studies**
        6 (1): 1-22.

Japanese management is analyzed using the Ecological-
Cultural-Historical-Institutional perspectives, which allow
for the unbiased study of cultural items. Japanese-style
managerial practices cannot be adopted by Americans unless
all dimensions are analyzed simultaneously. Since the U.S.

and Japanese societies and national characters are so
different, wide-scale transfers (Japan to the U.S.) of
useful managerial practices are unlikely.

0900   Cooney, Berry D. (1989) "Japan and America:
        Culture Counts," Training and Development
        Journal 43 (August): 58-61.

Japanese society is characterized as a militaristic society
structured along rank and authority, with a great concern
for group harmony and consensus. Americans wishing to
conduct business in Japan must take into account Japanese
culture and business practices. U.S. firms should become
more global in their outlook, develop closer links with the
educational institution, and develop more effective teamwork
practices.

0901   Cousins, Steven D. (1989) "Culture and Self-
        Perception in Japan and the United States," Journal
        of Personality and Social Psychology 56 (January):
        124-31.

Japanese and U.S. students exhibited different conceptions
of the self. Japanese students listed fewer abstract,
psychological attributes of the self and more social role
and behavioral attributes.

0902   Crump, Larry (1990) "Developing Effective
        Personnel for International Business,"
        Management Japan 23 (Autumn): 31-36.

Japanese corporations operating in foreign countries need to
establish training procedures for non-Japanese employees.
There should be stronger orientation programs for foreign
workers. Japanese personnel working overseas should become
more familiar with the local cultures and foreign
negotiation styles, management methods, and business meeting
styles.

0903   Cusumano, Michael A. (1991) Japan's Software
        Factories: A Challenge to U.S. Management.
        New York: Oxford University Press.

This study analyzes the efforts of four leading Japanese
firms to develop software factories during 1965-1985. Their
efforts are compared with those of several U.S. firms. There
are sections dealing with the Japanese strategy and values
which made these firms successful. Their managerial
practices gave these firms selected advantages. Japan's
"factory approach" is one policy U.S. firms should adopt.

0904   Davidson, William (1982) "Small Group Activity at
        Musaki Semiconductor Works," Sloan Management
        Review 23 (Spring): 3-14.

Field observations offer descriptions and analyses of small
group activities, training programs and mechanisms for

achieving management objectives in the Musashi Semiconductor Works in Tokyo. The reports are based on excellent field work in a work setting.

0905   Doktor, Robert (1983) "Culture and the Management of Time: A Comparison of Japanese and American Top Management Practice," Asia Pacific Journal of Management 1 (September): 65-71.

Japanese and U.S. CEO's and upper-level managers spend about the same amount of time working alone as opposed to working with others. Japanese CEO's spend 25% of their time working alone vs. 22% of their American counterparts. However, Americans spend shorter segments of time on separate activities. Half (49%) of their activities lasted less than nine minutes as compared to 18% for the Japanese.

0906   Doktor, Robert H. (1990) "Asian and American CEOs: A Comparative Study," Organizational Analysis 18 (Winter): 46-56.

Japanese and American CEOs use their workday time in very similar ways, except that the latter break their time into smaller segments. How meetings are used also differ.

0907   Doktor, Robert and Marvin Loper (1982) "A Comparative Study on the Nature of Managerial Work of Japanese and U.S. CEOs," Academy of Management Proceeding: 63-67.

The work patterns of Japanese and U.S. CEOs are similar in that no differences were found in the proportions of time spent with other people (72%-73%). Japanese CEOs spent a greater proportion of their working time in activities that lasted for one hour or more.

0908   Dollinger, Marc J. (1988) "Confucian Ethics and Japanese Management Practices," Journal of Business Ethics 7 (August): 575-84.

The ethics of Japanese management are based on the writing of Confucius. Modern Confucian thought, in terms of its code versus reality, is an early warning of social change. The author surveys the major Confucian statements related to business behavior, as well as their contradictions.

0909   Dore, Ronald P. (1973) British Factory-Japanese Factory. Berkeley: University of California Press.

One of the first empirical analysis of the organization of authority and management systems, workers' attitudes, and social relations in two Japanese factories. The Japanese firms are compared with two British factories.

0910   Dore, Ronald P. (1975) "Authority, Function
        and Status in British and Japanese Factories,"
        International Studies of Management and
        Organization 5 (Spring): 6-34.

This a reprint of sections of Dore's British Factory-
Japanese Factory (0909). The entries focus on the book's
analysis of the authority and status systems in two British
and two Japanese factories.

0911   Dunphy, Dexter (1987) "Convergence/Divergence: A
        Temporal Review of the Japanese Enterprise and its
        Management," The Academy of Management Review 12
        (3): 445-59.

The author summarizes the English language literature
dealing with whether Japanese and U.S. managerial behavior
are converging or diverging. The two models differ in terms
of many aspects, due to each country's values and culture.

0912   England, George W. and Jyuji Misumi (1986) "Work
        Centrality in Japan and the United states,"
        Journal of Cross-Cultural Psychology 17
        (December): 399-416.

The concept of work centrality (the importance working has
in the life of a person) is developed and measured using
4,228 workers in Japan and the United States in 1982. Work
was defined as "most important" more often in Japan (37%)
than in the U.S. (17%).

0913   Fallows, James (1990) "Conquering Japan,"
        Business Month (March): 54-57.

Kodak has been in Japan for over 100 years and currently
sells more supplies to Japanese professional photographers
than any other company. There are discussions of the
experiences and policy directives (quality, etc.) that have
make Kodak a success in Japan.

0914   Florida, Richard and Martin Kenney (1991)
        "Transplanted Organizations: The Transfer
        of Japanese Industrial Organization to the U.S.,"
        American Sociological Review 56 (June): 381-98.

The authors conduct an analysis of the degree to which
Japanese automobile manufacturers in the U.S. have adopted
American practices or whether they have instead transplanted
Japanese manufacturing practices to the U.S. These Japanese
organizations have transferred many organizational features
to the United States, essentially transforming their U.S.
environment to meet their needs and standards. Thus,
Japanese transplants are using work teams, high levels of
work rotation, fewer job classifications, and quality
control measures.

0915   Fox, William M. (1977) "Japanese Management,"
        Business Horizons 20 (August): 76-85.

Analyses of Japanese national character, traditional
Japanese business practices, and survey data indicate
changing social values and attitudes among Japanese young
adults during 1953-1968.

0916   Fukuda, K. John (1986) "What Can We Learn from
        Japanese Management?" Journal of General
        Management 11 (Spring): 16-26.

Japan's recent economic success has been in part due to its
being an acutely sensitive follower-borrower rather than a
leader-innovator. Western managers should become "effective
borrowers" of Japanese-style management rather than blind
imitators.

0917   Gelsanliter, David (1990) Jump Start: Japan Comes
        To the Heartland. New York: Farrar, Straus & Giroux.

This work is a journalistic report of the Nissan and Honda
operations in the United States from the perspectives of all
parties concerned, including politicians and labor union
officials. The two companies have different corporate
cultures and self-images. They are introducing their own
versions of Japanese-style management and worker relations
to the U.S. They are also learning from their U.S.
environment.

0918   Gregory, Gene (1985) "The Japanese Enterprise:
        Sources of Competitive Strength," Business and
        Society 24 (Spring): 13-21.

Japan's competitive strength is based on its unique cultural
and historical features. These characteristics are described
and analyzed.

0919   Grimes, Dale F. Jr. (1989) "Doing Business with the
        Japanese," Economic Development Review 7 (Summer):
        35-40.

Doing business in Japan involves a number of principles.
These include (1) stress face-to-face contact, (2) be
patient, and (3) dress conservatively. Communication
channels and methods in Japanese corporations differ from
those in U.S. firms, though their organizational structures
may be similar.

0920   Gundling, Enerst (1991) "Ethics and Working with the
        Japanese: The Entrepreneur and the "Elite Course,"
        California Management Review 33 (Spring): 25-39.

Japanese and Americans have different ethical systems based
on separate value systems and differences in national
character. Each group should not judge the other by its own
standards. Ethical differences are based in part on

differences in terms of self vs. group orientation, use of principles vs. case-by-case (depending on the relationship), and the dependency on administrative guidance vs. law and legal remedies.

0921   Hall, Ken (1985) "Japanese Management-Passing Fad or Model for the Future," Leadership & Organization Development Journal 6 (1): 17-24.

The author discusses the major elements of management ideology and work behavior in Japan. There are nine suggestions on how English-speaking managers can profit by adapting selected elements of Japanese-style management.

0922   Hamilton, Patricia W. (1988) "What American Managers Can Learn From the Japanese," D & B Reports 36 (March/April): 28-31.

Advantages of Japanese-style management include a commitment to quality, paying attention to workers' skills and needs, continuously upgrading skills, and the encouragement of intra-team cooperation. U.S.-style management practices are negatively contrasted to their Japanese opposites.

0923   Harber, A Douglas and Danny A. Samson (1989) "Japanese Management Practice: A Integrative Framework," International Journal of Technology Management 4 (3): 283-303.

The authors present a model which integrates Japanese-style managerial practices with cultural values and Japan's socio-economic objectives. This meta-level model can help those who wish to implement Japanese management practices by indicating the social values that underlie and reinforce such behavior.

0924   Hartmann, C. R. (1987) "Selling in Japan," D & B Reports 35 (May/June): 51, 53-4.

Foreign businesses offering high quality, difficult-to-duplicate products can be successful in Japan. The Japanese have different business customs than do Americans. Decision-making takes longer and is based on consensus. There are other significant protocols and work-related etiquette differences.

0925   Hatvany, Nina and Vladimir Pucik (1981) "An Integrated Management System: Lessons from the Japanese Experience," The Academy of Management Review 6 (July): 469-80.

The techniques of Japanese-style management are made possible by the maximum utilization of human resources through the use of three general strategies: (1) the development of an internal labor market, (2) a strongly defined company culture/philosophy, and (3) an intensive socialization of new employees. Specific Japanese management techniques can be adopted by foreign managers, some of which are already practiced in the U.S., such as lifetime employment and job rotation.

0926   Hayashi, Shuji (1988) Culture and Management in Japan. Tokyo: University of Tokyo Press.

The author discusses the cultural elements of Japanese-style management and work, including groupism, the Japanese sense of time, decision-making practices, familism and the high-context structure of the Japanese language.

0927   Helvoort, Ernest J. van (1979) The Japanese Working Man. Vancouver: University of British Columbia Press.

Based on surveys, economic data, and a review of the literature, the author presents comprehensive descriptions of corporate Japanese working patterns, career development, training, leadership and authority patterns, salary structure, etc.

0928   Hill, Roy (1977) "The Ideas Factory at Matsushita," International Management 32 (February): 36-9.

Employees at Matsushita Electric generate over 660,000 ideas a year, of which 10% are accepted. In some factories, the employees offered an average of 50 suggestion each. The article describes why workers were motivated to make suggestions, even though the financial rewards are slight.

0929   Hirschmeier, Johannes and Tsunehiko Yui (1981) The Development of Japanese Business, 1600-1980 Second Edition. Boston: George Allen & Unwin.

The authors trace the major elements of the Japanese economic institution from 1600 to the modern era. The last sections describe Japanese national character, modern business organizations, the social and educational characteristics of middle managers, and selected elements of Japanese corporation (training, recruitment, pay, etc.) practices.

0930   Hiwaki, Kensei (1990) "The Stable Long-Term Employment System of Japan: A Microeconomic Perspective," Human Systems Management 9 (1): 15-28.

The Japanese corporate policy of lifetime employment effects the time-perspective and career planning of employees. While this results in certain company-employee advantages, the system may become increasingly rejected by employees of stagnant, low-growth firms.

0931   Holstein, William J. (1990) <u>The Japanese Power</u>
        <u>Game: What it Means for America</u>. New York:
        Charles Scribner's Sons.

This work offers an expert review of the major institutional
features of contemporary Japan, its strengths and social
problems, and its global impact. One chapter deals with
Japan's exporting its managerial practices and work
ideology, including Honda's "joy of manufacturing" in the
states of Tennessee and Kentucky. There is also a discussion
of managerial strains and failures on the part of Japanese
in the United States. The author proposes a general U.S.
policy vis-a-vis Japan.

0932   Hou, Wee Chow (1984) "Japanese Management: American
        Egg, Oriental Bird?" <u>Singapore Management Review</u> 6
        (January): 1-24.

The author compares the Japanese and Western company systems
by reviewing the major works on Japanese-style management.
One can still learn from American management practices, even
from their mistakes. The author concludes both countries
have similar management tools. The use of these managerial
tools is superior in Japan, in part because of the mutual
support among business, government, and unions. The Japanese
value system also gives them an advantage.

933   Hull, Frank and Koya Azumi (1988) "Technology and
        Participation in Japanese Factories," <u>Work and</u>
        <u>Occupations</u> 15 (November): 423-48.

Fifty Japanese plants were studied in 1972 and during a 1982
restudy. Human relations factors were the major reasons
during both time periods why Japanese factories are so
productive. The U.S. practice is to sacrifice human
relations for efficiency; the Japanese stress human
relations first.

0934   Hull, Frank, Koy A. Azumi, and Robert Wharton (1988)
        "Suggestion Rates and Sociotechnical Systems in
        Japanese Versus American Factories: Beyond Quality
        Circles," <u>IEEE Transactions on Engineering Management</u>
        35 (February): 11-24.

The reward systems in Japanese and U.S. factories are
different. Japanese factories outperform their U.S.
counterparts. Japanese workers make more suggestions and
accept quality control circles better. Lifetime employment
is an indirect source of Japanese superiority in production.

0935   Imai, Masaaki (1975) <u>Never Take Yes for
an Answer: An Inside Look at Japanese
Business for Foreign Businessmen</u>. Tokyo:
The Simul Press.

One of the first books to offer detailed advice on how to
conduct business with Japanese, this work still provides
valid information.

0936   Imakita, Junichi (1989) "Management Through Creative
Confrontation in the United States and Europe,"
<u>Management Japan</u> 22 (Autumn): 3-7.

Japanese businesspersons will have difficulty in engaging in
face-to-face business dialogues with Europeans until they
understand European customs and confrontation behavior. Each
member of the work team should be culturally sensitive.

0937   Ishikure, Kazuo (1988) "Achieving Japanese
Productivity and Quality Levels at a U.S. Plant,"
<u>Long Range Planning</u> 21 (October): 10-17.

The Japanese firm Bridgestone Corporation achieved higher
levels of productivity and quality after taking over a
troubled plant. Using the same machines and workers, the new
management was able to double productivity and reduce the
number of defective tires by half by introducing Japanese-
style management.

0938   Iwata, Ryuahi (1982) <u>Japanese-Style Management: Its
Foundations and Prospects</u>. Tokyo: Asian Productivity
Organization.

The national character of the Japanese in relation to work
is explored in this work. The main goals of Japanese
managers are to motivate workers to submerge their
individuality and accept their groups' goals as their own.

0939   Jain, Hem C. (1990) "Human Resource Management in
Selected Japanese Firms, Their Foreign Subsidiaries
and Locally Owned Counterparts," <u>International Labour
Review</u> 129 (1): 73-89.

The traditional management practices of Japan and the U.S.
are described and compared. The personnel policies of eleven
Japanese firms in Canada, Singapore, Malaysia, and India are
described. Japanese managers in India and Malaysia work long
hours, their work is a central life interest, and they
expect their workers to feel the same. This is resented by
their workers. The Japanese find it difficult to adjust
their organizational practices and work values when working
abroad.

0940   Japan Information Center (1983) <u>What I Want
        to Know About Japan</u>. New York: Japan Information
        Center, third edition.

U.S. seventh graders were asked to list the questions they
had about Japan. The results are short summaries of 25
topics (diet, clothing, schools, games, customs, holidays,
etc.). This work is suited for secondary school students and
teachers, and forms a useful introduction to Japanese
culture.

0941   Japan Travel Bureau, Inc. (1989) <u>Illustrated
        "Salaryman" in Japan</u> (4th edition). Tokyo:
        Japan Travel Bureau, Inc.

A cartoon style is used as a guide to the "salaryman's"
(white-collar corporate employee) business and social
behavior patterns. The sections includes practical and
concise descriptions of daily activities, work behavior and
lifestyle of corporate lower and middle-level managers.
There are good sections on work-related vocabularies, and
meanings of gestures and proverbs. While in part trivial,
the work provides a comprehensive look at the life of a
salaryman. This book, and others dealing with all facets of
Japan and Japanese culture, can be found in the Kinokuniya
Bookstores of America, LTD., which are located in many of
the largest cities of the U.S., including San Francisco.

0942   Johnson, Chalmers (1978) <u>Japan's Public Policy
        Companies</u>. Washington, D.C.: American Enterprises
        Institute for Public Policy Research.

Japan's business elite enjoy a close relationship with
government ministries. Aside from government interventions
and support, Japanese corporations are influenced by
ministries through the practice of early retirement from
higher ministry positions. These persons are then hired by
corporations.

0943   Johnson, Chalmers (1988) "Japanese-Style Management
        in America," <u>California Management Review</u> 30
        (Summer): 34-45.

Japanese personnel policies of long-term retention and
training of American employees suggest that some aspects of
Japanese-style management can be used in the United States.
Such policies offer distinct advantages.

0944   Johnson, Sharon G. (1990) "Not Cut from
        the Same Bolt: Underneath the Management
        Fabric of Japan and the United States,"
        <u>Baylor Business Review</u> 8 (Summer): 18-21.

Christian businesspersons can learn from the dynamics
underlying Japan's economic success. There are similarities
between Japanese-style management and the Christian ethic,

including stress on the group, consensus decision-making, and teamwork.

0945   Jozsa, Frank P., Jr. (1988) "Establishing Effective
        U.S. Japanese Business Alliances," Business 38
        (April/May/June): 48-50.

Japanese-U.S. joint ventures are likely experience conflict because of different cultural values among participants. Americans stress short-term profits. Japanese firms look to long-term sales revenues. There are other differences.

0946   Jung, Herbert F. (1986) How to Do Business
        with the Japanese. Tokyo: The Japan Times, Ltd.

This work offers an extremely detailed and observant analysis of the Japanese way of business by a person with experience in Japan. This is a good introduction to Japanese workways.

0947   Kang, T. W. (1990) Gaishi: The Foreign Company in
        Japan. New York: Basic Books.

This informative work provides very knowledgeable descriptions of business activities in Japan, including customer-seller expectations, quality orientations, and employee-employer relations. The information is based on descriptions, anecdotes and secondary materials. Chapters include comments on globalization issues, expatriate problems, and joint ventures.

0948   Kaplan, David and Charles A. Ziegler (1985) "Clans,
        Hierarchies and Social Control: An Anthropologist's
        Commentary on Theory Z," Human Organization 44
        (Spring): 83-88.

William Ouchi argues that firms organized as industrial clans or families are more effective than those organized on the principle of hierarchy (Theory Z vs. Theory A). The authors feel that Japanese corporations are efficient for other reasons than their clan basis or organizational principles. In addition, the Japanese-style Z organizational structure may not encourage innovation.

0949   Kataoka, Hiroko C. with Tetsuya Kusumoto (1991)
        Japanese Cultural Encounters & How to Handle Them.
        Lincolnwood, Illinois: Passport Books.

The work consists of an analysis of Japanese national character and culture as illustrated by 56 situations with potentials for cultural misunderstandings and breaches of etiquette. The scenarios are described, and the reader must choose the correct responses. The responses are explained as to why each is proper or not. This work is an excellent tool for cross-cultural sensitivity training.

0950   Keys, J. Bernard and Thomas R. Miller (1984) "The
        Japanese Management Theory Jungle," The Academy of
        Management Review 9 (April): 342-53.

The authors review the theories which classify and clarify
the elements of Japanese style management. Each theory
offers a partial explanation of the effectiveness of
Japanese-style management, but a more integrated model is
needed.

0951   Khanna, Sri Ram and O.M. Agarwal (1984) "Japanese
        Management Style and Organisations Behaviour and its
        Interface with Host Cultures," Proceedings of the
        Academy of International Business: 730-41.

The authors list the major elements of Japanese managerial
practices. They indicate that these practices can be
partially successfully adapted to an Indian cultural
context, while American managerial practices cannot. The
authors criticize William Ouchi's theory Z concept of
blending Japanese and U.S. managerial practices.

0952   Kitao, S. Kathleen (1989) "The Group
        in Japan and the United States," World
        Communication 18 (Spring): 11-31.

One of the most important differences between Japanese and
U.S. societies is the nature of group interaction. Japanese
groups are more hierarchical, less individualistic, and
serve several purposes. Such differences are likely to cause
problems when Americans and Japanese work together in the
same groups. Japanese members, for example, may complete
tasks not specifically allocated to them or without being
asked to do so.

0953   Kline, Robert J. (1972) "Religious Influence on
        Japanese Businessmen," pp 172-90 in Lawrence Stessin
        (ed.), Managerial Styles of Foreign Businessmen.
        Series 9 Vol. 1. Hempstead, NY: Hofstra University.

Japanese society and business behavior are heavily
influenced by generally unrecognized religious values.
Shintoism and Buddhism underlie such practices as strong
worker loyalty to employers, the emphasis of sincerity over
absolute moral doctrines, corporation-government
cooperation, groupism at work, and decentralization of
authority. This article provides a unique interpretation of
Japanese business behavior.

0954   Kobayashi, Noritake (1990) "Comparison of
        Japanese and Western Multinationals-Part I,"
        Tokyo Business Today 59 (October): 50.

A comparison of Japanese and Western multinational showed
that Japanese firms stressed planning, training, and
supervision of expatriate managers. U.S. firms ranked higher
in terms of promotion of host nationals.

0955   Koike, Kazuo (1988) <u>Understanding Industrial</u>
<u>Relations in Modern Japan</u>. New York: St. Martin's
Press.

The author discusses the career paths of Japanese workers in
small and large firms, their enterprise unions, and the
careers of white collar workers. There are comparisons with
European and American data throughout the analysis.

0956   Kono, Toyohiro (1982) "Japanese Management
Philosophy: Can It Be Exported?" <u>Long Range Planning</u>
15 (June): 90-102.

Japanese management practices include both hard to transfer
and easy to transfer elements. Those that are difficult to
transfer to foreign management systems include job
ambiguity, group activity, life-time employment, and strong
identity with corporate philosophy. Transferable practices
include centralized negotiation units, respect for people,
job enlargement, and emphasis on quality control.

0957   Kotabe, Masaaki and Sam C. Okoroafo (1990) "A
Comparative Study of European and Japanese
Multinational Firms' Marketing Strategies and
Performance in the United States," <u>Management</u>
<u>International Review</u> 30 (1): 353-70.

36 Japanese and European firms in the U.S. are studied to
measure whether their marketing successes were due to
cultural or strategies of the firms. Japanese cultural
values encourage long-term planning and achieving market
shares. These factors made the Japanese firms more
successful than those of other countries.

0958   Kotler, Philip and Liam Fahey (1982) "The World's
Champion Marketers: the Japanese," <u>The Journal of</u>
<u>Business Strategy</u> 3 (Summer): 3-13.

Japan's post-war "economic miracle" is the result of (1)
good business practices, (2) unfair business practices, (3)
structural factors, and (4) happenstance. Japanese culture
underlies much of the reasons for Japan's competitive
success.

0959   Kudo, Hideyuki, Takeo Tachikawa, and Norikiko Suzuki
(1988) "How U.S. and Japanese CEOs Spend their Time,"
<u>Long Range Planning</u> 21 (December): 79-82.

U.S. CEOs spend more hours working and reading than their
Japanese counterparts. The authors compare length of
position, age, etc., of the two samples in terms of how time
is used. They also compare the meeting contents of the
respondents. U.S. meetings result in more decision-making
and discussions.

0960   Kumara, Upali Ananda, Yoshio Hara, and Masakazu
        Yano (1991) "On Understanding Behavior
        Characteristics of Japanese Manufacturing Workers:
        An Analysis of Job Climate," International Journal of
        Intercultural Relations 15 (2): 129-48.

A survey of 100 Japanese factory workers indicated that co-
worker support was a major priority and source of motivation
and job satisfaction. Supportive supervisors was important
only for socially awkward workers. The "groupism" value in
Japanese culture remains strong.

0961   Kumazawa, Makoto and Jun Yamada (1989) "Jobs and Job
        Skills under the Nenko Employment Practices," pp 102-
        26 in Stephen Wood (ed.) The Transformation of Work?
        Skill, Flexibility and the Labour Process. Boston:
        Unwin Hyman Ltd.

The post-war period in Japan established the existence of
lifetime employment, egalitarian values in terms of reward,
and enterprise unions. These reflect selected ideologies and
cultural values. Such practices were in part responsible for
Japan's "economic miracle." These practices operate best
under specific conditions which may not continue in the
future.

0962   Lansing, Paul and Randy Lee (1989)
        "Practical Business Etiquette in Japan:
        An Example and Explanation," International
        Journal of Management 6 (June) 154-60.

The authors illustrate what a U.S. business person feels and
experiences upon arrival in Japan and deals with a Japanese
counterpart. The scenario is then explained to point out
etiquette and practical errors made by the American.

0963   Laurie, Dennis (1990) "Yankee Samurai and the
        Productivity of Japanese Firms in the United
        States," National Productivity Review 9
        (Spring): 131-9.

According to a survey of 201 U.S. citizens working in Japan
("Yankee Samurai"), few Caucasians speak Japanese. Most
resented working long hours. Japanese consensus decision-
making was reserved for Japanese managers, as was lifetime
employment.

0964   Lazer, William, Shoji Murata, and Hiroshi Kosaka
        (1985) "Japanese Marketing: Towards a Better
        Understanding," Journal of Marketing 49 (Spring):
        69-81.

Japanese marketing principles differ from those in other
countries. The authors discuss the Japanese marketing
practices, including Japanese definitions of competition,
monopolies, and supervisors' responsibilities.

0965   Lewis, William H. (1989) "Doing Business in Japan,"
        Speaking of Japan 10 (September): 10-2.

There are eight aspects or trends in Japan which offer
foreigners the possibility of successfully entering the
Japanese market. The author also provides guidelines for
those wishing to enter this market, based on these eight
criteria. The advice includes selecting and training the
best persons for assignment in Japan and taking a long-term
view.

0966   Lincoln, James R. (1989) "Employee Work
        Attitudes and Management Practice in the
        U.S. and Japan: Evidence from a Large Comparative
        Survey," California Management 32 Review 32
        (Fall): 89-106.

Over 8,000 corporate employees were surveyed in Japan and in
the U.S. Japanese workers are less satisfied but more
committed. The article lists the reasons why Japanese
workers are more committed to their own companies. Japanese-
style management is effectively used in the U.S.

0967   Lokon, Elizabeth (1987) "Probing Japanese Buyers'
        Minds," Business Marketing 72 (November): 84-6, 88,
        90.

When marketing overseas, producers must take into account
local values and sensibilities, especially in terms of
communication. The author analyzes which methods are better
in determining the wants of Japanese consumers. Positive
questioning is necessary, as are non-directive comments. In
Japanese, 7% of a message is conveyed verbally, 38% is
communicated paralinguistically, and 55% through body
language.

0968   Lorsch, Jay (1987) "Baseball and Besuboru: A Metaphor
        for U.S.-Japan Misunderstanding," Speaking of Japan 8
        (November): 15-20.

The author illustrates the sources of Japanese-American
misunderstandings and conflicts through a comparison of the
different ways these two countries play baseball.

0969   Lu, David J. (1987) Inside Corporate Japan:
        The Art of Fumble-Free Management. Stamford,
        CT: Productivity Press.

Although there are a number of different types of Japanese
firms who compete with each other on the national level,
they all contain similar cultural values and corporate
cultures. They all stress familism and cooperation. The book
describes Japanese corporate values and practices. An
appendix details Japanese etiquette for foreigners.

0970   Ludlum, David A. (1988) "Living the Japanese
        Way of MIS," Computerworld 22 (May 23): 67, 72.

Management Information System (MIS) is based on the Japanese
practice of team work, commitment, job rotation, and quality
performance.   Japanese   subsidiaries   in   the   U.S.   are
developing a hybrid management style which combines U.S. and
Japanese elements of management.

0971   Lynn, Richard (1982) "More Brain Power Coming
        Down the Line from Japan," International Management
        37 (December): 37-41.

The Japanese population has the highest I.Q. average in the
world. Younger Japanese cohorts have higher I.Q. levels than
older groups. Thirty-five percent of Japanese youths score
over 115 points vs. 16% for a comparable U.S. population.
The Japanese will enjoy great advantages in terms of
entrepreneurship and innovations when the current group of
highly intelligent young Japanese become adults, beginning
in the 1990s.

0972   Lynn, Richard (1986) "Education in Japan: A
        Contributing Factor in Japanese Industrial
        Success?" The Journal of Social, Political
        and Economic Studies 11 (Winter): 379-91.

Over the last twenty years, a number of international
surveys of educational standards show Japanese children to
be well ahead of those in the West. Educational standards in
Japan are far higher than those in the U.S. Four factors are
responsible for Japan's educational successes: (1) a longer
school year, (2) centralization of curriculum, (3) powerful
cultural incentives for educational achievement, and (4) a
strong private educational sector.

0973   MacPherson, Mark F. (1987) "When in Tokyo...,"
        Business Marketing 72 (September): 83, 90, 92-3.

Americans know very little about selling products abroad.
They do not realize that marketing channels and business
customs are different in foreign countries. The author lists
cultural elements that are different in Asian countries,
focusing on Japanese customs.

0974   Maher, Thomas E. (1985) "Lifetime Employment in
        Japan: Exploding the Myth," Business Horizons 28
        (Nov/Dec): 23-26.

The Japanese policy of lifetime employment evolved within
unique cultural and time-limited contexts which may cause it
to be unadaptable in an American setting.

0975   **March, Robert M.** (1991) <u>Honoring the Customer:</u>
        <u>Marketing and Selling to the Japanese</u>. New
        York: John Wiley.

The author presents detailed and practical advice on how
foreigners should act when dealing with Japanese business
persons. In addition to Japanese protocol and business
practices, there discussions on what Japanese customers and
business associate expect in a business-related context.

0976   **March, Robert M. and Hiroshi Mannari (1981)**
        "Technology and Size as Determinants of the
        Organizational Structure of Japanese Factories,"
        <u>Administrative Science Quarterly</u> 26 (March): 33-57.

A sample of 50 Japanese factories were used to test the
relationship of size (number of personnel) and technology on
organizational structure. Size is a significant variable in
terms of differentiation and formalization. Technology is
significant for other variables. The findings conflict with
the work of the Aston group.

0977   **March, Robert M. and Hiroshi Mannari (1981)**
        "Divergence and Convergence in Industrial
        Organization: The Japanese Case," pp 447-61
        in Gunter Dlugos and Klaus Weiermair (eds.),
        <u>Managing Under Differing Value Systems: Political,</u>
        <u>Social, and Economical Perspectives in a Changing</u>
        <u>World</u>. Berlin and New York: Walter de Gruyter.

Critiquing those who stress alleged unique Japanese forms of
organization, especially lifetime employment, the authors
state that Japanese organizations are converging toward
their counterparts in other societies. Structural variables
are more significant than culture in explaining
organizational variables. 1969 and 1976 survey data indicate
that the value of lifetime commitment has no significant
effect on a respondent's chance of quitting. Modernization
factors are defined as more significant.

0978   **Masatsugu, Mitsuyuki (1982)** <u>The Modern Samurai</u>
        <u>Society: Duty and Dependence in Contemporary</u>
        <u>Japan</u>. New York: AMACOM Book Division.

Modern Japanese society and business behavior are analyzed
from the contexts of historical, linguistic and social
factors. There are also chapters on the "self" in Japanese
society, husband-wife relations, and Japanese-style human
resources control and development.

0979   McMillan, Charles J. (1981) "Social Values and
        Management Innovation: The Case of Japan," pp
        815-32 in Gunter Dlugos and Klaus Weiermair (eds.),
        Managing Under Differing Value Systems: Political,
        Social, and Economical. Berlin and New York: Walter
        de Gruyter.

There exist significant differences in organizational
structures among American and Japanese auto manufacturers.
Such contrasts are based on certain unique Japanese and U.S.
value and societal differences.

0980   McMillan, Charles J. (1984) The Japanese Industrial
        System. Berlin: Walter de Gruyter.

This book presents a very comprehensive analysis of Japanese
manufacturing and managerial practices, with some comparison
with firms in the U.S. and Europe. The emphasis is on levels
of analysis, which includes government and state policies,
the microeconomic sector, and specific managerial practices.

0981   Mehtabdin, Khalid R. (1986) Comparative Management:
        Business Styles in Japan and the United States.
        Lewiston, New York: The E. Mellen Press.

There is an overview of the differences in managerial
behavior in Japanese and American corporations. The chapter
contents are: Recruitment, Employment, Assignment, Career
Path, Evaluation, Communication, and Decision-making.

0982   Mendenhall, Mark E. and Gary Oddou (1986) "The
        Cognitive, Psychological and Social Contexts of
        Japanese Management," Asia Pacific Journal of
        Management 4 (September): 24-37.

After a review of the literature dealing with Japanese
national character and managerial practices, the authors
present matrixes indicating the mutual, direct, or indirect
influences among values, contextual elements, and managerial
practices.

0983   Mente, Boye De (1981) The Japanese Way of Doing
        Business. Englewood Cliffs, NJ: Prentice-Hall, Inc.

The author is a long-term resident of Japan and has written
a number of books on Japanese society. The current work
describes aspects of Japanese-style business behavior
through a description of selected business terms. This
approach describes the principles of Japanese business and
protocol.

0984   Mente, Boye Lafayette De (1989) Business Guide to
        Japan: Opening Doors...and Closing Deals!
        Tokyo: Charles E. Tuttle Co.

The work describes the business protocols practiced in
Japan. The author explains the values and behavior of

Japanese executives, and how foreigners can establish
personal relationships with potential colleagues.

0985   Mente, Boye Lafayette De (1990) Etiquette Guide to
        Japan: Know the Rules...that Make the Difference.
        Tokyo: Charles E. Tuttle Co.

This work describes the major elements of Japanese etiquette
and proper behavior. The discussions focus on social
etiquette, including gift giving, apologies, and general
public etiquette. The work prepares foreign visitors for a
visit to Japan and reduces culture shock of expatriates by
making Japanese customs more understandable.

0986   Miller, Laurence M. (1988) "The Honda Way,"
        Executive Excellence (March): 7-10.

Honda of America Manufacturing, Inc. uses its own Honda-
style management in its Ohio plant. Employees, called
associates, participate in profit sharing and are rotated
frequently from job to job. Peer review is part of the
discipline process. These practices are not completely
Japanese and could be adopted by U.S. managers.

0987   Miller, Peter D. (1991) "Getting Ready for Japan:
        What Not To Do," Journal of Business Strategy 12
        (Jan/Feb): 32-5.

The author presents guidelines on problems faced by
unprepared Americans going to Japan. Japanese sense of time
is different from that in the U.S., in part because there is
no future tense in the Japanese language. There are other
cultural and behavior differences between the two countries.

0988   Misawa, Mitsuru (1987) "New Japanese-Style
        Management in a Changing Era," Columbia Journal
        of World Business 22 (Winter): 9-17.

In spite of changes in organizational behavior in Japanese
firms, a number of elements remain constant, these include
bottom-up decision-making, a secretive attitude, and
consensus. Future changes will involve an emphasis of
creativity over efficiency.

0989   Misumi, Jyuji (1984) "Decision-Making in Japanese
        Groups and Organizations," pp 525-39 in Bernhard
        Wilpert and Arndt Sorge (eds.), International
        Perspectives on Organizational Democracy volume 2.
        New York: John Wiley & Sons.

Decision-making in Japanese organizations include formal and
informal aspects. Specific forms of decision-making, such as
nemawashi and ringi, work best when a consensus already
exists. The differences in decision-making in Japanese,
European, and U.S. settings lie in part in the fact that
work in Japan is conceptualized as organization-centered
rather than individual-centered.

0990   Misumi, Jyuji and Mark F. Peterson (1985) "The
         Performance-Maintenance (PM) Theory of Leadership:
         Review of a Japanese Research Program,"
         Administrative Science Quarterly 20 (June): 198-223.

There has been a thirty-year long research program on
leadership in Japan. This article reviews this program and
its findings. Autocratic leadership is less effective in
Japan than in the United States. Lower-level managers in
Japan exhibit more leadership capability than do their U.S.
counterparts.

0991   Mitsubishi Corporation (1988) Tatemae and Honne:
         Distinguishing Between Good Form and Real Intention.
         New York: The Free Press.

Mitsubishi Corporation has sponsored a "business glossary"
column for eight years in the "Tokyo Newsletter." This
volume includes the column's entries plus forty other terms.
Each entry is described in a paragraph and compared to other
terms. The vocabulary offers insights on Japanese business
culture. The term kangaete (I'll give it a thought) is a way
of saying "no." Sumimasen can mean "please," "I'm sorry,"
"excuse me," or "thank you."

0992   Miyeyima, Ritsuko (1986) "Organization Ideology of
         Japanese Managers," Management International Review
         26 (1): 73-6.

Ten Japanese managers working in the U.K. listed their
organizational values. The high-to-low ranking of roles was
(1) task, (2) role, (3) person, and (4) power. They
evaluated British colleagues as more power-oriented and less
person-oriented than themselves.

0993   Moffat, Gary A. (1990) "Japan vs. the U.S.: Tricks in
         the Trade," Telephone Engineer and Management 94
         (June 15): 65-8.

A conference dealing with conducting business in Japan
provided insights on Japanese business culture. Some of the
advice included (1) learning Japan's culture is important,
(2) decisions are made by consensus, and (3) much of
business is done after office hours.

0994   Morgan, James C. and J. Jeffrey Morgan (1991)
         Cracking the Japanese Market: Strategies for Success
         in the New Global Economy. New York: The Free Press.

There is an urgency in America becoming competitive vis-a-
vis Japan. The authors describe the Japanese national
character, business and social values, and worldview. There
are chapters offering advice on how to enter the Japanese
market and how to become a world-class competitor.

0995   **Morris, Rich editor (1987)** <u>The Economist</u>
        <u>Business Traveller's Guides: Japan</u>. **New York:**
        Prentice Hall Press.

This book is a superior tourist/business guide to Japan.   In
addition to lists of major hotels and restaurants, city
maps, shopping guides, etc., this guide contains essays on
Japanese economy, politics, business and culture, as well as
business and social protocols.

0996   **Morris-Suzuki, Tessa (1988)** <u>Beyond Computopia:</u>
        <u>Information, Automation and Democracy in Japan</u>. **New**
        York: Kegan Paul International.

Developed nations are becoming "information societies." This
is especially evident for Japan. The author describes this
new development, how related changes effect Japanese
society, and how Japanese society is changing in response to
an information revolution. The author develops a new
theoretical model of the information society.

0997   **Mroczkowski, Tomasz and Masao Hanaoka (1989)**
        "Continuity and Change in Japanese Management,"
        <u>California Management Review</u> **31 (Winter): 39-53.**

 Japanese companies have experienced changes in employment
policies as the population has changed.

0998   **Murabe, Tamotsu (1990) "Internal Communication in**
        Japan," <u>Communication World</u> **7 (December): 44-6.**

Japanese firms are characterized by high levels of internal
communication to set goals, allocate resources, etc. The
result has been consensus in terms of worker co-prosperity
and management-union cooperation. Japanese firms use three
channels for intra-firm communication: interpersonal, print,
and audiovisual.

0999   **Nakane, Chie (1970)** <u>Japanese Society</u>. **Berkeley:**
        University of California Press.

This work has become a classic and is one of the more
influential statement of Japanese national character and
social values underlying the structure of Japanese society
and behavior. The author's main thesis is that Japanese
society is group-centered and hierarchical.

1000   **Namiki, Nobuaki and S. Prakash Sethi (1988)**
        "Japan," pp 55-96 in Raghu Nath (ed.), <u>Comparative</u>
        <u>Management: A Regional View</u>. **Cambridge, Mass.:**
        Ballinger Publishing Company.

This essay consists of a general discussion of Japanese
society with an emphasis on work and management. Included
are analyses of Japanese social values, related business
practices, corporate structures, Japan's economy, and
infrastructures.

1001   **Negandhi, Anant R., Golpira S. Eshghi, and Edith
        C. Yuen (1985) "The Management Practices of Japanese
        Subsidiaries Overseas,"** California Management Review
        27 (Summer): 93-105.

A question exists whether or not Japanese managers modify
their managerial behavior when dealing with foreign workers.
An analysis of two different management styles (modified
local system and modified Japanese system) used by Japanese-
owned subsidiaries in the U.S., Europe, and less-developed
countries indicates less adaptability than that found in
other national corporations. The findings question the
Japanese MNCs' ability to adapt to local work customs.

1002   **Negandhi, Anant R. and Manuel G. Serapio, Jr.** (1991)
        **"Management Strategies and Policies of Japanese
        Multinationals: A Re-Examination,"** Management Japan
        24 (Spring): 25-32.

The present study continues the senior author's earlier
analyses of a number of managerial functions found in the
activities of Japanese multinationals firms and their
foreign subsidiaries. Headquarters make more decisions
concerning expatriate personnel and strategic and financial
matters than before. Power in general became more
centralized. A trend toward the nationalization of
management was evident, as was increased local procurement.

1003   **Nonaka, Ikujiro and Johnny K. Johanson** (1985)
        "Japanese Management: What About the "Hard" Skills?"
        The Academy of Management Review 10 (April): 181-91.

Most persons describing Japanese-style management focus on
"soft" skills. But the "hard" managerial skills of strategy,
structure, and systems have also contributed to Japan's
economic success. The "hard" skills, such as decision-
making, reflect Japanese social values.

1004   **Odaka, Kunio (1986)** Japanese Management: A
        Forward-Looking Analysis. **Tokyo: Asian
        Productivity Organization.**

The author describes the major elements of Japanese
management, stressing groupism and harmony. He then offers
criticisms of a number of Japanese managerial practices. The
major disadvantages are (1) suppressing creativity and
encouraging dependency, (2) discriminatory employment, (3)
harmful effects of Japanese promotion practices, and (4)
"work that gives no joy."

1005   **Ohmae, Kenichi (1982)** The Mind of the Strategist:
        The Art of Japanese Business. **New York: McGraw-Hill
        Book Company.**

The author is a consultant on a global scale and offers
detailed analyses on business strategies illustrated with
Japanese and other national examples. There are sections on

Japanese national character, economic planning (Ministry of International Trade and Industry), and Japanese consumer habits.

1006   O'Reilly, Brian (1988) "Japan's Uneasy U.S.
        Managers," _Fortune_ 117 (April 25): 245-64.

Japanese expatriates in America enjoy a higher standard of living than their co-workers in Japan, but they worry about fitting back into Japanese society. American business customs, such as being confrontational, make working in America difficult. A consequence of this culture shock is retreating into Japanese expatriate communities.

1007   Ouchi, William G. (1981) _Theory Z: How American_
        Business Can Meet the Japanese Challenge. Reading,
        Mass: Addison-Wesley.

Ouchi argues that American and Japanese managerial ideologies and cultural values influence each nation's dominant managerial styles, called Theory J (Japanese) and Theory A (American). He proposes Theory Z, which is a blend of both national systems, though closer to the Japanese model. Theory Z includes the features of lifetime employment, slow rates of promotion, concern for the total person, stress on general duties, and a high level of workers' involvement in the decision-making process.

1008   Ouchi, William G. and Jerry B. Johnson (1978)
        "Types of Organizational Control and Their
        Relationship to Emotional Well Being,"
        Administrative Science Quarterly 23 (June):
        293-317.

Types A organizations are America's traditional work organizational structures. They are characterized by highly specialized tasks, high turnover, and contractual relations among employees. Type Z organizational structures are a form of organization similar to Japanese-style structures. Types A and Z have different forms of organizational control and levels of worker satisfaction.

1009   Otsubo, Mayumi (1986) "A Guide to Japanese Business
        Practices," _California Management Review_ 28 (Spring):
        28-42.

This article includes specific illustrations on conducting business in Japan.

1010   Ozawa, Terutomo (1980), "Japanese World of Work:
        An Interpretive Survey," _MSU Business Topics_ 28
        (Spring): 45-55.

This analysis of the major features of Japanese national character (groupism, paternalism, etc.) includes discussions of the influence of Japanese culture on Japanese workways such as labor mobility and training, participative management and education of business leaders.

1011   Pascale, Richard T. and Anthony G. Athos (1981)
        **The Art of Japanese Management: Applications for
        American Executives**. New York: Simon & Schuster.

Taking a consultant's orientation, the authors present the major features of Japanese management through the "Seven-S" framework. Japanese managers stress the "soft-Ss" (human factors) such as over-all goals, staff, skills, and style (management's ways of dealing with subordinates). There are also good discussions of Japanese business practices.

1012   Peak, Martha H. and Julie A. Cohen (1991)
        "Tariffs and Taboos in Japan," **Management
        Review** 80 (February): 14-8.

Managers in U.S. firms located in Japan should be prepared to employ primarily Japanese in their labor force. Japanese will not want to change employers after being hired, so hiring mid-career managers will be very difficult. IBM-Japan has hired many women since most Japanese males do not want to work for a foreign company. Deal making and other behaviors differ in Japan from American customs.

1013   Pegels, Carl C. (1984) **Japan vs. the West:
        Implications for Management**. Boston:
        Kluwer-Nijhoff.

Significant aspects of the Japanese national character and society are the importance placed on group harmony and consensus. Such values have greatly influenced Japanese-style managerial practices.

1014   Perry, Tekla S. (1990) "When East Meets West,"
        IEE Spectrum 27 (August): 53-5.

There exist many communication problems when Japanese firms operate in the U.S. There are differences between Japanese and Americans in the amount of hours, worked, feedback, and socializing with workers. The adaptation process involves five stages.

1015   Picken, Stuart D.B. (1987) "Values and Value Related
        Strategies in Japanese Corporate Culture," **Journal
        of Business Ethics** 6 (February): 137-43.

Although there have been many discussions of specific Japanese business procedures, most discussions ignore the value system forming the context of Japanese-style management. The article presents a discussion of the values directing Japanese corporate behavior.

1016   Pierce, Milton (1987) "25 Lessons from the Japanese,"
        New Management 5 (Fall): 23-26.

Japanese-style work behavior and philosophy can be
summarized in twenty-five statements. These points are
sensitive to Japanese values. They include (1) avoid being
the first to try a new idea, (2) stability, image, and
reliability are vital, (3) be optimistic, (4) always show
respect for people, and (5) treat a team member's mistake as
the team's mistake.

1017   Putti, Joseph M. and Thomas Chong (1988) "Human
        Resource Management Practices of Japanese
        Organisation," Singapore Management Review 8 (July):
        11-19.

The authors examine the major features of Japanese-style
management. Most of these elements are not being transferred
to the Singapore environment without a high degree of
adaptation.

1018   Putti, Joseph M. and Atsushi Yoshikawa (1984)
        "Transferability - Japanese Training and
        Development Practices," Proceedings of the Academy
        of International Business: 300-11.

The authors describe in detail the training and personnel
development practices, and their underlying values, found in
Japanese enterprises. These policies are not being
transferred to Japanese-owned firms in Singapore.

1019   Rehder, Robert R. (1981) "What American and Japanese
        Managers are Learning from Each Other," Business
        Horizons 24 (March/April): 63-70.

The Japanese and American value systems are discussed in
terms of their organizational structure and management
systems. The two systems can be blended into a mixed
Japanese-American business culture.

1020   Rehfeld, John E. (1990) "What Working
        for a Japanese Company Taught Me,"
        Harvard Business Review 68 (Nov/Dec):
        167-176.

An American offers ten lessons he learned while working for
Toshiba America for nine years. Japanese corporate culture
encourages: staying focused on corporate goals, quantify
everything, emphasize the process-not the result, know the
whole person, visit customers, and build market share.

1021   Reichel, Arie and David M. Flynn (1983) "Values
        in Transition: An Empirical Study of Japanese
        Managers in the U.S.," Management International
        Review 23 (4): 63-73.

162 upper-level Japanese managers living in the U.S. were surveyed to measure whether their organizational values were being influenced by their foreign cultural environment. The results indicate that the sample did not fit an ideal "Japanese profile," though they also differed from an ideal American profile.

1022   Reitsperger, Wolf D. and Shirley J.
        Daniel (1990) "Dynamic Manufacturing:
        A Comparison of Attitudes in the U.S.A.
        and Japan," Management International Review
        30 (3):203-16.

Dynamic evolution (DV) and static optimization (SO) are models of policy-making in Japan and the U.S., respectively. Currently, DV is prevalent in both countries but at higher levels in the U.S. The DV model is quality-conscious, more efficient, and more flexible.

1023   Rosenberg, Larry J. and Gregory J. Thompson
        (1986) "Deciphering the Japanese Cultural Code,"
        International Marketing Review 3 (Autumn): 47-57.

Japanese executives understand how Westerners think. This is one reason for Japan's economic successes. Western executives, unfortunately, do not understand the Japanese or their values. This article explains key concepts of the Japanese national character.

1024   Saji, Keizo (1984) "Japanese Spirits: Whiskey
        and Work in Japan," Speaking of Japan 5
        (September): 13-18.

Japanese society is undergoing a rapid transformation. The Japanese national character is also changing. This change is illustrated in changing drinking styles among Japanese.

1025   Samiee, Saeed (1982) "How Auto Workers Look at
        Productivity Measures: Lessons from Overseas,"
        Business Horizons 25 (May/June): 85-91.

American workers' attitudes toward work improvement plans adopted from overseas are described. The findings indicate how and which work conditions can be imported for higher efficiency. There is a warning that workers must be carefully prepared before new work practices are introduced.

1026   Samiee, Saeed and Adam Mayo (1990) "Barriers
        to Trade with Japan: A Socio-Cultural Perspective,"
        European Journal of Marketing 24 (12): 48-66.

Trade between the European Community and Japan is hindered by "invisible barriers." These are social and cultural differences among the consumers and the exporters/importers. Successful entry into Japan demands a better understanding of the Japanese value system and market.

1027   Schwind, Hermann F. and Richard B. Peterson (1985)
        "Shifting Personal Values in the Japanese Management
        System," International Studies of Management and
        Organization 15 (Summer): 60-74.

Two schools of thought exist as to whether Japanese
management values will remain relatively stable or will
converge to those of western countries. Surveys of Japanese
managers who had graduated 10-12 years earlier from the
Institute for International Studies and Training (a Japanese
government-sponsored institute established to train
developing government and business leaders) indicate that
graduates generally maintained a "Japanese" managerial
ideology. Some differences were noted among more recent
graduates.

1028   Sengoku, Tamotsu (1985) Willing Workers: The
        Work Ethic in Japan, England, and the United
        States. Westport, Conn: Quorum Books.

The work ethic differs from country to country and by
national sub-groups, such as age cohorts. This book reviews
the attitudes of workers in three countries toward work and
the cultural basis for workers' behavior. It deals with
national character and the social, psychological, and
structural reasons why younger workers increasingly lack a
strong work ethic. There are also reports on surveys taken
in the U.S., Japan, and England comparing workers'
attitudes.

1029   Sethi, S. Prakash (1975) Japanese Business
        and Social Conflict. Cambridge, Mass: Ballinger
        Publishing Company.

Japanese values and practices in the general society and in
business in particular have allowed the development of a
number of social problems. The author discusses corporate
behavior within the context of cultures and how specific
problems have been reacted to by corporations and
government. A number of court cases and social problems are
analyzed from the perspectives of Japanese social character.

1030   Sethi, S. Prakash, Nobuaki Namiki, and Carl L.
        Swanson (1984) "The Decline of the Japanese
        System of Management," California Management
        Review 26 (Summer): 35-45.

The authors indicate that Japanese-style management is
capable of changing. They present discussions of changes in
managerial practices made by the Japanese in response to a
changing business environment.

1031   Shane, Scott (1988) "Language and Marketing
        in Japan," International Journal of Advertising
        7 (2): 155-61.

Foreign marketers wishing to be successful in Japan should be familiar with the verbal, non-verbal, and written Japanese communication styles. Spoken Japanese is ambiguous and pluralistic. Foreigners should also be familiar with the Japanese approaches to negotiation, packaging, correspondence, etc.

1032   Shapiro, Isaac (1983) "Cultural Barriers to Delivery of Services," chapter 8 in Parviz Saney and Hans Smit (eds.) Business Transactions with China, Japan, and South Korea. New York: Matthew Bender.

This chapter focuses on how and why the Japanese protect their legal institutions and commerce from foreign intrusion by erecting a number of informal and formal trade barriers. These barriers discriminate against foreigners and foreign goods, and they are based on certain social values and attitudes.

1033   Shenkar, Oded (1990) "'Japanology' in Organizational Sciences: The Myth and its Dangers," Human Systems Management 9 (1): 47-50.

Much discussion of Japanese-style management has taken place outside existing theoretical models. This has resulted in a confusion of ill-understood propositions.

1034   Shenkar, Oded (1988) "Uncovering Some Paths in the Japanese Theory Jungle," Human Systems Management 7 (3): 221-30.

The author traces the unique characteristics of Japanese management (seniority, job rotation, lifetime employment, consensus decision-making, etc.). These elements are highly interdependent and cannot be transferred singly to other cultural environments. The author concludes with a diagram indicating the interrelationships of environmental and managerial principles that form a system. The article is followed by a critique.

1035   Sheridan, John H. (1990) "Want to Work for the Japanese?" Industry Week 239 (March 19): 333-4.

51 American executives of Japanese-owned firms said they felt their decision-making abilities were restricted. The firms had overlapping authority lines. Long-term promotion career path were felt to be limited, in part because the Japanese owners expected their U.S. managers to leave their firms.

1036   Shimada, Haruo (1991) "The Desperate Need for New Values in Japanese Corporate Behavior," The Journal of Japanese Studies 17 (Winter): 107-125.

Japanese business activity stresses profit-driven competition and economically rational decisions on micro factors. Such attitudes have caused problems in terms of the level of happiness of workers, the Japanese standard of living, Japan's allies, and in other contexts. The author suggests Japanese companies reject their search for profits and concern themselves more with the quality of life of the Japanese population.

1037   Shimizu, Ryuei (1989) The Japanese Business Success Factors. Tokyo: Chikura Shobo.

The author, a former department head in the Ministry of International Trade and Industry, suggests that Japanese business success is based on an encouragement of employee creativity to develop new/better products. Managerial practices, by stressing trust and harmony, encourage business success. However, the author feels that managers and workers work best under conditions of limited tension, which can be maintained through job rotation, intra-firm competition, and corporate culture.

1038   Shioya, Ko (1988) "Courting the Japanese," Management Review 77 (March): 54-55.

There are more than 1,000 foreign-owned companies in Japan. The ways to succeed in Japan are to use intermediaries, use Japanese-language documents, have a skilled interpreter in negotiation, and have lots of patience.

1039   Simon, James H. (1991) "U.S.-Japanese Management Enters a New Generation," Management Review 80 (February): 42-5.

In U.S. Japanese-owned firms, many Japanese managers have become disillusioned with U.S. managers. The results have been poor performance and dismissals. A reason for the low level of American performance is poor communication with Japanese superiors. Americans also insist on managing American-style. The article lists a number of complaints made by American managers in Japanese-owned firms.

1040   Smith, Peter B. (1984) "The Effectiveness of Japanese Styles of Management: A Review and Critique," Journal of Occupational Psychology 57 (June): 121-36.

The author reviews studies on the performance and effectiveness of Japanese managers as compared with foreign managerial behavior. Japanese-style management contains a number of unique features which are ill-understood abroad. When seen through Western eyes, Japanese managerial behaviors are often mis-categorized and misinterpreted if Western-style models are used.

1041   Smith, Peter B. and Jyuji Misumi (1989) "Japanese
        Management-A Sun in the West?" pp 330-69 in Carl L.
        Cooper and Ivan T. Robertson (eds.), International
        Review of Industrial and Organizational Psychology.
        New York: John Wiley & Sons.

This is a sensitive review of major studies on Japanese
management. It points out exceptions to general assumptions
about Japanese management. There is a section on Japanese
working abroad. The bibliography is very good.

1042   Snodgrass, Coral H. (1988-89) "The New Japanese
        Challenge: Managing the Subcontractor Relationship,"
        Business Forum 14 (Fall/Winter): 17-21.

U.S. contractors dealing with Japanese firms need to be
aware of Japanese concerns for quality and communication.
Sub-contractors must be culturally sensitive in order to
deal effectively with the Japanese.

1043   Stening, Bruce W. and James E. Everett (1984)
        "Japanese Managers in Southeast Asia: Amiable
        Superstars or Arrogant Upstarts?" Asia Pacific
        Journal of Management 1 (May): 171-80.

1288 expatriates and local managers working in Japanese-
owned subsidiaries in Hong Kong, Indonesia, Malaysia, the
Philippines, Singapore, and Thailand were asked to evaluate
themselves, their foreign colleagues, and how they thought
they were seen by others. Three general stereotypes were
discovered: managerial, entrepreneurial, and congenial. The
Japanese were stereotyped as "efficient but not nice." The
Japanese evaluated the local employees very poorly.

1044   Sullivan, Jeremiah J. and Ikujiro Nonaka (1986) "The
        Application of Organizational Learning Theory to
        Japanese and American Management," Journal of
        International Business Studies 17 (Fall): 127-47.

Japanese managers indicated a greater commitment to
community establishment and information sharing than did
American managers. This results in Japanese managers being
more committed to a theory of action that facilitates
learning and strategy formation.

1045   Sullivan, Jeremiah and Ikujiro Nonaka (1988)
        "Culture and Strategic Issue Categorization
        Theory," Management International Review 28
        (3): 6-10.

The selective process of the labeling of issues as being
threats or opportunities effects managerial behavior and is
influenced by cultural background. Japanese and U.S.
executives exhibited different labeling behaviors. The
Japanese tended to label issues as problems. Americans
labeled issues as opportunities.

1046   Sullivan, Jeremiah and Richard B. Peterson (1982)
        "Factors Associated with Trust in Japanese-American
        Joint Ventures," Management International Review 22
        (2): 30-40.

Japanese managers perceive future trust when they (1) have a
position of power over joint-venture partners, (2) enjoy
positive interpersonal relations, (3) receive profits from
the joint venture, and (4) can initiate decisions. There is
a thorough review of the relevant literature.

1047   Sullivan, Jeremiah and Richard B. Peterson (1991) "A
        Test of Theories Underlying the Japanese Employment
        System," Journal of International Business Studies
        22 (1): 79-97.

A review of the relevant literature indicates that the
practice of lifetime employment in Japan will change (and is
changing) as Japan undergoes socio-economic changes. This
policy is dependent upon a stable workforce. Lifetime
employment offers corporations a high degree of control over
workers. A sample of Japanese managers and personnel
directors were asked their company's policies and gains
related to lifetime employment.

1048   Sullivan, Jerry and Coral Snodgrass (1991)
        "Tolerance of Executive Failure in American
        and Japanese Organizations," Asia Pacific
        Journal of Management 8 (April): 15-34.

A sample of 95 Japanese and American executives exhibited
the same level of tolerance of failure, though this
tolerance varied by economic condition and the degrees of
failure involved. The Japanese handle low-level failures
well and serious failures poorly. The reverse is true for
Americans.

1049   Sullivan, Jeremiah J., Terukiko Suzuki,
        and Yasumasa Kondo (1986) "Managerial
        Perceptions of Performance: A Comparison
        of Japanese and American Work Groups,"
        Journal of Cross-Cultural Psychology
        17 (December): 379-98.

Both Japanese and Americans accept a Rational Man theory of
the individual. But Americans see groups as helping to
increase the risk of poor performance. Japanese see groups
as enhancing good performance. Groups, to the Japanese,
bring out more from workers than would be otherwise. As a
result, the Japanese create incentives for increased group
participation.

1050   Sumiya, Mikio (1991) "Japan: Model Society of the
        Future?" The Annals of the American Academy of
        Political and Social Science 513 (January): 139-150.

Can Japan be considered a model society for the future? Japan's economic development, while keeping many of its traditional patterns and avoiding the negative consequences of modernization, makes it a unique society. The author feels that Japanese industrial practices are not unique. The basis of the Japanese economy's energy is the familial form of corporate structure. This cannot be a model for the future. Japanese values are currently too driven by economic aims.

1051   Suzuki, Norihiko (1985) "Workers' Perceptions of a
        Japanese Company's Song," Asia Pacific Journal of
        Management 2 (May): 189-98.

Japanese company songs are used to motivate workers and increase their loyalty to employers. Company songs generally have work and non-work related themes. Age and gender were significant variables in terms of workers' liking the non-business themes. Organizational status was significant in terms of perceptions of work-related themes.

1052   Takanaka, Akira (1985/86) "Some Thoughts on
        Japanese Management Centering on Personnel
        and Labor Management: The Reality and the Future,"
        International Studies of Management and Organization
        15 (Fall/Winter): 17-68.

Changing socio-economic conditions will force changes in Japanese managerial values and behavior. The author reviews the major features of Japanese-style management and suggests the directions of future changes.

1053   Tanaka, H. William and Nobuyuki Takashima (1986)
        Doing Business with Japan. New Canaan, CT:
        Business Books International.

The work begins with general descriptions of Japan's geography, economic institutions, trade controls, tourist information, and addresses of regulatory agencies. A short section is included on business protocol.

1054   Taniguchi, Kazuyoshi (1989) "Business Across
        a Cultural Void: Japan's Cultural Imperatives,"
        Business Marketing 74 (February): 63, 70-72.

Americans have lost many sales through ignorance of Japanese values and behavior patterns. Having a translator is an advantage. Americans should also learn the nature of Japanese decision-making, which is relatively time-consuming and built on consensus.

1055   Taylor, Jared (1983) Shadows of the Rising Sun.
        New York: Random House.

One of the themes of this well-informed work on the national character, modern trends, and the social institutions of Japan is the emphasis placed on the conformity and loyalty to group goals. These link subordinates and superiors into cooperative units. The author covers the main features and elements of the Japanese society within their historical contexts.

1056   Thian, Helene (1988) <u>Setting Up & Operating a Business in Japan. A Handbook for the Foreign Businessman</u>. Tokyo: Charles E. Tuttle Company.

Detailed information is offered on how foreigners can establish businesses in Japan. The clearly presented information is comprehensive and includes useful information on rent, leases, labor laws, employee relations, visa needs, and taxation/accounting policies. There are also lists of useful addresses.

1057   Tokuyama, Jiro (1987) "Strengths--and Weaknesses--of Japanese Management," <u>New Management</u> 5 (2): 27-31.

Although Japanese management practices have been influenced by U.S. style management, Japanese managers still exhibit traditional Japanese behavior patterns. There is more "learning by experience" in Japan, greater attention to develop generalist skills, and a wider knowledge of all of a company's facets. Younger Japanese refuse to stand out.

1058   Tracy, Lane (1985) "Is it Trust or WA: A Reply to Sullivan and Peterson," <u>Management International Review</u> 25 (2): 76-79.

Tracy extends and re-analyzes the work of Sullivan and Peterson who argue that Japanese partners of Japanese-American joint-ventures expected that "wa" (harmony) and trust would be achieved through positive personal relationships and decision-sharing. Tracy adds "trust" items to a similar study and suggests that the concepts of "trust" and "wa" should be kept methodologically separate.

1059   Trevor, Malcolm (1991) "The Overseas Strategy of Japanese Corporations," <u>The Annuals of the American Academy of Political and Social Science</u> 513 (January): 90-101.

The Japanese fear that the internationalization of their economy will result in diluting the Japanese-style managerial practices which led to Japan's economic global successes. Yet such managerial adaptation is also seen as necessary in the future.

1060   Tsuda, Masumi (1985-86) "The Future of the Organization and the Individual in Japanese Management," <u>International Studies of Management and Organization</u> 15 (Fall/Winter): 89-125.

The author defines the structures, major decision-making patterns, and authority channels in Japanese corporations. There are three types of hierarchical structures, some of which can lead to irresponsible management behavior under certain circumstances. The tendency toward autonomous management in Japan clashes with a traditional tendency of over-centralization, which is dysfunctional.

1061   Tsurumi, Yoshi (1982) "Managing Consumer and
        Industrial Marketing Systems in Japan," Sloan
        Management Review 24 (Fall): 41-49.

Unique Japanese national distribution systems as derived from selected aspects of Japanese culture are presented within a focus of Japan's complex marketing systems.

1062   Vaziri, M.T., Joe Won Lee, and Joseph L. Kreiger
        (1988) "Onda Moku: The True Pioneer of Management
        Through Respect for Humanity," Leadership &
        Organization Development Journal 9 (1): 3-7.

Onda Moku was Chief Finance Officer of the Matsushiro province 250 years ago. His managerial philosophy has had a great a impact on more modern Japanese managers. The principles of Moku's philosophy include (1) trust in people, (2) decision-making through consensus, and (3) the cooperative support of subordinates.

1063   Weisz, John R., Fred M. Rothbaum, and Thomas C.
        Blackburn (1984) "Standing out and Standing in: The
        Psychology of Control in America and Japan,"
        American Psychologist 39 (September): 955-69.

Japanese national character emphasizes the development of Secondary Control in which individuals increase their rewards by accommodating to existing realities and maximizing their fit with things and situations as they are. American culture emphasizes Primary Control, whereby the individuals receive social rewards by influencing or manipulating existing social realities (other people, circumstances, etc.). The authors investigate the consequences of each type of control in terms of each society's institutions, including work.

1064   Whenmouth, Edwin (1988) "Is Japan's Corporate Style
        Changing?" Industry Week 237 (October): 33-5.

Japanese work-related behavior and attitudes have changed drastically over the last two decades. Increasingly more Japanese make mid-career firm changes. Employers look for the ability of candidates to use individual judgement as well as being loyal. The affluence of the workforce and the experience of working in an international environment have caused these and other changes.

1065   Wilcox, John (1989) "Looking Beyond the Rising Sun,"
        Training & Development Journal 43 (March): 12-4.

The Japanese need to develop cultural norms that encourage
creativity and individual initiative. On a global level, the
Japanese must develop ways to become more culturally
sensitive.

1066   Wokutch, Richard E. (1990) "Corporate Social
        Responsibility Japanese Style," The American
        Academy of Management Executive 4 (May): 56-74.

The concept of corporate social responsibility in Japan is
very different from that in the United States. Some aspects
are superior to those found in the U.S., such as those
dealing with worker safety and labor-management-government
relations.

1067   Wolfe, John (1986) "Yank to Japan: U.S. Adman
        Reorients Skills with Dentsu," Advertising Age
        57 (September): 50-1.

The article describes the experiences of a copywriter living
in Japan. He had to adjust to language and cultural
problems. His employer treated him very well and his tax
liabilities were small. He learned Japanese business
customs.

1068   Wood, Stephen (1989) "The Japanese Management Model:
        Tacit Skills in Shop Floor Participation," Work and
        Organization 16 (November): 446-60.

A distinctive facet of Japanese-style management is the
greater amounts of group-based decision-making, the use of
knowledge among workers, and autonomy. The needs and talents
of the total worker are recognized.

1069   Woronoff, Jon (1982) Inside Japan, Inc.. Tokyo: Lotus
        Press Ltd.

This analysis of Japan's society, stressing its economic
institutions, is critical of a number of Japanese values and
practices. Japan's "miracle" is more fragile than is
generally admitted.

1070   Woronoff, Jon (1983) Japan's Wasted Workers.
        Totowa, New Jersey: Allanheld, Osmund & Co.,
        Publishers.

The author, a long-time resident of Japan, explains why many
Japanese workers, outside the largest corporations and their
factories, are low in job satisfaction, inefficient, less
well rewarded, and undervalued by their employers.

1071   Woronoff, Jon (1986) The Japan Syndrome: Symptoms,
        Ailments, and Remedies. New Brunswick: Transaction
        Books.

In spite of recent economic successes, Japan's population experiences a low level of quality of life compared with citizens of other industrialized nations. The author points out the society's failures and offers suggestions on how to improve the daily life of the Japanese.

1072   Yamada, Kiyotaka (1991) "Creativity in Japan,"
        Leadership & Organization Development Journal
        12 (6): 11-4.

There is a cultural bias against creativity in the Japanese language, the educational system, and society in general. Human resources management in Japanese companies stresses harmony and conformity and discourages innovation.

1073   Yamazaki, Masakuzu (1984) "A New Japanese
        Individualism: The Legacy of the 1970s,"
        Speaking of Japan 5 (June): 18-22.

The 1970 decade was a period of crisis for Japan's population, in part because of its economic prosperity. Younger Japanese became more concerned with the quality of their lives and became much more individualistic. Smaller groups--including occupational--are becoming the source for increased individual identity.

1074   Yoshida, Rosaku (1989) "Deming Management Philosophy:
        Does it work in the U.S. as Well as in Japan?"
        Columbia Journal of World Business 24 (Fall): 10-7.

Deming-style quality control works well in Japan because of Japanese work values and national character. The Japanese view a work process in a holistic manner while Americans are much more analytic. There are also a number of corporate policies that offer Japanese firms an advantage, including their personnel policies and encouragement of cooperation.

1075   Zemke, Ron (1981) "What's Good for Japan may not be
        Best for You and Your Training Department," Training
        18 (October): 62-5.

Too many managers are uncritically accepting selected elements of Japanese-style management. Many of these practices are too culture-bound to be useful in an American setting.

1076   Zimmerman, Mark (1985) How to do Business with the
        Japanese: A Strategy for Success. New York: Random
        House.

Descriptions of Japanese society and national character, detailed business protocols (business cards, gift giving, etc.), and general features of the Japanese economy are given for non-academic readers. A useful feature is an excellent analysis of Japanese society using Japanese language concepts and conventional patterns of conversation.

10

China and Related Areas

1077   Adler, Nancy J., Nigel Campbell, and Andre
         Laurent (1989) "In Search of Appropriate
         Methodology: From Outside the People's Republic
         of China Looking In," Journal of International
         Business Studies 20 (Spring): 61-74.

Results from surveys of managerial attitudes and behavior
may not translate easily from one cultural setting to
another. Many responses of Chinese managers were bi-modal in
distribution while reliable averages were obtained in twelve
other national samples. Western models of research are not
always transferable to other cultural environments.

1078   American Chamber of Commerce in Hong Kong, The
         (1982) Living in Hong Kong. Hong Kong: the
         American Chamber of Commerce in Hong Kong.

This is a useful guide to the problems and opportunities in
living in Hong Kong. There is advice on shopping for non-
tourist goods (household products), residential services,
medical facilities, etc. One chapter deals with living in
Beijing, China.

1079   Baird, Inga S., Marjorie A. Lyles, and Robert
         Wharton (1990) "Attitudinal Differences Between
         American and Chinese Managers Regarding Joint
         Venture Management," Management International
         Review 30 (Special Issue): 53-68.

Chinese and U.S. managers were asked to describe the ideal
characteristics of a joint venture and a supervisor, as well
as the elements of their management philosophy. Chinese
managers significantly preferred merit rewards and an

impersonal management style. The ideal supervisor was paternalistic.

1080   Battat, Joseph Y. (1986) **Management in Post-Mao China: An Insider's View**. Ann Arbor, Michigan: UMI Research Press.

This work is an analysis of managerial training, policies and behavior in post-Mao China, while focusing on computer technologies. Several chapters deal with Chinese management practices, including how managers balance needs and demands from various sources.

1081   Beemish, Paul W. and Hui Y. Wang (1989) "Investing in China via Joint Ventures," **Management International Review** 29 (1): 57-64.

Data on 840 joint ventures with Chinese and foreign partners indicate a preference for locating in Special Economic Zones and for manufacturing activities. Chinese business values and social cultures demand a long-term, flexible attitude on the part of foreigners.

1082   Bond, Michael Harris (1988) "Finding Universal Dimensions of Individual Variation in Multicultural Studies of Values: The Rokeach and Chinese Value Surveys," **Journal of Personality and Social Psychology** 55 (December): 1009-15.

A comparison of two measures of cultural values on the individual level indicates that cross-cultural measurement of values is possible. Chinese values center around two dimensions: cultural inwardness (values of tradition over individuals) and social integration (stress on harmony in interpersonal relations).

1083   Bond, Michael Harris and Geert Hofstede (1989) "The Cash Value of Confucian Values," **Human Systems Management** 8 (3): 195-99.

This article contains a re-evaluation of Hofstede's forty-country study of work values and an extension by correlating work values scores with economic growth. After an analysis of Confucian-related values, the authors compare Hofstede's work with the senior author's previous findings. They find an overlap in scale item definitions when focusing on Confucian values. Using Bond's Chinese Value Survey (CVS) items, the authors find some correlation between CVS and economic growth.

1084   Bond, Michael H., Kwok Leung, and Kwok
        Choi Wan (1982) "How Does Cultural Collectivism
        Operate? The Impact of Task and Maintenance
        Contributions on Reward Distribution," Journal
        of Cross-Cultural Psychology 13 (June): 186-200.

Americans are members of a more individualistic culture
while Chinese are more collectivist. Chinese and American
students differed in how to reward an individual's
contributions in various scenarios. Hong Kong Chinese were
more egalitarian in terms of assignment of rewards.

1085   Browning, Graeme (1989) If Everybody Bought One
        Shoe: American Capitalism in Communist China.
        New York: Hill and Wang.

This journalistic description of contemporary China includes
interviews with American expatriates and Chinese workers.
There are economic, political and social analyses. Wages for
working for foreign firms are determined by the state, and
are set at least fifty percent higher than comparable wages
in Chinese firms. There are also chapters on the Japanese in
China and the problems of training workers.

1086   Burnett, Robert S. (1990) "Ni Zhao: Good Morning
        China," Business Horizons 33 (Nov/Dec): 65-71.

A large Canadian enterprise brought eleven trainees from
China for a one-year stay to study North American management
methods. Both parties learned how different the two national
business practices were. Language became a major difficulty,
as were behavioral expectations.

1087   Butterfield, Fox (1982) China: Alive in a Bitter
        Sea. New York: Times Books.

This work is a superior journalistic account of post-Mao
Chinese society. The work is a good introduction for
foreigners expecting to work in China. There is a good
description of the basic segment of Chinese society: the
danwei urban work unit.

1088   Campbell, Nigel (1986) China Strategies:
        The Inside Story. England and Hong Kong:
        University of Manchester/University of
        Hong Kong.

Surveys, examples, quotes, and case studies are used to
describe China's business climate, operating costs,
negotiation strategies, staffing problems, etc.

1089   Casey, Terry W. (1978) "Attitudes
        Toward Work Behavior Amongst Chinese
        Managers: A Tale of Two Cities," Academy
        of Management Proceedings: 272-76.

Samples of Chinese managers in Hong Kong and Singapore were
interviewed concerning perceived work pressures, allocation
of time, the need to form different kinds of relationships,
and degree of uncertainty.   Both samples exhibited a
pragmatic orientation and a high degree of similarity of
scale scores across dimensions.

1090   Chang, Samuel K.C. (1985) "American and
        Chinese Managers in U.S. Companies in Taiwan:
        A Comparison," California Management Review 27
        (Summer): 144-56.

Two-hundred top-level Chinese and American managers of U.S.-
owned companies and joint ventures in Taiwan were surveyed
in terms of their attitudes toward work. Chinese managers
were more accepting of paternalistic leadership, although
the two national samples equally accepted other values.

1091   Chang, Xu Lian (1987) "A Cross-Cultural
        Study on the Leadership Behavior of
        Chinese and Japanese Executives,"
        Asia Pacific Journal of Management 4
        (May): 203-9.

This study tests the Performance Maintenance Theory of
Leadership using 16,260 respondents in 53 Chinese factories.
The results are compared to the findings by Misumi, who used
a comparable Japanese sample. The Japanese exhibited higher
efficiency scores in terms of meetings and communication of
information, although the two cultures have similar dynamics
of leadership.

1092   Chang, Y.N. (1976) "Early Chinese Management
        Thought," California Management Review 19
        (Winter): 71-6.

There were two general managerial policies in classical
China: the "do-nothing" practice and the emphasis on the
control of subordinates. These two contradictory policies
form the basis of managerial theory and practices in use
today in China.

1093   Chevrier, Yves (1990) "Micropolitics and
        the Factory Director Responsibility System,"
        pp 107-33 in Deborah Davis and Ezra F. Vogel
        (eds.), <u>Chinese Society on the Eve of
        Tiananmen: The Impact of Reform</u>. Cambridge,
        Mass: The Council on East Asian Studies/Harvard
        University.

Employees in declining organizations have the alternatives
of "exit, voice, loyalty, or micro- and macro-politics." The
possible emergence in China of more autonomous management in
industry will force managers to engage in macro-politics.
This may be a unsettling factor in many areas of Chinese
society. Foreigners dealing with Chinese managers will face
an even more complex business environment than in the past.

1094   Chinese Culture Connection, The (1987), "Chinese
        Values and the Search for Culture-Free Dimensions
        of Culture," <u>Journal of Cross-Cultural Psychology</u>
        18 (June): 143-64.

A list of forty Chinese values was developed. The resulting
list was administered to 100 university students in each of
22 countries. The methodologies used followed Hofstede's
ecological factor analysis. The responses in 20 countries
matched a subset of 53 in Hofstede's sample.

1095   Chiu, Hungdah (1978-87) "Chinese Attitudes
        Toward International Law in the Post-Mao Era,
        1978-1987," <u>International Lawyer</u> 21 (Fall):
        1127-66.

A survey of Chinese legal literature indicates a different
view of foreigners' rights than expressed in the West. While
the desire to modernize has forced Chinese officials to
adjust their legal system vis-a-vis foreigners and
international legal practices, legal interpretations still
reflect government policy.

1096   Chow, Irene Hau-Siu, Andres Inn, and Lorand
        B. Szalay (1987) "Empirical Study of the
        Subjective Meanings of Culture Between American
        and Chinese," <u>Asia Pacific Journal of Management</u>
        4 (May): 144-51.

Americans and Hong Kong and PRC Chinese listed 100 stimulus
words concerning their cultures through free association,
using the Associative Group Analysis technique. This
technique tests the subjective meanings of culture of
respondents. Effective management styles are influenced by
the subjective meanings given to such terms as family, work
employment, etc.

1097   Chu, Chin-Ning (1988) **The Chinese Mind Game:**
        The Best Kept Trade Secret of the East.
        Beaverton, Oregon: AMC Publishing.

The author uses examples to illustrate the major concepts
that explain Chinese values and business-related behavior to
Westerners. Examples from Chinese history and philosophy
offer insights on how foreigners should conduct their
business with Chinese as well as Chinese business strategies
and practices. There are 36 strategies promoting success.
The insights on Chinese behavior are based on psychology and
the personal experiences of the author.

1098   Clare, Tod O. (1986) "The Business Challenge in
        China: Separating the Yin from the Yang," **Vital**
        Speeches 53 (October 15): 18-20.

The joint venture of American Motors with a Chinese company
to build jeeps is described. The author lists the major
problems faced by American Motors.

1099   Clare, Tod O. (1988) "Yin and Yang--and Jeeps
        in China," **Financier** 10 (October): 24-9.

China's culture and bureaucracy are very frustrating to
foreigners. This article describes the early successes and
later frustrations of the China-U.S. joint venture to build
jeeps.

1100   Clarke, Christopher M. (1987) "Changing
        the Context for Policy Implementation:
        Organizational and Personnel Reform in
        Post-Mao China," pp 25-47 in David M.
        Lampton (ed.), **Policy Implementation in**
        Post-Mao China. Berkeley: University of
        California Press.

There is an extended discussion of Post-Mao reforms of
personnel policies in various institutions, including
business. Factories were placed under a system of
responsibility and expected to make profits. Programs were
established to train managers and increase their prestige in
Chinese society. In addition to overstaffing, many
bureaucrats in factories and elsewhere were appointed for
political reasons. Others had been traumatized by the
Cultural Revolution and therefore do not wish to express any
independence of thought or initiative.

1101   Crainer, Stuart and Nigel Campbell (1986)
        "Only Patience Pays in China," **Management**
        Today (December): 68-9.

A study of Chinese business behavior indicates the existence
of a number of problems when foreigners conduct business in

China. UK firms should adopt Japan's long-term approach. The Chinese are inconsistent when applying the law, and it is difficult to motivate workers. Negotiations with Chinese are time-consuming and complex.

1102   Davidson, William H. (1987) "Creating and Managing Joint Ventures in China," California Management Review 29 (Summer): 77-94.

An analysis of the experiences of 35 persons involved in U.S.-China joint ventures points out a number of special problems faced by foreigners who wish to deal with the Chinese. Foreign participants need to write and exchange notes constantly with their hosts in order to avoid misunderstandings. Those wishing to deal with PRC personnel must be extremely patient.

1103   Davis, Deborah (1990) "Urban Job Mobility," pp 85-108 in Deborah Davis and Ezra F. Vogel (eds.), Chinese Society on the Eve of Tiananmen: The Impact of Reform. Cambridge, Mass: The Council on East Asian Studies/Harvard University.

The unique features of post-Mao labor practices are influenced by policy shifts that maintain the individual's dependence on the Chinese Communist Party and the state. Hiring procedures handicap foreign employers.

1104   Dennis, Robert and Shipley Munson (1983) "Trading with China: A Boom for Some—A Disappointment with Many," Management Review 72 (May): 13-20.

Persons who have engaged in trade with China offer their advice. The result is a series of points on doing business in China. There is information on sources of profitability, institutional arrangements, the Chinese negotiating styles, and the political context of business in China. Negotiation elements in China include (1) the need to be invited to enter negotiations, (2) all communications are monitored, (3) there is a Chinese home-court advantage, (4) the time factor, and (5) the superior ability of Chinese negotiators.

1105   Earley, P. Christopher (1989) "Social Loafing and Collectivism: A Comparison of the United States and the People's republic of China," Administrative Science Quarterly 34 (December): 565-81.

Managerial trainees from China and the U.S. were compared in terms of their amount of social loafing behavior under different tasks accountability settings. Social loafing refers to reduced performance of individuals acting as part of a group. Social loafing was observed for the American participants, defined as individualistic, but not for the Chinese (collectivistic) participants. An individualist's performance in a group setting was less than that when working alone. Collectivists did not exhibit social loafing: performance was highest for collectivists in a high shared-responsibility setting.

1106   Eliasoph, Ellen (1987) **Law and Business Practice in Shanghai**. Hong Kong: Longman group (Far East) Ltd.

Shanghai is China's major commercial center whose businesspersons are the most familiar with Westerners and Western behavior. This work offers practical advice on conducting business in China.

1107   Engholm, Christopher (1989) **The China Venture: America's Encounter with the People's Republic of China**. Glenview, Il.: Scott, Foresman.

Doing business with China demands the application of three general principles: (1) a long-range commitment, (2) the development of political alliances, and (3) the establishment of a small niche at first. Case studies and surveys of U.S. executives involved in business in China explain the social, political, and business environments of China.

1108   Farh, Jiing-Lih, Gregory H. Dobbins, and Bor-Shiuan Cheng (1991) "Cultural Relativity in Action: A Comparison of Self-Ratings Made by Chinese and U.S. Workers," **Personnel Psychology** 44 (Spring): 129-42.

Self-ratings of performance using 982 leader-subordinate dyads from nine organizations in Taiwan indicated that subordinates rated their job performance less favorably than their supervisors, resulting in a "modesty bias." This result, uniform across gender, age, and educational levels, is contrary to that found using U.S. samples. Chinese employees are more reluctant than Americans to promote their own effectiveness and talents.

1109   Farh, Jiing-Lih, Philip M. Podsakoff, and Bor-Shiuan Cheng (1987) "Culture-Free Leadership Effectiveness Versus Moderators of Leadership Behavior: An Extension and Test of Kerr and Jermier's Substitute for Leadership Model in Taiwan," **Journal of International Business Studies** 18 (Fall): 43-60.

195 employees of the Ministry of Communications of Taiwan were surveyed to measure the effect of situational factors on leaders' influence on the performance of subordinates. Situational factors were found to be less significant than

the perception that leaders administered rewards appropriate to the behavior of subordinates.

1110   Foster, Lawrence W. and Lisa Tosi (1990)
        "Business in China: A Year After Tiananmen,"
        Journal of Business Strategy 11 (May/June): 22-27.

Westerners and Chinese hold different views of the world and of their business goals. The political and cultural contexts of the Chinese also differ from those in other nations. Overlooking these differences will result in business failure when dealing with the Chinese.

1111   Frankenstein, John (1990) "The Chinese Foreign
        Trade Environment," International Studies of
        Management and Organization 20 (Spring/Summer):
        135-48.

The article includes an analysis of responses from a 1984 survey of Chinese business practices, attitudes, and policies as compared to the findings in a 1988 study. The "spiral model" of behavior is found to be still useful. This model includes continuous engagement and negotiation while deepening commitment. A comparison of two surveys indicates that Chinese business goals are in transition.

1112   Garratt, Bob (1981) "Contrasts in Chinese
        and Western Management Thinking," Leadership
        & Organization Development Journal 2 (1): 17-23.

Chinese management thought is a blend of Confucianism and Maoism. Chinese values dealing with time, causality, the lesser importance of the individual over the collective, and free will of persons differ from their Western counterparts.

1113   Gold, Thomas B. (1990) "Urban Private Business and
        Social Change," pp 157-78 in Deborah Davis and Ezra
        F. Vogel (eds.), Chinese Society on the Eve of
        Tiananmen: The Impact of Reform. Cambridge, Mass:
        Council on East Asian Studies/Harvard University.

The recent emergence of private businesses in post-Mao China exacerbated certain already-existing conditions in China, such as corruption and income inequality. Private businesses may lose their relative independence as China's leaders struggle to maintain their power and control. Such trends have implications for foreign business persons in China.

1114   Graf, Lee A., Masoud Hemmasi, John A. Lust,
        and Yusua Liang (1990) "Perceptions of
        Desirable Organizational Reforms in Chinese
        State Enterprises," International Studies of
        Management and Organization 20 (Spring/Summer):
        47-56.

Cultural values underlie work expectations and job
attitudes. The changing business-related value systems in
China (from a Soviet to a more free-enterprise system) are
in turn changing work-related attitudes and perceptions. A
sample of 239 managers from nine research institutes
indicates that work-related attitudes are changing in some
respects while traditional values are maintained in others.
Cooperation is still promoted and should be both increased
and rewarded. Superior work should be rewarded through
individual bonuses if wage differentials are kept minimal.

1115   Granick, David (1990) Chinese State Enterprise: A
        Regional Property Rights Analysis. Chicago: The
        University of Chicago Press.

China's urban state-owned industrial enterprises are
described in terms of their organizational structures, means
of control, means of appointment of cadres, and allocation
of wages and labor. Based on twenty case studies conducted
during 1981-85, qualitative and quantitative data were
collected that test a number of hypotheses related to
production, quota-meeting factors, etc. There are
discussions of the selection and duties of foremen and other
cadres. The Chinese enterprise model is compared with the
Soviet and other models.

1116   Grieves, Robert (1986) "A Very Costly Business
        for Foreigners in China," Asian Business 22 (May):
        60-1.

Doing business in China is very costly. Hotel charges can
be up to $90,000 per year plus a management fee and charges
for utilities. Expatriates must be paid hardship bonus for
working in China. High costs may result in low profits.

1117   Griffiths, Robert D. (1986) "'Guanxi' is
        the Secret to Success for American Companies
        in Southern Taiwan," Business America 9
        (November): 12-13.

Southern Taiwan is an area eager to import U.S. goods.
Successful business demands knowledge of the local customs
and values; promotion material should be printed in the
local language. An expatriate presence is necessary for a
number of reasons.

1118   Grub, Phillip D. (1987) "A Yen for Yuan:
        Trading and Investing in the China Market,"
        Business Horizons 30 (July/August): 16-24.

The article offers descriptions of the Chinese business environment. There are also detailed information on the Chinese business style and protocols.

1119   Henderson, Gail E. and Myron S. Cohen (1984)
        The Chinese Hospital: A Socialist Work Unit.
        New Haven: Yale University Press.

This is a thorough report of fieldwork conducted during 1979-80 in Central China of a large hospital complex of 830 persons, including medical staff, construction workers, cooks, child care personnel, etc. The complex, an administrative work unit called a "danwei," controls all aspects of a member's life, including food, housing, education, and work. Most Chinese workers "loaned" to foreign employers maintain their prime identity and loyalty to their original danwei. The danwei unit dominates their members' lives. Someone expecting to use mainland Chinese labor would gain insights on workers' orientations and motivations from the first half of this work. See also Butterfield (1087).

1120   Hendryx, Steven R. (1986) "The China Trade:
        Making it Work," Harvard Business Review 64
        (July/August): 75, 81-84.

Chinese organizational practices include a lack of cooperation/coordination among different units and a fear of decision-making.

1121   Ho, Alfred Luo-liang (1990) Joint Ventures
        in the People's Republic of China: Can Capitalism
        and Communism Coexist? Westport, Conn: Praeger.

The author describes the Chinese legal structure for establishing and maintaining joint ventures in China. There are also discussions of the complex political and cultural environments related to business. The author identifies and describes the major joint ventures in China.

1122   Holton, Richard H. (1990) "Human Resource
        Management in the People's Republic of China,"
        Management International Review 30 (Special
        Issue): 121-136.

Foreign managers working in China must realize the importance of the danwei work unit, the value of economic egalitarianism, and the pervasiveness of the government bureaucracy. When beginning a new venture, there should be contractual clauses allowing for the dismissal of workers after a probationary period, and the ability to set wages and establish bonuses.

1123   Hsu, Paul S.C. (1984) "The Influence of Family
        Structure and Values on Business Organizations
        in Oriental Cultures: A Comparison of China and
        Japan," Proceedings of the Academy of International
        Business: 754-68.

Chinese and Japanese enterprises differ in many respects. Many of these differences reflect national differences in cultural and family values. Inheritance values encourage Chinese firms to be shorter lived than Japanese firms.

1124   Huo, Y. Paul and Donna M. Randall (1991)
        "Exploring Subcultural Differences in Hofstede's
        Value Survey: The Case of the Chinese,"
        Asia Pacific Journal of Management 8
        (October): 159-73.

Hofstede's Value Survey Module (VSM) is used to compare four subcultural groupings in Chinese-populated regions. The VSM scores revealed substantial sub-cultural differences in how subjects viewed the world. The social and economic conditions in each region influenced VSM scores.

1125   Hwang, Dennis and Michael Blue (1991) "A
        Comparative Analysis of the Requirements to
        Become a CPA in China, Taiwan and the
        United States," Journal of Global Business 2
        (Spring): 35-42.

The criteria in China, Taiwan, and the United States for becoming a CPA differ from one country to another, indicating different cultural values. In China and Taiwan, qualified instructors may be exempt from taking the CPA exams. There are no specific college course requirements in those two nations.

1126   Jacobs, J. Bruce (1982) "The Concept
        of Guanxi and Local Politics in a Rural
        Chinese Setting," pp 209-36 in Sidney L.
        Greenblatt, Richard W. Wilson, and Amy
        Auerbacher Wilson (eds.), Social Interaction
        in Chinese Society. New York: Praeger Publishers.

Although this book chapter deals with political power and influence in a small Chinese township, its discussion of the guanxi relationship illustrates its central importance underlying most social relationships. No one can deal effectively with the Chinese without understanding the nature and dynamics of the guanxi relationship.

1127   Jamal, Mohammad and Jia-Lin Xie (1991) "The
        Relationship Between Managerial Style and
        Job Involvement, Job Satisfaction, Perceived
        Job Stress and Turnover-Motivation in China,"
        International Journal of Management 8 (September):
        682-94.

The participative style of management in China leads to
higher levels of job involvement, job satisfaction, and
higher commitment, and lower levels of perceived job stress.
These findings based on 307 Chinese managers and workers are
similar to findings based on Western samples.

1128   Jones, Kay M. (1990) "China Syndrome: Westerners
        Learn to Read the Tea Leaves," Management Review
        79 (April): 46-9.

It is very easy to misinterpret the validity of China's
reforms, the encouragement of foreign business, and the
potentials of the Chinese market. The author provides tips
on successful dealing while in China. Few U.S. consumer
products, for example, will be sold in China.

1129   Joy, Robert O. (1989) "Cultural and Procedural
        Differences that Influence Business Strategies and
        Operations in the People's Republic of China,"
        Advanced Management Journal 54 (Summer): 29-33.

There are many differences between the Chinese and American
cultures. Ways of being polite and negotiating differ, as
does the concept of responsibility. The author recommends
joint ventures as the best way to conduct business in China.

1130   Kirkbride, Paul S. and Shae Wan Chaw (1987) "The
        Cross-Cultural Transfer of Organization Cultures:
        Two Case Studies of Corporate Mission Statements,"
        Asia Pacific Journal of Management 5 (September):
        55-66.

Mission statements of two foreign firms located in Hong Kong
are compared to the cultural values dominant in Hong Kong.
Their statements of general principles and goals are
compared to Hong Kong dominant values in terms of Hofstede's
four cultural dimensions. There exist large gaps between
foreign corporate culture statements and the local value
system. Hong Kong values include preferences for
centralization and autocracy. The two foreign companies are
low on these values.

1131   Kotkin, Joel (1987) "The Chinese Way of Business,"
        Inc. 9 (June): 66-70.

This article describes a company in Thailand owned by an
ethnic-Chinese. It is a family-run business in which

relatives are sent to foreign countries to obtain citizenship and manage local divisions.

1132   Kung, Lydia (1983) <u>Factory Women in Taiwan</u>. Ann Arbor: UMI Research Press.

The author conducted research in Northern Taiwan during 1974 and focused her attention on women working in light industry. The employment careers of Chinese women are influenced by the Chinese values related to women and daughters. There are sections dealing with the respondents' values and worldview, dating and marriage patterns by industry, relations in the workplace, control of income, and women's position in society and in relation to their parents.

1133   Laaksonen, Oiva (1977) "The Power Structure of Chinese Officials," <u>International Studies of Management and Organization</u> 7 (Spring): 71-90.

Chinese and capitalist forms of managerial/bureaucratic organizations are compared in terms of selected structural factors. The article focuses on national differences in the relative degrees of five dimensions of power (ideological, economic, coercive, normative, and communicative).

1134   Laaksonen, Oiva (1984) "The Management and Power Structure of Chinese Enterprises During and After the Cultural Revolution; With Empirical Data Comparing Chinese and European Enterprises," <u>Organization Studies</u> 5 (1): 1-22.

The author describes the changing power and reward systems in Post-Mao China, as influenced by various power centers. The Chinese industrial power structure is compared to those in European firms using a comparable questionnaire.

1135   Laaksonen, Oiva (1988) <u>Management in China During and After Mao in Enterprises, Government, and Party</u>. Berlin and New York: Walter de Gruyter.

Beginning with an essay on China's human and material resources and Chinese culture, the author reviews the traditional schools of management followed before Mao. Modern managerial values and behavior are presented and compared to their counterparts in Japan and Europe. There are included studies on decision-making and other empirical analyses.

1136   Lee, Peter N.S. (1987) <u>Industrial Management and Economic Reform in China, 1949-1984</u>. Hong Kong: Oxford University Press.

The author reviews major industrial and development policies in China during 1949-84. Several chapters deal with the process of managerial policy-making in relation to cultural values and government policy. Leaders in China are expected to be powerful and faction-oriented. Command management reflects and is similar to China's command economy.

1137   Lingnan University Research Institute (1982) "Principles of Management in a Socialist Economy," <u>International Studies of Management and Organization</u> 12 (Summer): 20-44.

A unit of a Chinese research institute offers its members' view of "democratic centralism": the official managerial philosophy of the Chinese Communist Party and its ideal characteristics at all organizational levels. This policy promises to be a dominant factor in all managerial activities in China, whether national or foreign, for some time.

1138   Lockett, Martin (1987) "China's Special Economic Zones: The Cultural and Managerial Challenges," <u>Journal of General Management</u> 12 (Spring): 21-31.

Special Economic Zones in China are increasing in size and number. They offer challenges and advantages to foreign managers due to China's values and workways. There are several ways of ensuring success in China.

1139   Lockett, Martin (1988) "Culture and the Problems of Chinese Management," <u>Organization Studies</u> 9 (4): 475-96.

This article details Chinese organizational structure and presents an innovative model of a response to an actual machinery failure in a factory. The latter describes the organizational dynamics of a Chinese bureaucracy in action. Chinese cultural values are unlikely to accept Western managerial practices, though some adoption of Western methods may reduce some of China's managerial problems.

1140   Mann, Jim (1989) <u>Beijing Jeep: The Short, Unhappy Romance of American Business in China</u>. New York: Simon and Schuster.

The frustrations of doing business in China and dealing with Chinese corporate culture are thoroughly recounted in this journalistic case study of the AMC-China joint venture to build American jeeps in Beijing. One finding was that loyalty ties of workers were stronger to their danwei than to the foreign-owned company. The most powerful person in the plant was the local representative of the Chinese Communist Party rather than the American director.

1141   Macleod, Roderick (1988) China, Inc.: How to Do Business with the Chinese. New York: Bantam Books.

A practical guide on conducting business in China, the work also includes ten case histories. Business conflicts and misunderstandings are presented and analyzed from the Chinese perspective. There are also sections on negotiations, how to establish contact, and the special problems faced by expatriates living in China.

1142   McDonald, Gael and Raymond A. Zepp (1988) "Ethical Perceptions of Hong Kong Chinese Business Managers," Journal of Business Ethics 7 (November): 835-45.

97 middle level Chinese managers in Hong Kong who enrolled in the MBA program at the University of East Asia, Macau, were surveyed in terms of their reactions to thirteen situations. They perceived their peers as less ethical than they. There was little consistency among responses by ethical situation.

1143   McGuinness, Norman, Nigel Campbell, and James Leontiades (1991) "Selling Machinery to China: Chinese Perceptions of Strategies and Relationships," Journal of International Business Studies 22 (2): 187-207.

Chinese perceptions of suppliers (Germany, Switzerland, U.K., Italy, Japan, and France) of machinery indicate that strategies based on quality and service are preferred. Friendship feelings are less important than expected. Product quality was perceived to be highest in Swiss and German firms. Japanese were evaluated as highest in terms of early entry into China and service efforts.

1144   Mente, Boye Lafayette De (1989) Chinese Etiquette & Ethics in Business. Lincolnwood, Illinois: NTC Business Books.

The author describes the values, national character, and business-related behavior of Chinese. Although focusing on business relations, there are discussions of material useful for tourists and expatriates. Appendices list useful phrases, addresses, and sources of information.

1145   Montagu-Pollock, Matthew (1991) "All the
        Right Connections: China Management Has
        Amazing Advantages Over "Modern" Methods,"
        Asian Business 27 (January): 20-4.

Typical Chinese business practices include an emphasis on
guanxi (personal relations), entrepreneurship, and low
capitalization businesses. Chinese managers will succeed
when (1) speed of response is necessary and (2) where deal-
making skills are important.

1146   Myers, Howard (1987) "The China Business Puzzle,"
        Business Horizons 30 (July/August): 25-28.

Chinese business culture is described in terms of the values
of the China-first orientation, group connections, the noncompetitive ethic, and the control imperative.

1147   Negandhi, Anant R. (1973) Management and Economic
        Development: The Case of Taiwan. The Hague:
        Martenus Nijhoff.

Managerial practices in Taiwan among local enterprises and
Japanese and U.S. subsidiaries are compared and contrasted.
The author also compares his Taiwanese data with those from
India, the Philippines and three Latin American countries.
Japanese and local firms were adopting selected American
managerial practices, such as the consultative leadership
style. U.S. subsidiaries achieved higher levels of
corporation among various units.

1148   Nevis, Edwin C. (1983) "Cultural Assumptions and
        Productivity: The United States and China," Sloan
        Management Review 24 (Spring): 17-29.

The author presents the Chinese and U.S. cultural values and
their influence on those two countries' managerial behavior.
The comparisons are done through a Hierarchies of Needs
model as well as a survey of motivational factors among
Chinese workers. The Needs ranks of American workers are:
individual development, self-esteem, belonging, safety, and
physiological. The Chinese Need rankings are: self-
actualization through the service of society, safety,
physiological and belonging. The article concludes with a
discussion of the causes and implications of Needs rankings
of values for Americans.

1149   Oh, Tai K. (1976) "Theory Y in the People's
        Republic of China," California Management Review
        19 (Winter): 77-84.

China's contemporary managerial official ideology is
analyzed within the framework of McGregor's Theory Y of
management.

1150   Osland, Gregory F. (1990) "Doing Business
        in China: A Framework for Cross-Cultural
        Understanding," Marketing Intelligence and
        Planning 8 (4): 4-14.

The author develops a conceptual model of communication
based on three dimensions. The model is used to describe the
Chinese way of doing business, including the practices of
guanxi and deference to age and rank. The Communist Party is
an all-pervasive element in all facets of business policy
and activities. Foreign companies that establish long-term
relationships and exhibit commitment gain preferential
treatment.

1151   Overgaard, Herman O.J. (1983) "Marketing in the
        People's Republic of China," pp 459-89 in Herman
        O.J. Overgaard et al. (eds.), International Business:
        The Canadian Way. Dubuque, Iowa: Kendal/Hunt
        Publishing Company.

Although the Canadian-oriented export-import data (1968-71)
with China are dated, the chapter includes still-useful
advice on Chinese business protocols, selection of proper
bureaucratic channels, etc.

1152   Pegels, C. Carl (1987) Management and Industry
        in China. New York: Praeger.

This book provides an overview of business in general in
China. A number of chapters deals with Chinese managerial
practices and summaries of surveys dealing with Chinese
perceptions and comparisons. Chinese managers viewed
themselves as relatively aggressive Pioneer and Conqueror
managerial types. Half of the Chinese managers defined
themselves as Pioneers (flexible, creative, extroverted,
intuitive, restless). The same proportion of a sample of
American managers defined themselves as Diplomats (inspired
confidence, steady but flexible within acceptable limits,
strategic directed).

1153   Piturro, Marlene C. (1991) "US West in China:
        A Case Of Innocents Abroad," Management Review
        80 (July): 54-7.

US West executives believed they had won the world's largest
cable TV Franchise in Hong Kong, although the $1 billion
contract collapsed 18 months later. The failure was due in
part to US West's lack of knowledge of how business is
conducted in Hong Kong. A source of confusion was the Asian
view that a contract is open to change as circumstances
dictate.

1154   Pratt, Daniel D. (1991) "Conceptions of Self
        Within China and the United States: Contrasting
        Foundations for Adult Education," International
        Journal of Intercultural Relations 15 (3): 285-310.

The Chinese construction of the self emphasizes family,
societal roles, hierarchical relationships, and maintenance
of stability. The U.S. concept of self is quite different.
These cultural differences have important consequences for
educational programs of adults, including business-related
programs.

1155   Ram, Jane (1987) "Asia Conjures Wind and Water
        to Boost Business," International Management
        42 (July/August): 57-60.

Accepting Asian values and traditional patterns of beliefs
in Hong Kong can increase productivity and profits. Using as
consultant an expert in fung shui (wind and water) is often
necessary to cure workers' illnesses, for correctly placing
the front door of a business, and to determine when to
inaugurate a company in order to give it good luck. In one
office, an expert's suggestion to "put something red on the
wall up there" cured a secretary's neck and back pains.

1156   Redding, S. Gordon (1990) The Spirit of Chinese
        Capitalism. Berlin and New York: Walter de Gruyter.

Overseas Chinese play an important part in national and
international commerce throughout the Pacific Rim. This work
describes the values of the overseas Chinese (Confucianism
and familism). The distinctive aspect of Chinese enterprises
is that they are usually small family businesses managed by
paternalistic leaders. Much of the work's information is
based on the accounts of Chinese-ethnic businessmen in four
Pacific Rim countries.

1157   Redding, S. Gordon and Michael Ng (1982) "The
        Role of 'Face' in Organizational Perceptions of
        Chinese Managers," Organization Studies 3 (3):
        201-20.

The concern for face (need for comfortable interaction and
to avoid embarrassment) is especially strong in Asian
cultures. A study of Chinese managers in Hong Kong indicates
all (100%) respondents felt shame as a result of loss of
face. The threat of a loss of face or respect was a major
motivator and concern among managers. Business behavior was
heavily influenced by this concern.

1158   Redding, S. Gordon and Michael Ng (1983) "The Role
        of 'Face' in the Organizational Perceptions of
        Chinese Managers," International Studies of
        Management and Organization 13 (Fall): 92-123.

The concept of "face" is central in Chinese culture. It is
as significant in Chinese organizational behavior. "Face"
includes the concepts of (1) moral character and integrity
and (2) one's reputation based on one's efforts and personal
success. Findings are presented from a survey of 102 Chinese
middle-level executives in Hong Kong. All of the sample
indicated "face" as greatly influencing their daily business
activities.

1159   Schell, Orville (1986) To Get Rich is Glorious:
        China in the 80s. Revised Edition. New York:
        New American Library.

While not a book on business in China per se, the work is an
excellent introduction to Post-Mao China and Chinese
culture. Those expecting to travel to China or live there
will find this book a good preparation.

1160   Schermerhorn, John R., Jr. (1987) "Organizational
        Features of Chinese Industrial Enterprise: Paradoxes
        of Stability in Times of Change," The Academy of
        Management Executive 1 (3): 345-9.

Chinese business practices are very different from those in
America. The social, economic, and political environments
are very different in China. There are great differences in
terms of an organization's concern for the welfare of its
members. The authority structures have no U.S. equivalent.

1161   Schermerhorn, John R., Jr. and Michael H.
        Bond (1991) "Upward and Downward Influence
        Tactics in Managerial Networks:"
        A Comparative Study of Hong Kong Chinese
        and Americans," Asia Pacific Journal of
        Management 8 (October): 147-58.

203 part-time MBA students in Hong Kong and the U.S. were
asked to evaluate scenarios describing preferred managerial
interpersonal strategies. There were slight cultural
differences in preferred strategies. Chinese subjects were
more likely to praise and flatter subordinates, while
Americans were more likely to prefer ingratiation with
superiors.

1162   Schermerhorn, John R., Jr. and Mee-Kau Nyaw (1990)
        "Managerial Leadership in Chinese Industrial
        Enterprises," International Studies of Management
        and Organization 20 (Spring/Summer): 9-22.

The authors develop several models in this essay on the
paradoxical nature of management demands and behavior in
modern China. Enterprises operate both as independent profit
centers and parts of a centralized plan controlled by
political appointees. Enterprises consist of "simultaneous
systems" of which business is only one sub-system. In the
First Automobile Works, 80% of all workers are employed in
ways totally unrelated to car production.

1163   Seligman, Scott D. (1989) Dealing with
        the Chinese: A Practical Guide to Business
        Etiquette in the People's Republic Today.
        New York: Warner Books, Inc.

This is one of the most complete books on Chinese culture
and business protocol available. The author discusses all
aspects of Chinese-style business (seating arrangements,
banquet behavior, presentations, use of interpreters, etc.)
and social behavior (saving face, showing respect, body
language, etc.). The sections on "Getting Things Done" and
on negotiations are also superior.

1164   Silin, Robert H. (1976) Leadership and Values:
        The Organization of Large-Scale Taiwanese
        Enterprise. Cambridge, Mass: Harvard University
        Press.

This study of a large manufacturing enterprise in Taiwan
describes the dominant values and patterns of behavior
discovered during fieldwork conducted in 1970. The focus
includes managerial styles and national character. There was
a great reluctance to report negative news, which tended to
isolate the administrative leaders. Their awareness of this
pattern forced them to develop informal and other channels
of information. One result was the managers' support of
"communication brokers" whose role is to informally pass on
information to leaders. Cliquishness is extremely common
among members of a work division or section, making
universalistic standards of rewards difficult. Numerous
quotes from workers and managers illustrate the author's
main findings.

1165   Sin, Yat-Ming and Hon-Ming Sin (1984)
        "Businessmen's Attitudes Towards Advertising:
        A Cross-Cultural Study," Proceedings of the
        Academy of International Business: 89-99.

Chinese-ethnic managers and expatriates in Hong Kong
differed in terms of their attitudes toward advertising.
Chinese managers were much more critical of advertising
practices than were foreigners.

1166   Smith, Larry A. and Joan Mills (1988)
        "Implementing Project Management in China,"
        International Journal of Management 5
        (December): 347-53.

U.S. project management techniques will not easily transfer
to a Chinese environment. Chinese managers avoid risk,
since there is no reward for successful risk taking. Envy
is a powerful motivator, and Chinese co-workers will prevent
others from achieving personal goals. The Chinese are not
used to working as teams. Other Chinese values and
practices make the successful transfer of U.S.-style
management unlikely.

1167   Specter, Christine Mielsen and Janet Stern
        Solomon (1990) "The Human Resource Factor in
        Chinese Management Reform," International
        Studies of Management and Organization 20
        (Spring/Summer): 69-84.

The attitudes and motivations of future managers in Shanghai
and in two U.S. universities are measured in terms of nine
factors in predicting managerial success. Shanghai students
were lower in terms of need for occupational achievement,
self-description of the level of their intelligence, self-
assurance, decisiveness and initiative. They were higher on
their need for security.

1168   Stewart, Sally and Chong Chung Him (1990)
        "Chinese Winners: Views of Senior PRC
        Managers on the Reasons for Their Success,"
        International Studies of Management and
        Organization 20 (Spring/Summer): 57-68.

Chinese managers of an electronic company were asked to
explain the reasons for their organizational success. This
measurement of managerial self-concept illuminates cultural
values of Chinese managers. Training was seen as the most
significant element in those successes, in addition to
planning and reading official documents. Attending meetings
was seen as less productive but necessary. The Chinese
managers had success ratings similar to those of an American
sample.

1169   Stross, Randall E. (1991) **Bulls in the**
        China Shop: And Other Sino-American
        Encounters. New York: Pantheon.

Doing business in China is a unique experience. There are
many Sino-U.S. cultural misunderstandings of procedures,
goals, and definitions of means. While much of the book
deals with political issues, there are a number of very
instructive business-related sections.

1170   Tai, Lawrence S.T. (1988) "Doing Business in the
        People's Republic of China: Some Keys to Success,"
        Management International Review 28 (1): 5-9

Doing business in China demands knowledge of Chinese culture
and customs, including how the Chinese deal with foreigners.
Often, the objectives of Chinese and foreigners are
different. A long-term perspective is necessary.

1171   Tung, Rosalie L. (1981) "Patterns of Motivation
        in Chinese Industrial Enterprises," **The Academy**
        of Management Review 6 (July): 481-9.

Chinese workers are motivated through rule enforcement,
external rewards, and internalized motivation. In addition,
there are a number of nonmaterial incentives that must be
utilized if foreign manufacturers expect to be successful in
China.

1172   Tung, Rosalie L. (1982) "Reforms of the
        Economic and Management Systems in China,"
        International Studies of Management and
        Organization 12 (Summer): 3-19.

The author surveys the economic and managerial reforms in
China based on the "Four Modernization" program. These are
still official policy.

1173   Turner-Gottschang, Karen and Linda A. Reed
        (1987) **China bound: A Guide to Academic Life**
        and Work in the PRC. Washington, D.C.: National
        Academy Press.

A general review of life in China is presented from a
Western perspective. There are also detailed descriptions of
how foreigners live while working in China.

1174   Walder, Andrew G. (1984) "Worker Participation
        or Ritual of Power? Form and Substance in the
        Chinese Expatriate," pp 541-58 in Bernhard Wilpert
        and Arndt Gorge (eds.), International Perspectives
        on Organizational Democracy Vol II. New York: John
        Wiley & Sons.

Post-Mao China has organized work and workers in unique
ways. The Communist Party controls the decision-making and
reward processes through extensive record keeping and
control of resources (housing, food, education, job
classification). While the structures of organization appear
to be democratic and worker-controlled, rewards are
available only to those who express "correct" political
opinions and official ideology.

1175   Walder, Andrew G. (1986) Communist Neo-
        Traditionalism: Work and Authority in Chinese
        Industry. Berkeley: University of California
        Press.

Modern Chinese organization of work in large enterprises
differs from comparable Soviet, Japanese, and U.S. models.
Chinese workers are more dependent upon their superiors,
vertical and personalistic ties are stronger and allocation
of reward is extremely particularistic. Party ideology is
paid lip service while patron-clients ties are used to
allocate scarce resources (such as housing and education).
Patronage and clientism have become the keys to the
understanding of Chinese work patterns. The author calls
these new relationships "neo-traditionalism."

1176   Wall, James A, Jr. (1990) "Managers in the People's
        Republic of China," The Academy of Management
        Executive 4 (May): 19-32.

175 interviews with Chinese managers and workers indicate
that managers are in a "low power" situation. Managerial
power is based on interpersonal attraction, offering favors,
and selectively enforcing rules. Management success is
strongly based on guanxi ("back door") relationships and
abilities.

1177   Warner, Malcolm editor, (1987) Management
        Reforms in China New York: St. Martin's Press.

There are a number of managerial issues in post-Mao China.
Included are accounts of teaching quality performance,
marketing concepts, and the value of service excellence to
Chinese workers and cadres. One chapter contains detailed
descriptions of work incentives strategies in an industrial
enterprise: bonuses, wage differentials, and motivational
factors. Material incentives in the forms of wage increases

and bonuses were found to be prime motivators among a sample of workers and cadres.

1178   **Wenzhong, Hu and Cornelius L. Grove (1991)**
        Encountering The Chinese: A Guide for Americans
        Yarmouth, Maine: Intercultural Press.

This work offers concrete and detailed advice on Chinese business protocol and behavior. Chapter topics include Chinese national character, social values, time use, titles, and banquet behavior.

1179   **Wheeler, Ladd, Harry T. Reis, and Michael**
        Harris Bond (1989) "Collectivism-Individualism
        in Everyday Social Life: The Middle Kingdom and
        the Melting Pot," Journal of Personality and
        Social Psychology 57 (July): 79-86.

American students reflect their culture's emphasis on individualism while Chinese students in Hong Kong are more collectivist in their orientation. The Hong Kong students had half as many interactions over a two-week period with fewer persons.

1180   **Whyte, Lynn T. III (1978) Careers in Shanghai:**
        The Social Guidance of Personal Energies in a
        Developing Chinese City 1949-1966. Berkeley:
        University of California Press.

A study of career and work patterns in China's most commercial city indicates an economic system subordinate to the political institution. This work includes descriptions of how government policies influence which jobs are made available (or unavailable) to applicants. These policies lead to overstaffing, selected motivational/reward strategies and unique productivity and job distribution problems.

1181   **Whyte, Martin King (1973) "Bureaucracy and**
        Modernization in China: The Maoist Critique,"
        American Sociological Review 38 (April): 149-63.

Chinese bureaucratic forms are influenced by China's social contexts (culture, ideology) as well as structural elements (size, hierarchy, and division of labor).

1182   Whyte, Martin King and W.L. Parish (1984)
        Urban Life in Contemporary China, Chicago:
        University of Chicago Press.

This book offers a general description of urban life in
modern China. It includes extended discussions of the
organization and control of person's activities by their
danwei work units.

1183   Wickman, Michael editor (1975) Living in Hong
        Kong. Hong Kong: Amcham Publications Hong Kong
        Limited.

While dated, this work offers useful advice for expatriates
and tourists on living and working in Hong Kong. The advice
covers issues that must be faced in other foreign locations.

1184   Wilson, Richard W. and Ann Wang Pusey (1982)
        "Achievement Motivation and Small-Business
        Relationship in Chinese Society," pp 195-208 in
        Sidney L. Greenblatt, Richard W. Wilson, and
        Amy Auerbacher Wilson (eds.) Social Interaction
        in Chinese Society. New York: Praeger.

Achievement motivation theory predicts that children
socialized to be less individualistic and more group-
oriented would have low achievement successes. But previous
studies indicate that Chinese are as achievement oriented as
Anglo American subjects. Success for the Chinese is a group
enterprise. This chapter concludes with a description of
fieldwork conducted in a Chinese restaurant in the U.S. The
workers were high in loyalty, sharing, and familism.

1185   Wing-Yue, Leung (1988) Smashing the Iron Rice Pot:
        Workers and Unions in China's Socialism. Hong Kong:
        Asia Monitor Resource Center.

Focusing on trade union and organized labor, this book
contains discussions of lifelong employment and its future,
China's labor problems in general, special economic zones,
workers' incomes, and living conditions.

1186   Winkler, Edwin (1987) "Statism and Familism on
        Taiwan," pp 173-206 in George C. Lodge and Ezra
        F. Vogel (eds.), Ideology and National
        Competitiveness: An Analysis of Nine Countries.
        Boston: Harvard Business School Press.

The author discusses the national character and values of
Taiwanese. The national ideology, based on international
politics and statism, constrains business-oriented values.

1187   Yao, Esther Lee (1987) "Cultivating Guanxi
        (Personal Relationships) with Chinese Partners,"
        Business Marketing 72 (January): 62, 64 and 66.

The Chinese have distinct views of leadership and social
relationships. Personal relationships are very important but
take a long time to establish. The article contains other
advice on how to manage Chinese subordinates and deal with
Chinese peers.

1188   Yao, Esther Lee (1988) "Venturing Through
        China's Open Door'," Business Marketing 73
        (February): 63-6.

Those hoping to conduct business in China must keep a number
of China's social/cultural values in mind. Group/societal
welfare is more important than individual gain. Class, rank,
and age are respected. Accountability is at the group rather
than the individual level. Non-verbal and casual
communications are taken very seriously.

1189   Yau, Oliver H.M. (1988) "Chinese Cultural
        Values: Their Dimensions and Marketing
        Implications" European Journal of Marketing
        22 (5): 44-57.

Chinese values can be classified along the dimensions of
man-to-nature, man-to-man, time, and activity. The Chinese
stress past-time and have a high-risk aversion. The extended
family is important. Fate is often blamed for failure in
products or services.

1190   Yeh, Ryk-Song (1988) "On Hofstede's Treatment of
        Chinese and Japanese Values," Asia Pacific Journal
        of Management 6 (October): 149-60.

The author reviews Hofstede's four dimensions of work-
related values and notes that they are culture-bound. As a
result, Hofstede's value profiles of his Japanese and
Chinese samples are inadequate.

1191   Yeh, Ryk-Song (1991) "Management Practices of
        Taiwanese Firms: As Compared to Those of American
        and Japanese Subsidiaries in Taiwan," Asia Pacific
        Journal of Management 8 (April): 1-14.

Locally-owned Taiwanese firms are using a Japanese-American
mix of management practices. Taiwanese firms have
successfully adapted foreign influences to their advantage,
and will continue to do so.

1192   Zamet, Jonathan M. and Murray E. Bovarnick
        (1986) "Employee Relations for Multinational
        Companies in China" Columbia Journal of World
        Business 21 (Spring): 13-9.

There is a summary of a survey dealing with the major human
resource management problems of expatriates working in
China.   Pay premiums are among the highest in the world.
There are no recreational facilities for foreigners, as
China resembles a third-world country in many aspects.

1193   Zhao, Jie (1991) "Doing Business with China:
        Cultural Aspects," East Asian Executive Reports 13
        (January 15): 10-11.

Knowing the proper Chinese business protocols will make
success in business in China more likely. Chinese managers
are still developing their own business styles, and the
legal system must be changed to respond to new business
conditions. The Chinese see business relations as personal
ones which bring tangible and intangible benefits.

11

*Pacific Rim and
South East Asia*

1194   Agarawal, Rekha and Girishwar Misra (1986) "A
        Factor Analytic Study of Achievement Goals and
        Means: An Indian view," International Journal
        of Psychology 21 (6): 717-31.

The concept of "achievement" varies across cultures and
within cultures (rural vs. urban, etc.). The urban Indian
sample was much more individualistic and "Western" in its
concept of achievement.

1195   Agrawal, Govind Ram (1980) Management in Nepal.
        Kathmandu, Nepal: Curriculum Development
        Centre, Tribhuvan University.

The author describes the major elements, and their cultural
contexts, of Nepalese-style managerial practices. These are
defined as "crisis-oriented" decision-making and "management
by manasaya." The latter is defined as determining what
one's superiors want done. Management is authoritarian and
risk-avoiding. Ad hoc and crisis decisions are the norm.
"Chakari" (getting favors from powerful people through
flattery, yes-manship, etc.) is common. The work is
sensitive to 1970s Western managerial theories.

1196   Agrawal, Govind Ram editor (1982) Emerging
        Concepts in Nepalese Management. Kathmandu,
        Nepal: Centre for Economic Development and
        Administration, Tribhuvan University.

This book contains 46 articles on Nepalese management. Many
articles deal with the socio-economic contexts and
background of management and managers. An article (pp. 29-
35: "Social and Cultural Factors in Management and the Role
of Nepalese Managers") deals with the national character of
workers and their social values. Work-related values are
influenced by Nepal's caste system, religious systems, and
family values. Another article (pp. 36-51) deals with

Nepalese decision-making, which is influenced by determining the "manasaya" (wishes and desires) of superiors, as well as postponing decisions until "bholi" (tomorrow), which never comes.

1197   Ainsworth, W. Murray and Quentin F. Willis
        editors (1985) <u>Australian Organizational</u>
        <u>Behavior: Readings</u>. South Melbourne:
        Macmillan Company of Australia.

This collection of material is well-rounded and balanced. There are selections on workers, managers, groups, job satisfaction, work values, and organizational change. Australians exhibit a high labor turnover, signifying a society-wide malaise and value crisis.

1198   Allen, Tim, Louis Lucas, Philippe Marthet,
        and Cyril Rocke (1988) <u>Sales and Distribution</u>
        <u>Guide to Malaysia</u>. New York: Pergammon Press.

While the work focuses primarily on investment, economic, and financial opportunities in Malaysia, there are short sections that deal with population, geography, ethnic composition, consumption patterns, etc. There are also segments dealing with the cultural aspects of business in Malaysia, such as the "bumiputra" approach to business.

1199   Alvi, Shafiq A. and Syed W. Ahmed (1987)
        "Assessing Organizational Commitment
        in a Developing Country: Pakistan, A Case
        Study," <u>Human Relations</u> 40 (3): 267-80.

Employees in Pakistan exhibit a relatively high degree of organizational commitment, with the degree of female commitment higher than that of male workers. Younger workers were more highly committed to their employers than older workers.

1200   Aryee, Samuel and Thomas Wyatt (1989) "Central Life
        Interests of Singaporean Workers," <u>Asia Pacific</u>
        <u>Journal of Management</u> 6 (April): 281-91.

A sample of 268 Singaporeans were surveyed concerning their central life interests. Workers (69%) indicated a dual commitment to both work and non-work areas, though there were variations by organizational ranks. A review of similar studies indicates that greater proportions of Singaporeans value non-work areas of life than do workers from Japan and five English-speaking countries. The majority in each sample nevertheless chose non-work as a central life interest.

1201   Basu, Mihir K. (1988) <u>Managerial Performance</u>
        <u>Appraisal in India</u>. New Delhi: Vision Books.

The author surveys 60 Indian companies to determine managerial performance. Appraisal reports were seen as useless and ignored for promotion purposes.

1202   Bhatt, Bhal and Edwin L. Miller (1984) "Industrial
        Relations in Foreign and Local Firms in Asia,"
        Management International Review 24 (3): 62-75.

A sample of 1,223 respondents working in subsidiaries of
foreign-owned enterprises and local companies in India,
Thailand, Singapore, and the Philippines were interviewed in
terms of their socio-economic profiles, wage levels,
unionization, and grievances. The duration of strikes was
lowest in Singapore and highest in locally-owned enterprises
in Thailand.

1203   Birnbaum, Philip H. and Gilbert Y.Y. Wong
        (1985) "Organizational Structure of
        Multinational Banks in Hong Kong,"
        Administrative Science Quarterly 30
        (June): 262-77.

An investigation of twenty multinational banks in Hong Kong
indicated that the determinants of work satisfaction among
93 Hong Kong Chinese managers were similar to those found in
managers in other countries. The preference for centralized
decision-making was the only non-culture-free variable.

1204   Blunt, Peter (1988) "Cultural Consequences
        for Organization Change in a Southeast
        State: Brunei," Academy of Management
        Executive 2 (August): 235-40.

45 members of an educational organization in Brunei were
interviewed to determine their values. Using Hofstede's four
dimensions of culture, the respondents were defined as high
in power distance, high in uncertainty avoidance, low in
individualism (generally), and medium in masculinity. This
profile differs somewhat from the one developed by Hofstede
of the region.

1205   Bordow, Allan editor (1977) The Worker in
        Australia: Contributions from Research.
        St. Lucia, Queensland: University of
        Queensland Press.

The contributors describe various aspects of the Australian
work force, including entrepreneurs, work satisfaction, and
evaluation of superiors on the part of miners.

1206   Boulgarides, James D. and Moonsong David Oh
        (1985) "A Comparison of Japanese and Korean
        Managerial Decision Styles: An Exploratory Study,"
        Leadership & Organization Development Journal 6
        (1): 9-11.

A model of managerial decision-making is developed,
resulting in four styles: analytic, conceptual, directive,
and behavioural. Cultural origin influences managerial
decision-making.

1207   Brandt, Vincent S.R. (1987) "Korea," pp 207-239 in
        George C. Lodge and Ezra F. Vogel (eds.) Ideology
        and National Competitiveness: An Analysis of Nine
        Countries. Boston: Harvard Business School Press.

Economic behavior and values are shaped by a number of
factors. The traditional value system of Korea stressed a
form of communitarianism and modern circumstances encourage
a strong unity between government bureaucracies and
business. The chapter also discusses Korean national
character and modern values.

1208   Chang, Chan Sup (1988) "Chaebol: The South Korean
        Conglomerates," Business Horizons 31 (March/April):
        51-7.

The driving force of South Korea's economy has been its
chaebols, or conglomerates. They account for one-fourth of
that nation's GNP. This article describes the social and
political characteristics of the ten largest chaebols. Most
(70%) chaebol's top executives attended Seoul National
University and are professional career managers, though
family owners retain most corporate powers.

1209   Chatterjee, Bhaskar (1990) Japanese Management:
        Maruti and the Indian Experience. New Delhi:
        Sterling Publishers.

The Indian firm Maruti Udyog Limited developed a joint
venture with Suzuki Motor Co., Ltd. This book is a case
study of the degree of transferability of Japanese work
practices to India. The Japanese practices of consultative
decision-making and job rotation/mobility did not transfer
into the Indian firm. The Indian "babu" mentality of
buckpassing, lack of information-sharing, and delaying
decisions continued.

1210   Cheek, Malcolm (1990) "Doing Business in Thailand:
        A U.S. Firm's Perspective," East Asian Executive
        Reports 12 (February 15): 21-2.

Americans working in Thailand must recognize that the Thais
have their own business culture.

1211   Choy, Chong Li (1987) "History and Managerial
        Culture in Singapore: 'Pragmatism,' 'Openness'
        and 'Paternalism,'" Asia Pacific Journal of
        Management 4 (May): 133-43.

Management ideology in Singapore has always been
multinational in origin with a strong family-oriented
Chinese influence. Management practices remain fluid and
easily assimilate foreign influences. Yet Singaporean
management remains "pragmatic," "open," and "paternalistic."

1212   Chung, Kae H. and Hak Chong Lee (1989) "National
        Differences in Managerial Practices," pp 163-80
        in Kae H. Chung and Hak Chong Lee (eds.), Korean
        Managerial Dynamics. New York: Praeger.

The authors discuss the managerial ideologies, corporate
structures, and organizational goals among employees in
U.S., Japanese, and Korean firms.

1213   Clark, Nicolas (1986) "Central Life Interests of
        Australian Workers," Work and Occupations 13
        (February): 67-76.

252 male workers in Australia completed Dubin's Central Life
Interest (CLI) questionnaire. Australian workers were much
less committed to work than their American, Canadian,
British, and Japanese counterparts. Australians were equally
committed to both work and leisure.

1214   Cohen, Erik (1985) "Sociocultural Change
        in Thailand: A Reconceptualization," pp 82-94
        in Erik Cohen, Moshe Lissak, and Uri
        Almagor (eds.) Comparative Social Dynamics.
        Boulder: Westview Press.

Thai culture exhibits great adaptability in which the major
features of Thai tradition can be maintained in the face of
modernization.   Thai   culture   promotes   a   form   of
"individualism"   that   differs   from   the   related   Western
concept. Thai individualism is rooted in the present and is
more anarchistic.

1215   Danandjaja, Andreas (1987) "Managerial Values in
        Indonesia," Asia Pacific Journal of Management 5
        (September): 1-7.

979 Indonesian managers are interviewed as to their personal
values. The findings are compared to similar studies using
samples in five other countries. Indonesian managers (71%)
tended to be defined as "pragmatic" types as were the
Japanese (66%) and Koreans (61%). Half (58%) of Americans
were pragmatic types.

1216   Das, G.S. and Chester C. Cotton (1988)
        "Power-Balancing Styles of Indian Managers,"
        Human Relations 41 (7): 533-51.

412 managers of Indian enterprises were asked to discuss how
they handled situations when administrative power had to be
shared. Four dominant styles were determined. The managerial
power-balancing style correlated with six dimensions.

1217   Doktor, Robert H. (1990) "Asian and American
        CEOs: A Comparative Study," Organizational
        Analysis 18 (Winter): 46-56.

Korean, Japanese, Hong Kong Chinese and American CEO's were
observed in terms of their use of time. Asian CEO's spent
more time on problem solving and had longer meetings. All
CEO's spent most of their time in group activities. The
Korean and Japanese CEO's spent more time on each unit of
time use.

1218   Dowling, Peter J. and Trevor W. Nagel
        (1986) "Nationality and Work Attitudes:
        A Study of Australian and American Business
        Majors," Journal of Management 12 (Spring):
        121-8.

American business majors placed greater emphasis on self-
fulfillment, responsibility, and other intrinsic rewards.
Australians had higher scale scores on income and job
security interests. These differences have implications for
cross-cultural managerial settings.

1219   Dowling, Peter J. and Denice E. Welch (1988)
        "International Human Resource Management: An
        Australian Perspective," Asia Pacific Journal
        of Management 6 (October): 39-65.

The authors provide an extensive review of the literature
dealing with international human resource management. They
then use case studies of Australian enterprises, both
locally-owned and foreign subsidiaries, to test the
literature's major findings. The Australian expatriate
failure rate is extremely low compared to that in U.S.-owned
firms, although the Australian-owned firms are highly
ethnocentric.

1220   Enriquez, Virgilio editor (1986) Philippine
        World-View. Singapore: Institute of Southeast
        Asian Studies.

This work consists of six essays on different aspects of the
Filipino national character, including how eating behavior
exhibits social relationships and social solidarity. There
are chapters on core values that dominate social behavior,
art and society, and the mass media.

1221   Fieg, John Paul, revised by Elizabeth Mortlock (1989)
        A Common Core: Thais and Americans. Yarmouth, Maine:
        Intercultural Press, Inc.

This work is one of the better treatment of all aspects of
Thai national character, cultural expectations, and behavior
patterns. Thai values are at times contrasted with American
cultural patterns.

1222   Filella, Jaime (1987) "Management Development in
        India and Spain," pp 123-35 in Bernard M. Bass and
        Pieter J.D. Drenth (eds.), Advances in Organizational
        Psychology. Newbury Park, CA: Sage Publications.

India and Spain have similar cultural features. Both are
oral cultures with preferences for face-to-face interaction.
People show "traces" of idealist temperament in that once a
problem is solved mentally, the person may assume the issue
no longer exists. People in managerial positions have a
"clerical" mentality and are "stabilizers," thereby
resisting change.

1223   Foxall, Gordon R. and Adrian F. Payne (1989)
        "Adaptors and Innovators in Organizations:
        A Cross-Cultural Study of the Cognitive Styles
        of Managerial Functions and Subfunctions," Human
        Relations 42 (7): 639-49.

238 British and Australian mid-career managers were tested
in terms of their managerial styles, defined as either
"adapters" or "innovators." Most of the sample were
classified as "innovators," with the British sub-sample
slightly more concentrated in that category.

1224   Fukuda, K. John (1987) "Japanese-Style Management
        in Hong Kong and Singapore," Journal of General
        Management 13 (Autumn): 69-81.

In spite of Singapore's and Hong Kong's cultural and
geographic proximity to Japan, Japanese-style management has
not been well-received in those two city-states. The author
lists the major elements of Japanese-style management and
cultural items (dependency, duty, obligation, feeling) and
surveys local attitudes toward Japanese management in Hong
Kong and Singapore. Japanese-style managerial features not
employed in Japanese subsidiaries and local firms include
job rotation, promotion, welfare programs, and training.
Hong Kong and Singaporean management practices differed from
each other and from Japanese practices.

1225   Gochenour, Theodore (1990) Considering Filipinos.
        Yarmouth, Maine: Intercultural Press, Inc

Filipino national character and daily customs are described
through a contrast with their U.S. counterparts. Short case
studies illustrate the basic concepts discussed in the first
half of the work.

1226   Government of India (1984) "Toward Organizational
        Development in Government: An Empirical Study,"
        International Studies of Management and Organization
        14 (Summer/Fall): 30-45.

The Human Resource Development Unit of the Department of
Personnel and Administrative Reforms conducted a survey of
government workers' levels of satisfaction, skills

utilization, flows of communications, etc. This article summarizes the major findings of this survey. The findings indicates that the respondents feel there were too much specialization and departmentalization, thereby reducing inter-office cooperation. The higher the rank, the higher the level of work satisfaction.

1227   Greenwald, Ruth (1986) "Lessons in Productivity
        Improvement from Nations in the Pacific Rim,"
        Industrial Engineering 18 (May): 14-6.

Pacific Rim nations are culturally diverse, though many have been economically successful in recent decades. A major variable common to all successful nations is the willingness to learn from foreigners, including managerial knowledge. This managerial knowledge must be adapted to the local cultural context. The business elites remain too conservative. U.S. businesspersons could learn valuable lessons from these rapidly developing nations.

1228   Griffin, Trenholme J. (1988) Korea: The Tiger
        Economy. London: Euromoney Publications PLC.

This very informative book contains chapters on the history, population, and government of South Korea. Other chapters deal with foreign relations, domestic politics, and financial and economic institutions. One chapter describes the Korean business and managerial styles. A final chapter offers information on foreign businesses in Korea, including several case studies.

1229   Hackman, Dahlia and Brian H. Kleiner (1990) "The
        Nature of Effective Management in Singapore,"
        Leadership & Organization Development Journal 11
        (4): 28-32.

Singaporean managers have adopted many U.S. management practices. Managers have become more individualistic and masculine, as defined by Hofstede. Singaporeans still differ from Americans on the dimension of power distance.

1230   Hall, Richard H. and Weiman Xu (1990) "Run Silent,
        Run Deep-Cultural Influences on Organization in
        the Far East," Organization Studies 11 (4): 569-76.

Although China and Japan have Confucian-based cultures, they exhibit very different organizational forms. While both nations stress family relations, each defines the concept in different ways.

1231   Handley, Paul (1990) "Talking Back:
        Thais Begin to Question Japanese Management,"
        Far Eastern Economics Review 148 (May): 54-5.

Japanese-owned subsidiaries in Thailand offer short-term training programs for Thai nationals, though these programs do not lead to promotion into the managerial ranks. Thais exhibit little company loyalty and they change employers easily.

1232   Harwood, R. Frank (1991) "An Oriental Management
        Philosophy Transplanted to Alabama, U.S.A.,"
        International Journal of Management 8
        (June): 484-92.

Korean-style managerial practices stress "inhwa," or harmony of relationships. This leads to a family atmosphere among workers, managers, and the market. These practices were successfully introduced to U.S. workers of a Korean-owner business.

1233   Hitt, Michael A., Beverly B. Tyler, and
        Daewoo Park (1990) "A Cross-Cultural Examination
        of Strategic Decision Models: Comparison of
        Korean and U.S. Executives," Academy of
        Management Proceedings: 111-15.

U.S. and Korean strategic decision-making differ, indicating the importance of cultural values in strategic management. However, personal factors have a stronger effect on U.S. executives' decision-making. U.S. executives exhibited more homogeneity of thought and background. Both national samples placed strong weight on objective criteria in their strategic decisions.

1234   Hofstede, Geert and Michael Harris Bond (1988)
        "The Confucius Connection: From Cultural Roots to
        Economic Growth," Organizational Dynamics 16
        (Spring): 3-21.

Neo-Confucian social and managerial ideologies are shown to be major contributors to the recent economic growth of Confucian-based societies in the Pacific Rim. Measures indicate a widely-followed East-West division in philosophy and world outlook. Factors associated with Confucian dynamism are values encouraging persistence, the ordering of relationships by status, thrift, and having a sense of shame. Other Confucian values are shown to be relatively unimportant.

1235   Hsu, Paul S. (1987) "Patterns of Work Goal
        Importance: A Comparison of Singapore and
        Taiwanese Managers," Asia Pacific Journal
        of Management 4 (May): 152-66.

There exists significant differences in work goals among Singapore and Taiwanese managers. A cluster analysis identified four patterns of work goal importance: passive stoics, moralistic enthusiasts, aloof turned-offs, and pragmatists. Seventy-eight percent of Singapore managers were defined as moralist enthusiasts. The largest (40%) category of Taiwanese were aloof turned-offs.

1236   Hurst, G. Cameron III (1984) "Getting a Piece
        of the R.O.K.," UFSI Reports number 19: 1-11.

Included is a discussion of the Korean national character,
its fear of foreign domination, view of contractual
obligations, and influence of Confucianism on business-
related values and behavior. There are also detailed
descriptions of Korean bureaucratic structure and the
important place of patronage and bribery in business. Basic
personality attributes of Koreans are described, and they
are characterized as "the Irish of the Orient."

1237   Hwa, Chia Hock and A. Pecotish (1988) "Multinational
        Management Strategy and ASEAN Regional Development,"
        Asia Pacific Journal of Management 6 (October): 161-
        74.

A study of 128 senior managers of multinational corporations
in Singapore indicates that country of origin is a
significant variable in determining perceptions related to
policy, planning, and goals.

1238   Jacobs, Norman (1985) The Korean Road to
        Modernization and Development. Urbana:
        University of Illinois Press.

The author analyzes various aspects of Korean values,
significant historical events, and selected institutions
from which are derived the Korean national character,
leadership styles, and their implications for the directions
of Korea's economic and social developments. South Korea's
modernization is likely to follow a unique direction guided
by a patrimonial value system.

1239   Jain, Sagar C. (1971) Indian Manager: His Social
        Origin and Career. Bombay: Somaiya Publications,
        PVT LTD.

This work describes the attitudes, social origins, and
career development of 2,158 senior Indian managers in 116
corporations.

1240   Jain, Uma (1989) "Values of Computer
        Professionals: Implications for Institutional
        Building," International Studies of Management
        and Organization 19 (Spring): 53-73.

A study of values was conducted using 142 computer
professionals in India. The existential values were ranked
highest (concern for experience, expression, dignity of
people, goal orientation, and a longer time perspective).
Five value dimensions were measured. Some items in each
scale were ranked highly.

1241   Kapoor, Ashok (1976) "The Indian Manager Looks at
        The American Technician," pp 221-9 in Ashok Kapoor
        (ed.) Asian Business and Environment in Transition:
        Selected Readings and Essays. Princeton, NJ: The
        Darwin Press.

The author offers a number of case studies to illustrate the
difference in behavior and business values among Indians and
Americans. In India, no relationship is purely professional
or impersonal, and family interests are more important than
business interests.

1242   Katayame, Frederick H. (1982) "Analyzing Cultural
        Stereotypes in Multinational Business: United States
        and Australia," Journal of Management Studies 19
        (July): 307-25.

This study surveys the attitudes and values of Australians
and Americans taking part in Hawaii's Advanced Management
Programs over a 26-year period (N=491). The two samples
differed on a number of selected values. Australians were
pro-unions, felt that their work organizations suppressed
individuality, felt workers had little ambition or drive,
and were more cynical about being moral in a managerial
position.

1243   Katayame, Fredrick H. (1989) "How to Act Once
        You Get There," Fortune 120 (Fall): 87-8.

Doing business in Asia requires different behavior than that
expected in the U.S. The author offers advice on how to
behave correctly while in Asia. The advice includes using
titles and surnames, avoiding physical contact, dressing
conservatively, and being punctual.

1244   Kearney, Robert P. (1991) The Warrior Worker: The
        Challenge of the Korean Way of Working. New York:
        Henry Holt and Company.

Korean workers are treated paternalistically by their
employers. In return, Korean managers expect workers to be
hard   working,   obedient,   and   grateful.   Korean-style
management is a blend of Korean-U.S.-Japanese practices.
Corporate paternalism is comprehensive in return for
obedience. The book contains case studies of individuals, a
historical essay of Korea, and well-crafted detailed
descriptions of work and workers in the corporate and
industrial sectors. The book's style is journalistic.

1245   Kelley, Lane, Arthur Whatley, Reginald
        Worthley, and Harry Lie (1986) "The Role
        of the Ideal Organization in Comparative
        Management: A Cross Cultural Perspective
        of Japan and Korea," Asia Pacific Journal
        of Management 3 (January): 59-75.

Although people discuss the "Confucian Work Ethic," the
authors find significant differences in managerial
practices--both factual and ideal--between Japan and South
Korea. Middle managers in Japanese and Korean banks were
asked to rank a series of statements dealing with power
distance, time, materialism, power, uncertainty avoidance,
etc.

1246   Kelly, Brian and Mark London (1990) "Seoul
        Searching," Business Month (February): 61-66.

There are descriptions of South Korea's factory
organizational structure and management. There are also
descriptions of Korean industrial workers. The focus is on
the Samsung Group.

1247   Keys, Bernard, Tom Case, and Alfred C. Edge
        (1989) "A Cross-National Study of Differences
        Between Leadership Relationships of Managers
        in Hong Kong with Those in the Philippines,
        Korea and the United States," International
        Journal of Management 6 (4): 390-404.

The "Managerial Relationships Inventory" scale measures
relationships among superiors, subordinates, and peers. U.S.
and Hong Kong managers were the most similar. The Korean and
Filipino managers were the most different. U.S. and Korean
managers also significantly differed from each other.

1248   Khan, A. Farooq and Adrian Atkinson
        (1987) "Managerial Attitudes Toward
        Social Responsibility: A Comparative
        Study in India and Britain," Journal
        of Business Ethics 6 (August): 419-32.

89 top executives in Britain and India were surveyed in
terms of their notion of corporate responsibility. Nearly
all (94%-98%) of the respondents agreed that social
responsibility was relevant to business. Other findings
dealing with ethical standards in business are presented.
Some of the findings are compared to data based on U.S.
samples.

1249   Khandwalla, Pradip N. (1985) "Pioneering
        Innovative Management: An Indian Excellence,"
        Organization Studies 6 (2): 161-83.

A scale (PI) is developed which measures attitudes toward
pioneering innovation, acceptance of change, risk-taking,
flexibility, and creativity. High scale values are

positively correlated with firm growth. PI scores are
relatively context free, indicating such positive attitudes
toward innovation and change could be encouraged and
developed even in government-run bureaucracies.

1250   Kim, Hwang-Joe (1987) "Labor and Management
        Strategies Toward Technological Changes in Korea,"
        Journal of East and West Studies 16 (Fall/Winter):
        23-41.

Current management policies in Korea do not take advantage
of South Korea's abundant, educated and well-motivated human
resources. There is also an urgent need to minimize labor-
management disputes over technological development.

1251   Kim, Kyong-Dong (1984) Man and Society
        in Korea's Economic Growth: Sociological
        Studies. Seoul: Seoul National University Press.

This work offers a systematic presentation of the historical
aspects of South Korea's economic development and its
relationship to Korean values, including those of managers,
entrepreneurs, general-level workers, and occupational-
educational groups. Fairly high levels of frustration and
felt grievances exist among workers. A survey of managers
(N=225) showed that managers were highly pragmatic and
positive in their values toward a greater acceptance of
merit over ascription for hiring and promotion. Managers
listed "high productivity" as highest in importance in terms
of their value goals while employee and social welfare were
rated lowest.

1252   Kim, Kyong-Dong and On-Jook Lee (1985)
        "Middle-Class Perceptions of Economic
        Development and External Relations in Korea,"
        Journal of East and West Studies 14
        (Fall/Winter): 35-65.

The last twenty-five years have witnessed a rapid growth of
the Korean economy. This modernization of the economy has
been accompanied with complex changes in the Korean society.
The perceptions, attitudes, and values of the population
have also changed.

1253   Kyi, Khin Maung (1988) "APJM and Comparative
        Management in Asia," Asia Pacific Journal of
        Management 5 (May): 207-224.

The editor-in-chief of the Asian Pacific Journal of Asia
reviews the results of that journal's five years of
publications. He summarizes the methodologies used, the
biases and characteristics of the authors' orientations, and
provides a summary of finding on the major characteristics
of Asian-style management.

1254   Kyi, Khin Maung, Ang Swee Hoon, and Tan Ching
        Ling (1984) "Patterns of Job Mobility of
        Singapore Managers," Proceedings of the Academy
        of International Business: 574-91.

The job mobility patterns of 254 managers in Singapore are
presented. Age and education are major factors, as is having
a father who is a self-employed professional. Sons of blue
collars also had a high upward mobility rate. The image of
Singaporean job-hopping is a myth. Interfirm mobility is at
the same level as found in Japan and the U.S.

1255   Lee, Hak-Chong (1989) "Managerial Characteristics
        of Korean Firms," pp 147-62 in Kai H. Chung and Hak
        H. Chung (editors) Korean Managerial Dynamics. New
        York: Praeger.

The chapter analyzes findings based on a survey of Korean
managers. The results measure managerial values and
corporate strategies of managers. There are also discussions
of formal and informal organizational behavior.

1256   Lee, Hak-Chong (1989) "Structure and Behavior of
        Korean Business," Journal of East West Studies 18
        (March): 1-30.

Attitudes and values (power, informal structure, patterns of
interpersonal communications, motivation, etc.) are surveyed
using a sample of Korean workers in 86 large Korean
enterprises, excluding chaebols. The research is in part
guided by Peters and Waterman's (In Search of Excellence,
1982) 7-S framework of American companies exhibiting
excellent performance.

1257   Lee, Sang M. and Sangjin Yoo (1987) "The K-Type of
        Management: A Driving Force of Korean Management,"
        Management International Review 27 (4): 68-77.

This article contains an excellent description of the major
features of South Korean society and management style that
influenced Korea's rapid economic growth in recent decades.
The Saemaul Movement prepared the rural areas for economic
development and became the model for urban and factory
modernization. Korean corporations tend to be family
enterprises and supported by governmental policies that
promote exports. Korean management style includes a number
of unique features.

1258   Lee, Sang M., Sangjin Yoo, and Tosca M. lee
        (1991) "Korean Chaebols: Corporate Values
        and Strategies," Organizational Dynamics 19
        (Spring): 36-50.

The authors feel that South Korea's Chaebols are undergoing
changes, and that each must review its own values and
corporate strategies. There are data on the largest
Chaebols' personality criteria for new members.

1259   Leon, Corrina T. De (1987) "Social Categorisation
in Philippines Organisations: Values Toward
Collective Identity and Management Through
Intergroup Relations," Asia Pacific Journal
of Management 5 (September): 28-37.

Although traditional Filipino values differ from American
values, it is possible to blend these countries' managerial
practices, resulting inn a "synchronic synergy" convergence.
Filipino values of cooperative relationships and group
cohesion will be integrated in the new system of management.

1260   Leppert, Paul (1987) Doing Business with the
Koreans: A Handbook for Executives.
Chula Vista, CA: Patton Pacific Press, Inc.

This brief guide to the history and culture of Korea is an
excellent introduction. There are sections on business
etiquette, bargaining and negotiation behavior, travel tips,
and useful addresses.

1261   Lie, John (1990) "Is Korean Management
Just Like Japanese Management?" Management
International Review 30 (2): 113-8.

The author compares characteristics of managers in Korea and
Japan in terms of their socio-economic backgrounds. The
author predicts a convergence of personal characteristics
between the two sets of managers in the near future.

1262   Limdingan, Victor Simpao (1986) The Overseas
Chinese in Asean: Business Strategies and
Management Practices. Manila, Philippines:
Vita Development Corporation.

Overseas Chinese have been extremely successful economically
in the South East Asian Nations (ASEAN), in spite of the
lack of a trading tradition in China. The author analyzes
the factors of overseas Chinese successes in ASEAN, which
include a favorable economic environment, entrepreneurship
values, and a Chinese-style system of managerial control.

1263   Ling, Tan Ching and Joseph M. Putti (1989) "The
Relationship Between Personality and Management Style
in India-An Empirical Investigation," International
Journal of Management 6 (March): 91-9.

A sample of 155 Indian managers in two firms indicated that
personality traits did not determine managerial style. The
modal managerial types were defined as "initiating of
structure" type (one who clearly defines his role and lets
his followers know what is expected of them) and the "active
leader" type.

1264   Longton, Peter A. and Bruce W. Stening (1988)
        "The Cultural Milieu of Management: A
        Comparative Study of the Role of Management in
        ASEAN," Asia Pacific Journal of Management 6
        (October): 91-104.

Business is never context-free, and the ambience of doing
business in Asia changes from one cultural milieu to
another. The author provides a set of ideal types of
cultural milieus for ASEAN nations. The ideal types of
cultural contexts correlate with a traditional-industrial
continuum. Management education should take into account
various cultural contexts.

1265   Low, Peter S. (1984) "Singapore-Based Subsidiaries
        of U.S. Multinationals and Singaporean Firms: A
        Comparative Management Study," Asia Pacific Journal
        of Management 2 (September): 29-39.

983 respondents describe their managerial ideologies.
Singaporean managers are authoritarian and favor centralized
decision-making. Such values result in higher absenteeism
and turn-over rates than in the U.S.

1266   Masters, Robert and Manton Gibbs (1990)
        "Risk-Taking Influences on Managerial Decision
        Making: An Indian-United States Comparison,"
        International Journal of Management 7 (June):
        215-222.

Indian male managers were found to be more risk averse than
U.S. males and females and female Indian managers. Indian
males and European managers exhibited similar levels of risk
averseness.

1267   McCormick, Ian A. and Cary L. Cooper (1988)
        "Executive stress: Extending the International
        Comparison," Human Relations 41 (January): 65-72.

The stress levels of 220 executives from seven countries
were measured. Executives from less developed countries had
higher levels of stress and dissatisfaction. The article
focuses on a New Zealand sample. This sample has the second
lowest levels of stress and job dissatisfaction.

1268   Mente, Boye De (1988) Korean Etiquette &
        Ethics in Business. Lincolnwood, Illinois:
        NTC Business Books.

This book is one of the best practical guides to the South
Korean way of doing business, the Korean national character,
and general societal features of Korea. One chapter deals
with significant Korean historical events. Other chapters
cover problems and tensions faced by foreign businesspersons
who deal with Koreans. A glossary illustrates major cultural
and business values.

1269   **Miller, Joan G., David M. Bersoff, and
Robin L. Harwood (1990) "Perceptions
of Social Responsibilities in India and
in the United States: Moral Imperatives
or Personal Decisions?"** <u>Journal of
Personality and Social Psychology</u> 58
(January): 33-47.

400 Indian and U.S. respondents were asked to make moral
decisions about a series of hypothetical situations. Indians
tended to make evaluations in moral terms in all situations.
The results suggest Indians view social responsibilities in
a broader ethical context than do Americans.

1270   **Mole, Robert L. (1973)** <u>Thai Values and Behavior
Patterns</u>. **Rutland, Vermont: Charles E. Tuttle
Company.**

The national character of Thais and their basic social values are described, including their views of individualism,
patronage, and foreigners. Sections include advice to foreigners on proper behavior and Thai authority (in a business
context) patterns.

1271   **Mukhi, Suresh K. (1982) "Leadership
Characteristics Required of Australian
Managers,"** <u>Leadership & Organization
Development</u> 3 (4): 9-12.

A study of the success values/experiences of 420 Australian
managers stresses work experience, long working hours, and a
university degree in finance or accounting. 70-80% of work
time is spent meeting with others. Ranked success elements
were (1) having a need to achieve results, (2) the ability
to work with a variety of people, and (3) having the ability
to influence others and negotiate.

1272   **Namsirikul, Suraphol (1986) "Employee Benefits in
Thailand,"** <u>Benefits and Compensation International</u>
18 (July): 18-26.

Wage policies in Thailand are underdeveloped, and most
employees prefer immediate financial rewards rather than
long-range benefits, such as retirement benefits or
disability insurance. Modern types of benefits are being
introduced in Thailand.

1273   **Nirenberg, John editor (1979)** <u>Aspects of
Management in Malaysia</u>. **Athens, Ohio:
University of Ohio. MARA Institute of
Technology.**

This well-rounded collection of articles deals with the
characteristics of management and work values in Malaysia,
its social structure, and social values. There are
presentations on the cultures of the major cultural groups
of Malaysia.

1274   Nirenberg, John (1986) "Work Values of Singapore
        Employees Revisited," Singapore Management Review
        8 (January): 1-11.

Singaporean workers have strong, positive work ethic values,
but the workplace environment frustrates these attitudes.
The respondents valued most the dignity of labor and pride
in work.

1275   Olanvoravuth, Ninnat and Andrew Kakabadse
        (1981) "Tips from Thailand: A SE Asian
        View of Western Consultants," Leadership &
        Organization Development Journal 2 (2): 24-7.

The national character of Thais includes an acceptance of
change, a respect for western education, a preference for
family-controlled businesses, and selection of workers on a
personal basis. Decision-making does not stress consensus
but avoids conflict. Two-way, non-interactive, communication
is the norm. Other aspects of Thai personality are
discussed.

1276   Onedo, A.E. Ojuka (1991) "The Motivation and Need
        Satisfaction of Papuan New Guinea Managers," Asia
        Pacific Journal of Management 8 (April):
        121-9.

This article compares five levels of need satisfaction of
Australian and Papua New Guinea (PNG) executives. PNG scores
are similar to those in developing countries. Australian
values stress "individualism." PNG values center around
"wankoism," or "one-talk/language." This concept refers to
the intense loyalty to those from the same linguistic-
ethnic-village group. Wankoism creates a system of social
obligations on an on-going basis.

1277   Park, Chunoh, Nicholas P. Sovrich, and
        Dennis L. Soden (1988) "Testing Herzberg's
        Motivation Theory in a Comparative Study of
        U.S. and Korean Public Employees," Review of
        Public Personnel Administration 8 (Summer): 40-60.

100 Korean and U.S. respondents recognized achievement and
recognition as two most favorable responses of needs met.
This pattern supports Herzberg's two-factor theory.

1278   Park, Heung-Soo (1985) "Sex-Role Values and
        Television in Korea," Journal of East and West
        Studies 14 (Fall/Winter): 1-34.

The dominant values of Korea remain traditional in spite of
the rapid expansion of the Korean economy in recent decades.
Television is reinforcing the traditional values of male-
dominated paternalism, and the young reflect traditional
values. This is retarding the transformation of Korea into a
more egalitarian society.

1279   Phillips, Herbert P. (1966) **Thai Peasant Personality**.
        Berkeley: University of California Press.

This work is an anthropological field study of the patterns
of interpersonal relations in a Thai village. Such patterns
reflect the national character of Thais in urban areas. Included are descriptions of the power structures that dominate Thai culture.

1280   Popp, Gary L. and Herbert J. Davis (1984) "American
        and Australian Work Reward Preference Patterns,"
        Asia Pacific Journal of Management 2 (September):
        62-4.

A survey of Australian and U.S. MBA students indicated that
both samples ranked "opportunity for growth" and
"achievement" highest in terms of reward. The Australian
students ranked "hobbies" higher than Americans, though
overall national differences were small.

1281   Posner, Barry Z. and Peter S. Low (1990)
        "Australian and American Managerial Values:
        Subtle Differences," **International Journal of
        Management** 7 (March): 89-97.

Two national samples of managers rated organizational
effectiveness as most important in terms of a set of values.
However, Australians rated higher the importance of
leadership, high morale, organizational reputation, and
value to the community. The Americans rated profit
maximization higher. In terms of personality traits,
Americans ranked in descending order: ability, achievement,
job satisfaction, cooperation, and skill. The Australian
rankings were: ability, job satisfaction, achievement,
success, and skill.

1282   Putti, Joseph M. (1989) "A Comparative
        Study of Work Values of Employees in
        Japanese and American Companies,"
        International Journal of Management 6
        (June): 125-9.

The work values of East Asian workers in U.S.- and Japanese-
owned subsidiaries indicated differences by the national
ownership of employment enterprises. The employees of
Japanese companies were more involved in their work, less
interested in their earnings, and preferred to be kept busy
while at work. There were no significant differences in
terms of pride in work, upward striving, or social status.
The workers' values reflected in part the values of the
parent employers' cultures.

1283   Redding, S. Gordon (1967) "The Study of Managerial
        Ideology Among Overseas Chinese Owner-Managers,"
        Asia Pacific Journal of Management 4 (May): 167-
        77.

Chinese-owned enterprises in East Asia exhibit a high degree
of cooperation. The author provides a conceptual framework
to operationalize managerial ideology in order to understand
this inter-organizational cooperation.

1284   Redding, S. Gordon and S. Richardson (1986)
        "Participative Management and its Varying Relevance
        in Hong Kong," Asia Pacific Journal of Management 3
        (January): 76-98.

The participative-style of management results in higher
productivity in Singapore but not in Hong Kong. The reason
for this difference is that the work context in Hong Kong is
less foreign and more traditional. The authors describe managerial beliefs and practices in eight Southeast countries,
Japan, the U.S., and Nordic and Latin Europe. There are also
Hong Kong-Singapore contrasts in terms of cultural values,
labor productivity, age population distributions, etc.

1285   Reeder, John A. (1987) "When West Meets East:
        Cultural Aspects of Doing Business in Asia,"
        Business Horizons 30 (Jan/Feb): 69-74.

Involvement of U.S. businesspersons in Asian countries will
increase as more countries in that region experience
economic development, including China and Indonesia. Asian
cultures contain some similarities of values and behavior
patterns. These similarities include a concern for a
person's dignity (face) and a shame (vs. guilt) dimension of
social control. The author concludes with specific advice on
how to behave while in Asia.

1286   Renard, Patrice, Jean-Stephane Arcis,
        Sylvie Lacoste, and Odile Perraguin (1988)
        Sales and Distribution Guide to Thailand.
        New York: Pergamon Press.

Although the focus is on marketing, shipping, financial,
political, and economic issues, this work contains
discussions of cultural items, such as the Thai concepts of
partnership and proper business relations.

1287   Renwick, George W. and revised by Reginald Smart
        and D. L. Henderson (1991) A Fair Go For All:
        Australians and North Americans. Yarmouth, Maine:
        Intercultural Press, Inc.

The Australian national character, work attitudes, language
patterns, and work-related behavior (leadership, decision-
making, family, work, etc.) are described in this 96-page
work. The writer, a respected cross-cultural training

consultant, offers sensitive advice on developing proper
relationships with Australians.

1288   Rew, Alan (1986) "Institutional Culture and
        Persistent Structures in Papua New Guinea,"
        Public Administration and Development 6
        (Oct/Dec): 391-400.

The distribution and allocation of administrative resources
in Papua is dependent upon cultural values of officials and
public. Cultural values encourage conflicts in how "besena"
(tribe or nation) is defined.

1289   Rhee, Yang-Soo (1981) "A Cross-Cultural
        Comparison of Korean and American Managerial
        Styles," Journal of East and West Studies 10
        (Fall/Winter): 45-63.

This article compares the interrelationships between socio-
cultural factors and managerial behavior in South Korea and
the United States. A series of propositions is presented.
Managerial behaviors should be studied in terms of not only
their socio-cultural factors but also in terms of their
individual, situational, and organizational dimensions.

1290   Runglertkrengkrai, Somokao and Suda Engkaninan
        (1986) "The Motivation and Need Satisfaction of
        Thai Managerial Elite," Asia Pacific Journal of
        Management 3 (May): 194-97.

77 chief executive officers of Thai firms answered a questionnaire of 13 items dealing with need satisfaction of managers. The study replicates other studies of Thai respondents and those from other countries. Thai senior managers
have higher need satisfaction levels than managers in other
countries.

1291   Runglertkrengkrai, Somokao and Suda Engkaninan
        (1987) "The Patterns of Managerial Behavior in
        Thai Culture," Asia Pacific Journal of Management
        5 (September): 8-15.

Dominant themes in Thai culture include (1) personalism, (2)
fun-loving, (3) merit accumulation, (4) present-time consumption, (5) the middle way of life, and (6) individualism.
These traditional patterns are contrasted with "modern" values. The study presents data using the Least Preferred Co-
Worker test among senior Thai managers.

1292   Saha, Arunoday (1990) "Traditional Indian
        Concept of Time and its Economic Consequences,"
        International Journal of Sociology and Social
        Policy 10 (7): 58-79.

Time is a culturally-based concept and its definitions vary
from culture to culture. The Indian concept of time tends to
reject commonsense definitions of time as irrelevant and

results in static thinking. This view of time encourages high absenteeism and low productivity among Indian factory workers, as well as overstaffing.

1293   Saha, Arunoday (1990) "Cultural Impediments to
        Technology Developments in India," International
        Journal of Sociology and Social Policy 10 (8): 25-53.

Indian cultural values encourage a certain type of mysticism which denigrates technology and its users. Such attitudes alienate workers from their work. This is expressed in high absenteeism rates, low quality performance, etc.

1294   Saiyadain, Mirza (1985) "Personal Characteristics
        and Job Satisfaction: India-Nigeria Comparison,"
        International Journal of Psychology 20 (2): 143-53.

1,398 Indians and Nigerians were measured in terms of the relationship between job satisfaction and personal characteristics. Age was an important variable for the Nigerian sample in a linear fashion. The relationship was curvilinear for the Indian sample. Indian males were much happier than Nigerian males. The industrialization level in each country influenced the results.

1295   Sarachek, Bernard, Aziz Abdul Hamid,
        and Zakaria bin Ismail (1984) "An Opinion
        Survey of Malaysian Middle Level Managers and
        Professionals," Asia Pacific Journal of
        Management 1 (May): 181-189.

234 Malaysian manager-training course trainees were examined to see if, like the Japanese, they could be modern in work-related attitudes but traditional in others. The authors contrast modern, Chinese, and Malay values along ten dimensions. Ethnic Chinese Malay trainees seemed more "modern" in terms of many issues, such as religion, work, nepotism, and superior-subordinate relationships.

1296   Savery, Lawson K. and Pamela A. Swain
        (1985) "Leadership Style: Differences
        Between Expatriates and Locals," Leadership
        & Organization Development Journal 6 (4): 8-12.

This article describes the conflict between leadership style and employees' reception of that style in an Australian firm located in Papua New Guinea. Papuan preferred leadership style stresses consensus decision-making, extrinsic rewards, mobility through merit, decentralized authority, and group over individual responsibility. The Australians preferred a managerial style stressing a very low trust level in others, centralization, individual decision-making, and intrinsic rewards.

1297   Sekaran, Uma and Coral R. Snodgrass (1987)
        "Impact of Culture on Organization Members'
        Style of Interactions with the External Environment,"
        Asia Pacific Journal of Management 5 (September):
        38-54.

A sample of 156 Malaysian and Singaporean nationals studying
in the U.S. indicated a preference for close, personal ties
with clients, irrespective of the nature of the mechanisms
of relationships (bureaucratic, market, or clan). This is
contrasted with the more Westernized client-worker
relationship guided by standards of impersonality and
individualism.

1298   Sin, Gregory Thong Tin (1987) "The Management of
        Chinese Small-Business Enterprises in Malaysia,"
        Asia Pacific Journal of Management 4 (May): 178-86.

The author examines the sources of success among Chinese enterprises in Malaysia. The enterprises are small and family-
owned, and management principles derive from the sixteen
"Principles of Good Business Practices" which originated in
China during the fifth century B.C. These principles may become dysfunctional should Chinese businesses become larger
and modernized.

1299   Singh, Joginder P. (1990) "Managerial Culture
        and Work-Related Values in India,"
        Organization Studies 11 (1): 75-102.

The author replicates Hofstede's findings using the Values
Survey Module. The VSM scores vary when using four Indian
sub-samples. Indian managers were low on all four
dimensions. Age, education, type of superior, and type of
work were significant variables. The findings disagree with
Hofstede's. Hofstede has a rejoinder at the end of Singh's
article.

1300   Sinha, Jai B.P. (1984) "A Model of Effective
        Leadership Styles in India," International
        Studies of Management and Organization 14
        (Summer/Fall): 86-98.

Leadership styles can be conceptualized as authoritarian,
nurturant-task, and participative. This article reports on
surveys and experiments which operationalize these leadership styles among Indian samples. The nurturant-task style
is preferred by managers while subordinates prefer a dependent and personalized relationship with leaders. The findings are correlated with a number of variables to test a
series of hypotheses. There is a comprehensive reference
section of related works.

1301   Stoever, William A. (1988) "India: The Long Slow
        Road to Liberalization," Business Horizons 31
        (Jan/Feb): 42-6.

The values of India's bureaucrats are hindering efforts to
modernize India's economy. In spite of the encouragement of
India's current leaders, foreign investors will continue to
experience difficulties in doing business in India.

1302   Stone, Eric (1989) "The Delicate Art of the
        Dealmaker," Asian Business 25 (December): 22-8.

A new breed of dealmakers is emerging in Southeast Asia.
These persons are young, creative, secretive, and willing to
take risks. The author describes some of these new Asian
entrepreneurs.

1303   Springer, J. Fred and Richard W. Gable (1980)
        "Dimensions of Sources of Administrative Climate
        in Development Programs of Four Asian Nations,"
        Administrative Science Quarterly 25 (December):
        671-88.

Interviews on perceptions of the work environment in
Indonesia, Korea, Philippines, and Thailand indicate that
administrators in each culture experienced different
organizational climates. Organizational climate was defined
in term of six dimensions, including feelings of pathology,
futility, and effectiveness. Korean personnel perceived
relatively high levels of pathology and low levels of
flexibility.

1304   Steers, Richard M., Yoo Keun Shin, and Gerardo
        R. Ungson (1989) The Chaebol: Korea's New Industrial
        Might. New York: Harper & Row, Publishers.

South Korea's chaebols dominate that country's industrial
and export/import sectors. The authors explain the chaebol's
structure within the context of Korean national character.
The chaebols are contrasted to Japan's Keiretsu. There are
chapters on Korean management, personnel policies, and the
work environment.

1305   Stening, Bruce W., James E. Everett, and Peter
        Longton (1983) "Managerial Stereotypes in
        Singaporean Subsidiaries of Multinational
        Corporations," Asia Pacific Journal of
        Management 1 (September): 56-64.

Expatriate and local managers of British, Japanese, and U.S.
firms located in Singapore were asked to profile the
stereotypes each group holds of the others. The British and
Singaporean managers were in general agreement about the
British stereotype. The Japanese expatriates exhibited the
highest amount of disagreements with other stereotypes and
their own self-image.

1306   Swierczek, Fredric William (1988) "Culture
        and Job Satisfaction: An Obtrusive Approach,"
        Management Decision 26 (6): 37-41.

160 Thai managers from three surveys selected job
satisfaction items as most important. Respondents defined as
important the fit between person and organization, as well
as good relationships at work. Valued traits at work
included challenge, accomplishment, and variety.

1307   Swierczek, Fredric William (1988) "Culture
        and Training: How do They Play Away From
        Home?" Training and Development International
        43 (November): 74-80.

Differences in behavior between Thai and U.S. managers are
relatively few, except in terms of communications, conflict
resolution, and interpersonal relations. Some managerial
techniques cannot be transferred from one cultural context
to another.

1308   Tayeb, Monir (1987) "Contingency Theory
        and Cultures: A Study of Matched English
        and Indian Manufacturing Firms," Organization
        Studies 8 (3): 241-62.

Fourteen matched organizations in England and India were
compared in terms of their contextual variables (size,
ownership and control, product technology, etc.). The
purpose was to test the contingency model, which predicts
that organizations must adapt appropriately to their
environments. The main features of the Indian and English
cultures are contrasted, and the model is found to be
inadequate. Delegation, formalization, and communication
patterns were not influenced by contextual factors. Cultural
factors are assumed to be influential.

1309   Tayeb, Monir (1988) Organizations and National
        Culture: A Comparative Analysis. Beverly Hills,
        CA: SAGE Publications.

The author discusses the major models for analyzing
organizations and develops a third model for studying
organizations on a comparative basis. This model is based on
a number of dimensions using decision-making as its
framework. The dimensions include motivation, trust,
communication, and tolerance for ambiguity. A sample of
British and Indian organizations (seven manufacturing
companies in each country) is used to measure national
character and other dimensions, such as centralization. The
"culturist" position is shown to have some support.

1310   Thiagarajan, Karumuthu M. (1968) <u>A Cross-Cultural</u>
        <u>Study of the Relationships Between Personal Values</u>
        <u>and Managerial Behavior</u>. Ph.D. Dissertation,
        University of Pittsburgh.

A survey of the values of U.S. and Indian managers and students found large cultural differences between the national
samples and occupational groups. The Indian respondents were
more moralistic and less accommodative. Indian managers con-
formed more than American managers; the reverse was true for
students. The study is based on the work of G.W. England.

1311   Thompson, Allan G. (1989) "Cross-Cultural
        Management of Labour in a Thai Environment," <u>Asia</u>
        <u>Pacific Journal of Management</u> 6 (April): 323-38.

Thai cultural values result in a unique work environment.
While Thais recognize power differences among persons in the
same enterprise, they also assume a coincidence of interests
which should result in harmonious relationships with peers
and superiors. These values result in on-going dialogues and
a distrust of formalized procedures.

1312   Torres, Amaryllis Tiglao (1988) <u>The Urban</u>
        <u>Filipino in an Industrializing Society</u>.
        Quezon City, Philippines: University of the
        Philippines Press.

A sample of Filipino workers in a garment factory is studied
in terms of their adaptation to a new socio-economic, urban,
industrialized environment. This excellent study deals with
all aspects of workers' values, such as performance and work
satisfaction.

1313   Turner, Mark M. (1989) "'Trainingism' Revisited in
        Papua New Guinea," <u>Public Administration and</u>
        <u>Development</u> 9 (Jan/March): 17-28.

The concept of "trainingism" explains the resistance of
persons to improve their work-related behavior. This concept
is culture-bound and is oriented toward the latent functions
of educational and training programs. Training someone in
the latest Western techniques of decision-making will not
change a manager's behavior if such knowledge does not fit
local social structures and values. The discussion uses
examples from the author's experiences in Papua.

1314   Useem, John and Ruth Hill Useem (1955)
        <u>The Western-Educated Man in India</u>. New York:
        The Dryden Press.

Indians educated in the United States find themselves culturally marginal when they return to India. The authors interviewed U.S.-educated Indians and reported on their
attitudes, feelings, and values. Quotes and interpretations
also expose the major features of Indian national character
within a business context.

1315   Westwood, Robert G. and James E. Everett (1987)
        "Culture's Consequence: A Methodology for
        Comparing Management Studies in Southeast Asia,"
        Asia Pacific Journal of Management 4 (May): 187-202.

Hofstede's four dimensional model of culture is tested using
170 managers from Hong Kong, Malaysia, and Singapore. The
study takes into account the methodological criticisms of
Hofstede's work. The conclusion is that, although individual
responses are not amenable to a factor analytical treatment,
some similarities in value distributions between the
authors' findings and Hofstede's work exist. Hofstede's work
should be used as a starting point for further studies.

1316   Whitehill, Arthur M. editor (1987) Doing
        Business in Korea. New York: Nichols Publishing
        Company.

Selected chapters deal with Korean national character, the
banking, legal and government institutions, and with Korea's
trade policy. The first chapter covers the Korean way of
conducting business, how to make contacts, who should be
contacted, Korean business values, national character, and
how to establish valuable personal relationships.

1317   Whitely, Williams (1981) "Sources of Influence on
        Managers' Value Dimension Structure, Value Dimension
        Intensity, and Decisions," pp 481-535 in Gunter
        Dlugos and Klaus Weiermair (eds.), Managing Under
        Differing Value Systems: Political, Social, and
        Economical Perspectives in a Changing World.
        Berlin and New York: Walter de Gruyter.

There is a presentation of a well-developed theoretical
model of the nature of value orientation based on the
dimensions of structural factors and degree of value
integration. Based on samples of Australian and Indian
managers, the study finds that cognitive differences
(pragmatism vs. moralism) strongly influence the solution of
problems even when objective conditions are constant. There
is an excellent review of the relevant literature.

1318   Whitley, Richard D. (1990) "East Asian Enterprise
        Structures and the Comparative Analysis of Business
        Organization," Organization Studies 11 (1): 47-74.

Evidence indicates that a single pattern of business
organization across nations does not exist. This indicates
that cultural context imposes certain features on social
structures. The author develops a framework for the
comparative analysis of organizations based on eight
dimensions. The differences among dominant forms of business
organization in East Asia are analyzed.

1319   Whitley, Richard D. (1991) "The Social Construction
        of Business Systems in East Asia," Organization
        Studies 12 (1): 1-28.

There exist very different systems of business organizations
in Japan, South Korea, Taiwan, and Hong Kong. These forms
reflect differences in national character and cultures,
especially in terms of specialization, authority patterns,
trust and loyalty, strategic preferences, and inter-firm
coordination.

1320   Williams, Claire (1981) Open Cut:
        The Working Class in a Australian Mining
        Town. Sidney: George Allen & Unwin.

This is an extensive study of the workers' social patterns,
values, and attitudes (job satisfaction, family, etc.) based
on several methods (observation, surveys, interviews) using
a Marxist-Feminist theoretical framework. Management was
autocratic and top-to-bottom in decision-making.

1321   Williams, Geoff (1983) "Managing Diverse
        Work Groups: The Implications for Management
        Education," Leadership & Organization
        Development Journal 4 (1): 20-25.

Managerial theories generally assume a culturally uniform
workforce. This is no longer true in Australia. The author
describes changing work values and attitudes, the changing
cultural background of workers, and the implications of such
diversity for management education.

1322   Wimalasiri, Jayantha (1984) "Correlates of Work
        Values of Singaporean Employees," Singapore
        Management Review 6 (January): 51-75.

A sample of 275 Singaporean workers indicated that intrinsic
work values such as pride in work, activity preference, and
job involvement were highly scored. Monetary rewards and
social status associated with position were the least
desired values.

1323   Wimalasiri, Jayantha (1988) "Cultural Influence on
        Management Aspects: The Experience of the Chinese
        in Singapore," Asia Pacific Journal of Management
        5 (May): 197-206.

A random sample of 306 ethnic Chinese Singaporeans reacted
to twenty-two true-to-life situations. The responses were
analyzed in terms of four general value structures:
relational, temporal, mastery over nature, and activity. In

the first category, collectivism was preferred over individualism. The article concludes with a discussion of the implications of the findings.

1324   **Worthy, Ford S. (1989) "When Someone Wants a Payoff," Fortune 120 (Fall): 117-22.**

East Asian nations have ethical standards that accept the existence of payoffs and bribes. U.S. managers in Asia can begin by becoming familiar with the Foreign Corrupt Practices Law. It is often possible to maneuver around corrupt officials. In Asia, business relationships are often more important and more effective than money.

1325   **Wyatt, Thomas A. (1988) "Quality of Working Life: Cross-Cultural Considerations," Asia Pacific Journal of Management 6 (October): 129-40.**

The study of quality of working life (QWL) on a cross-cultural basis is a recent phenomenon, yet it promises great benefits to organizations and business enterprises. QWL levels change according to culture, and multinational enterprises must take into account the various socio-economic contexts of their workers from different countries. The author analyzes Hofstede's four dimensions in context to their usefulness for studies using respondents from Southeast Asia nations.

1326   **Zabid, A.R.M. (1987) "The Nature of Management Work Roles in Malaysian Public Enterprises," Asia Pacific Journal of Management 5 (September): 16-27.**

Public enterprise managers in a Malaysian sample of 105 respondents evaluated their perceptions of different aspects of work roles. They perceived the role of entrepreneur as the most important.

Subject Index

Note: numbers refer to entry numbers (for example, 1=0001), not page numbers.

Author Index

Note: numbers refer to entry numbers (for example, 1=0001), not page numbers

About the Compiler

JON P. ALSTON, Ph.D., is Professor of Sociology at Texas A&M University. He has been involved in international research for over a decade and has published, most recently, *The Intelligent Businessman's Guide to Japan* (1990), and *The American Samurai: Blending American and Japanese Managerial Practices* (1986).